Extraordinary Synergy

Measure the Unmeasurable

Extraordinary Synergy

Measure the Unmeasurable

Written by Human Intelligence.
Please Pardon Imperfection.

Dr. Hairong Gui, Ph.D., MBA

www.extraordinarysynergy.com

EXTRAORDINARY SYNERGY:
Measure the Unmeasurable

This book is not generated from any Artificial Intelligence tools or platform. The valuation model in this book is developed and configured by the author. The author wishes to apologize in advance for any syntax mistakes.

Printed in the United States of America
ISBN 979-8-89633-994-6 (hc)
ISBN 979-8-89633-992-2 (sc)
ISBN 979-8-89633-993-9 (e)

This book is printed on acid-free paper.

2025.12.12

Page Solutions
124 Rock Crystal Ln,
Lakeside Park,
KY 41017A
United States

PAGE
SOLUTIONS

Extraordinary Synergy –
Measure the Unmeasurable

By Hairong Gui, Ph.D., MBA
2nd Edition
Book Summary & Why 2nd Edition

Why bring 2nd edition? With AI upon us, now is a critical time to demonstrate the human "gut feelings" could and can make wise investment decisions. In addition, the digital commerce was thought to take over. However, in-person experience is reviving. We are social beings after all.

The *Extraordinary Synergy—Measure the Unmeasurable* answers:

How do we measure the holistic value of flagship investments that includes the intangible values, such as brand impact, cultural capital, and leadership vision?

This book presents a breakthrough valuation model - the Synergistic Option Model (SOM) - to quantify instinctive decision values, the "gut feeling". These values won't necessarily be shown on the traditional spreadsheets; however, carry the long-term vision and strategic timing. SOM captures not just what a business is *worth today*, but what it *could become* under the right leadership and conditions.

From **Chicago to Beijing**, From **London to Paris** - this book takes you around the globe. It reads like a global business travelogue. You will see the actual Flagship scenes in different countries back in the early 2000s. From NikeTown Chicago's original Jordan Air Sneaker with his signature to the Beijing NikeTown spectacular glamor; from Kobe's indoor display to London NikeiD Studio, you will have the first hand inside of Brand's global expansion and the sportswear industry: the real time insights you won't find in any annual report.

Nobel laureate Dr. Robert Merton and Nike's legendary founder Mr. Phil Knight: directly advised and influenced on the Synergistic Option Model (SOM) in profound ways.

Real Stories, Real Impact, Actual data: making it not just a story, but real cases story telling. Featuring exclusive real case studies from Nike's global flagship investments, this book demonstrates how controversial decisions, once dismissed as irrational, became billion-dollar brand moves. This is extremely counterintuitive, however in the hindsight, proved to be right.

Reconfiguring Nobel Prize Winning Black-Scholes Option Pricing Model: SOM goes beyond accounting formulas. It captures not just what a business is *worth today*, but what it *could become* under the right leadership and conditions.

For Entrepreneurs and Leaders: how to balance online scale with offline brand experience, this book offers both analytical modeling and strategic prediction tool.

This book is the result of over a decade of on-the-ground fieldwork. No Artificial Intelligence is involved. Please pardon my imperfect writing.

Contents

List of Tables

List of Figures

Author Introduction

At the age of 4, on a stormy day, filled with fear, I creatively climbed out of the house through the hole in the wall (the entrance for our rooster) and sprinted to my mother's office. I knew then that I would be a rule breaker or a system outlier at least. The idea of becoming a System Scientist seemed as improbable as reaching the moon. Life, however, has a peculiar sense of humor.

Over the years, I discover fascinating dynamics in systems. My passion led me to delve deep into the study of various "systems," unraveling the intricate connections between financial valuation systems, business enterprises systems, and broader economic and socio-cultural systems they intertwine with.

By the time I turned 12, I was inspired by a Nike commercial that ignited a dream—to come to the United States, a place where hard work is truly rewarded. The dream is a "mission impossible". My family is in academia with little power or wealth. BUT, I was undeterred and embarked on an extraordinary journey.

I landed in Boston to study MBA; then began in the financial investment industry, specializing in quantitative research. I just always remember Nike. After hundreds applications to Nike, I started writing letter to the executives. Finally one executive picked up my letter and I started as a Finance Analyst at the Asia Pacific Geography. It was during this time that I witnessed the "extraordinary synergy" in the investment decisions made by the leadership—sometimes relying on their "gut feelings" rather than the traditional valuation models, and the results proved them right! I began incubating the Synergy Option Model. Subsequently, I had the privilege to work at Nike's European Middle East Africa Headquarters in the Netherlands, allowing me to travel extensively and visit numerous retail stores I returned to North America in 2009 to complete my dissertation.

I am fortunate to have studied, worked, and lived in over thirty countries, spanning almost every continent. In each of these places, I immersed myself in thousands of retail stores, traversed bustling high streets, surveyed countless customers, and engaged in insightful conversations with executives, store managers, and staff. These firsthand experiences exposed me to the embedded values that extend beyond mere financial considerations. Combined with extensive research, calculations, and advice, these encounters have given birth to an unconventional valuation methodology, further refined, and applied in the dynamic arena of investment valuation.

I have always been an educator at heart. Fast forward to today, I find myself in academia, much like my father, to pass on the valuable knowledge and experiences I've gained throughout my journey.

Book Introduction

Have you been to Nike Flagship stores? You might think these significant investments were made based on careful financial calculations. Yes and No. They were actually made based on the financials and on the leaders' instinctive beliefs in their assessments. Quite interestingly, these decisions turned out to be right! This book is not an academic textbook. It is a global sportswear market eye-opening read.

This book presents a groundbreaking valuation method, showcased through real-world case studies of Nike's flagship store investments worldwide. Dr. Gui's Synergistic Option Model (SOM) serves as a valuable complement to conventional valuation approaches by effectively quantifying the hidden synergistic value of strategic investments.

The SOM reveals that experienced leaders' decisions driven by gut feelings are often both strategic and financially viable in the long term, provided their instincts are accurate. By extending the renowned Black Scholes Option Pricing Model (BSOPM), the SOM allows for the quantification of leaders' gut feelings prior to making substantial investments. Developed using Nike's proprietary data in an unbiased manner, the SOM demonstrates its capability to provide precise forecasts for strategic financial decisions that were previously challenging to quantify accurately.

Abstract

A deep gratitude is dedicated to Mr. Phil Knight, a leader who, in essence, shaped the sportswear industry for my generation and for future generations. Mr. Knight inspired and continues to inspire me to challenge the "conventional wisdom." I am very fortunate to have had Mr. Knight as one of my advisors in this research, and I am grateful for his coaching on Nike's heritage, an unwavering and lasting legacy. Without his guidance, this research would likely never have been realized.

I am fortunate to have had the opportunity to meet with Nobel Prize winner Dr. Robert Merton on several occasions. He and I discussed many aspects of Black Scholes Option Pricing Model (BSOPM). The insights he shared with me opened up a new vision for me, which significantly enhanced and deepened my understanding of the Model. In many ways, his direct teaching unveiled the "secret".

This book is an extension of my dissertation in 2011. Since then, I have continued extending this model to other industries and other types of investments, such as head-to-toe glass fancy Apple Stores in main cities, glamourous Louis Vuitton flagship stores, the SpaceX "Tesla-to-Space" event, and so on. The unexpected global Covid pandemic hit the world in a way no one would have foreseen. It is evident that extraordinary events disrupt normal business operations, (re)shape industries, and create new business opportunities.The synergy associated with such events is extraordinary.

Most business financials show outlier performance in 2020, 2021, and part of 2022. Using conventional valuation methodology, such as Discounted Cash Flow (DCF) and its core calculation method Net Pricing Model (NPV), the financial results would be over of the place. This leads to a new and unique utilization of the Black Scholes Option Pricing Model (BSOPM) to quantify the synergistic value generated by high investment/high risk-return (HI/HRR) investments. This synergistic value is invisible to standard bookkeeping methods, but is visible to the method I devised—a new application of the BSOPM. I have named my application the "Synergistic Option Model" (SOM).

My original dissertation presented a mechanism that applied the Black Scholes Option Pricing Model (BSOPM) and its principles to quantify hard-to-measure risks and rewards of significant investments. We analyzed four Nike flagship stores in New York, Chicago, Paris, and Beijing. Conventional valuation methods for all four flagship stores showed negative returns. Our BSOPM analysis, capturing the synergistic value of these strategic investments, showed positive returns for all four of these strategic investments. The forecasted results from the model were then compared to the actual results of the investments to confirm the accuracy of the risk/reward analysis. My dissertation used the sportswear industry[1] (in particular, the retail sector) to test whether the BSOPM could measure synergistic value not measured by conventional financial accounting methods.

Nike's internal proprietary data was used to evaluate whether the SOM constitutes an accurate forecasting method that enables strategic financial decisions (this is also the reason it took 10 years before this book could be published). Over the years, Nike has adapted more Direct-to-Consumer strategies through Nike-owned retail stores (vs. through sporting goods retailers stores. Whether Nike will keep its dominant position in the sportswear industry remains to be seen, as the competition is firing up fiercer than ever. To continue Mr. Phil Knight's legacy, it will be critical for Nike to continue staying as a learning and growing Company.

Nike's "Just Do It" motto always inspires me. Do The Right Thing Right.

---

[1] Not all sportswear industry investments require upfront investments as large as in other HI/HRR risk-return industries. My dissertation focused on significant investments in flagship stores by Nike, which were made with the understanding that standard accounting practices showed negative NPV figures.

Acknowledgements

I would like to gratefully and sincerely thank my dissertation Committee members for their advice, patience, and, most importantly, their mentorship during my graduate studies. Without the strong support and guidance of Dr. John Oh, Dr. Janet Hamilton, Dr. Tom Gillpatrick, and Dr. Wayne Wakeland, and Mr. Phil Knight and Dr. Michael Wrinn, I would not have been able to complete this work.

The most important person in this research effort, and the person who made completion of this work and my study possible, is my Committee Chairman, Dr. John Oh. Not only did he bring this research to life and steer me through this PhD journey, but also he cultivated, evolved and enhanced my professional, academic, and personal growth. "Once teacher, lifetime mentor." I am indebted to Dr. Oh.

A very special appreciation must be dedicated to Mr. William Bloom, my chief editor, friend, and mentor. Through this long and sometimes lonely tunnel, we have built strong mentorship and friendship. He encouraged me to become a noble educator, a bold entrepreneur, and an optimistic, resilient, never-give-up individual with an open mind and a humble heart. I would not be here today without the inspiration, motivation and encouragement of my honorary "Uncle Bill."

I would like to thank my parents and my sister. They have given me steadfast support, encouragement, patience and unconditional love. Their tolerances of my obsession of continuous learning, their faith and confidence in me, and their willingness to allow me to be as ambitious as I wanted to be, have been unwavering. Because of them, I have endless drive, energy, and motivation to tackle whatever lies ahead of me.

Finally, this part of my life-long learning journey started with a dream, a dream that someday I can become a great inspirational educator like my father. My father has been my guiding light in this research throughout this long journey and in life. He is my source of wisdom and strength of mind in life.

I have asked all of the people who helped and contributed in this study, "How I can thank you?" They all simply tell me to "Pass it on."

Thank you all. I have been and I shall continue.

Dissertation Committee

John Oh, Chair, School of Business, Portland State University

Janet Hamilton, School of Business, Portland State University

Thomas Gillpatrick, School of Business, Portland State University

Wayne Wakeland, School of System Science, Portland State University

Timothy Anderson, School of Engineering and Management, Portland State University

Phil Knight (external advisor) Michael Wrinn (external advisor) Portland State University, © 2011

Main Contributors to this Research

Phil Knight (Chairman & Co-Founder, Nike, Inc.)

Robert Merton, Ph.D. Nobel Prize Winner (Harvard University / MIT)

William Bloom (Advisor, Chief Editor, faculty Professor)

Tim Hershey (CEO/Founder of Centricity Consulting, LLC, former VP Nike Global Merchandizing)

Charlie Wadsworth (Business Advisor, former Nike Central East Europe CFO)

Trevor Vigfusson (CFO EXOS, former CFO Nike Golf)

Interviewees (in the order of interviews)

Keith Fitz-Gerald (Investment Director Money Map Press, Founder CEO)

Charlie Wadsworth (retired CFO, Former Europe Finance Director, Nike Inc.)

David Sanderson (Europe Retail Finance Director, Nike Inc.)

Ryan K. Smith (CFO, Nike Golf)

Simon Kemmett (Sr. Director Business Planning, Former CFO, Nike Europe)

Lisa McKillips (Executive Assistant to Mr. Phil Knight, Nike Inc)

Eunan McLaughlin (Former President Nike Affiliates Brands)

Victor Williems (LEAN Business Solutions, European Director)

Sonia de Paolis (Treasury Director, TomTom, former Sr Treasury Analyst, Nike Inc)

Maximo Alfonsi (Founder, MaxieWeb)

Olivier Pennetier (Counselor, One Plus Investment, France; Former NikeTown Paris, GM)

Sean Ghouse (Head of Home Retail Alfred Dunhill, Former NikeTown London GM)

Orences Christian (Jordan Brand Sales Rep, Former NikeTown Chicago GM)

Rob Weerts (Niketown Project Manager, Nike Inc.)

Jean-Philippe Sauvageot (Director of Stores Western Europe)

Nicola Chardon (Former European Retail Finance Director)

Jon McCathy (former UK Retail Development Manager, Nike Inc)

Paul Klein (West Europe Merchandizing Manager, Nike Inc)

Raymond Gregor (Window Dresser, De Bijenkorf Department Store, Amsterdam)

Dale Frakes (Senior Supply Chain Analyst, Nike Inc)

Philip Hatton (Golf Club Business Manager, Nike Inc)

Bill Mullen (LEAN Director, Nike Inc)

Ronald Tracey (Enterprise Architecture Director, Nike Inc)

Arnie Gardner (Director Global Financial Planning, Nike Inc)

Tambert Lau (Retired Nike Senior Product Engineer)

Allan Brovo (Niketown Chicago original store design project lead)

Dan Burris (GM Action Sports, Nike Inc)

Janet Callahan (Emerging Market Retail Operation Manager, Nike, Inc)

Kelly Heiden (Process Manager, Nike Inc)

Nelson Farris (Nike Communication Director)

Richard McDaniel (Retail Concept Director)

Marshall McCauley (Nike Planning/Allocation Director)

1. Opening—Narrative

Do you wonder why many flagship stores on 5th Avenue in New York City are so extravagantly ever lit? Don't they know the electricity cost? Why did Mr. Elon Musk (the founder of Space-X and CEO of Tesla) rocket a Tesla into Space with his own spaceship? Didn't he know the cost? Why did Mr. Bernard Jean Étienne Arnault build a stunning atrium in his of Louis Vuitton flagship store on the Avenue des Champs-Elysees in Paris? Didn't he know the cost? Many costs incurred by flagship stores and other extravagant venues cannot be justified by conventional accounting; sometimes, expenditures like these in fact can cause flagship stores to actually lose money in terms of day-to-day operations.

From my work at Nike, I witnessed the leadership's ability to see beyond the standard accounting data in strategic decision- making. Mr. Philip Knight personally told me that he did the return- on-investment analysis on the back of an envelope. He and other Nike leaders understood that sometimes investments (such as flagship retail stores) have strategic value that is not reflected by standard book-keeping. Mr. Knight sparked my interest in the quantification of such strategic values.

While working for the Nike European & Middle East areas overseas, I visited many flagship stores and walked in many "high streets" in many countries (Yes, many "*manys*") to personally experience and observe the "non-financial" embedded values. I surveyed thousands of customers in the stores and on the streets. I interviewed hundreds of store managers and staff. These personal experiences and first-hand real feedback reinforced my belief that some of the flagship stores' strategic merits are not fully captured or measured by standard accounting numbers. In seeking managerial insights as to why these investments were made, I was privileged to interview practitioners in the field, seeking their practical insights. These indispensable discussions provided exceedingly valuable input to this breakthrough in measuring the "invisible return" from unconventional investments.

It took me a solid four years to do these trips. In 2009, I came back from Europe and started writing the dissertation. In 2011, I graduated from Portland State University with a joint Philosophy Doctoral Degree in System Science & Strategic Finance. On May 14, 2022, I defended my dissertation in front of the Committee and public. Since then, I have continued this study. Together with Dr. Tom Gillpatrick and Mr. William Bloom, we wrote and published a few research papers and presented them in conferences. I left Nike and joined a consulting firm, where I got exposed to varieties of industries. Afterwards, I started my own consulting company in order to apply what I have learned. Then I go back to the higher education to service, research, and teach. I am inspired to pass on my learning. It amazed me how broad and deep our "Synergistic Option Model" (SOM) can be and should be used.

I started using the SOM (Synergistic Option Model) to quantify extreme events such as Elon Musk's "shooting a Tesla into space" or Red Bull sending Austrian skydiver Felix Baumgartner to the stratosphere to set a 128,000 feet (about 24 miles above Earth's surface) parachute jump. What synergistic values, if any, did these costly campaigns generate?

I began looking into the Apple flagship store investments. They are glamorous, with top to bottom entry doors, in major cities, on high streets—all of which are very expensive. Why does the company see value in opening such extravagant Apple stores?

I once visited the Starbucks flagship store in Shanghai. The store is actually a small coffee factory! Such an investment just to sell coffee? What did Howard Schultz see as the return on that extravagant investment, which does not sell enough coffee to make a profit according to conventional accounting methods?

The examples in this book—the four NikeTown Flagship Stores

- investments are higher than the present value of the projected cash flows. Had Nike's leadership followed the traditional valuation methods, none of these investments would have proceeded. On August 3, 2007, just one year ahead of the 2008 Beijing Olympics, NikeTown Beijing opened. Nike brand President Charlie Denson attended the grand opening: "China is one of Nike's biggest growth opportunities, Our Beijing flagship store creates a strong brand statement... As we head toward the Olympics, we're extending our brand leadership, deepening our consumer relationships...." Nike's decision-makers intuitively understood that NikeTowns could create synergistic values, even if they could not quantify those values. The Synergistic Option Model (SOM) results validate these leaders' foresights. SOM enables decision makers and/or investors to detect what the synergistic options are and how such values can create benefits that may not be reflected in the traditional valuation methods.

NikeTown Beijing achieved what was it was created to achieve during the Olympics[2]. Nike started the second stage expansion shortly after. I was fortunate to be able to verify the NikeTown Beijing's financial and strategic success after 2008 Olympics and thereby validate the SOM results.

Similar results were also verified and validated in the case of NikeTown Paris (for the 2010 World Cup and 2011 French Football Association sponsorship launch). As the 2012 London Olympics approached, Nike leadership anticipated the opportunity and started the most expensive renovations in NikeTown London—remodeling top floors and building a "black box" NikeiD[3] studio hanging in the middle of the Store. The valuation results from the traditional methods show a significant negative present value of this investment while SOM results show positive. Nike went ahead despite the negative net present value of the project. However in hindsight, had the Synergistic Options Model been in place, NikeTown London could have received the resources needed for the renovation in a more timely fashion.

---

[2] Nike brand President Charlie Denson: "China is one of Nike's biggest growth opportunities, and one of the most dynamic retail markets in the world. Our Beijing flagship store creates a strong brand statement with a compelling world-class shopping experience. As we head toward the Olympics, we're extending our brand leadership, deepening our consumer relationships and building what we expect soon to be a $1 billion business and Nike's second-largest market in the world."

[3] NikeiD (renamed as "Nike By You") was first conceded in 1999 in the American market. It is a service provided by Nike allowing customers to personalize and design their own Nike merchandise, most specifically footwear but also sportswear.

3

In sum, the Synergistic Options Model is a valuation game changer—it goes beyond providing just a valuation result based on accounting numbers. It incorporates multiple internal & external market risks, factoring in opportunity costs, and facilitating the coherent strategic allocation of resources. It enables businesses and investments to create holistic strategies and to identify future growth potential[4].

---

[4] Below are few examples:

1. Growth & Expansion

   a. Explosive entry strategy or steadily easing into the market

   b. First-mover or second-mover strategy

   c. Grow existing business territory

2. Sustaining

   a. Build upon existing infrastructure

   b. Build new infrastructure

3. Delay or Staging

   a. Wait until the uncertainty is mitigated

   b. Test new markets by stages

4. Abandonment:

   a. Abandon one or more new investment opportunities

   b. Divest existing non-performing assets

NikeTown London, UK, by the author

London Oxford Shopping Area, by the author

Paris Champs-Élysées Street, by the author

Paris Champs-Élysées Street, by the author

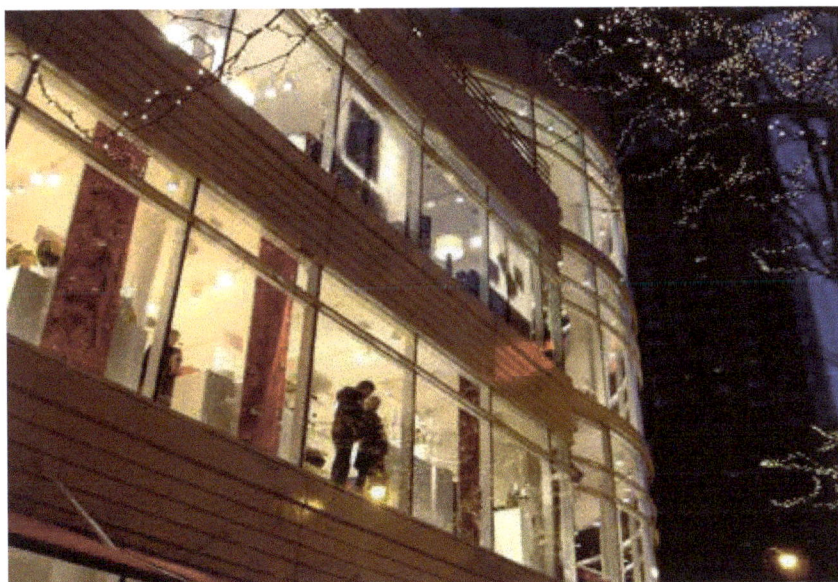

NikeTown Chicago, USA, by the author

NikeTown Chicago, USA, Jordan Shoe, by the author

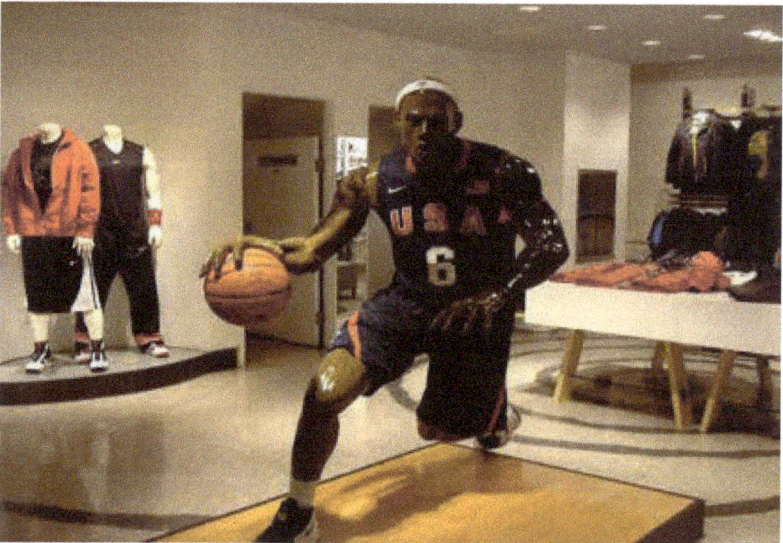

NikeTown Chicago, USA, by the author

NikeTown Beijing by Donghua Ma, 2024

2. Opening—Technical

In 1973, economists Fischer Black and Myron Scholes created the Black-Scholes Option Pricing Model (BSOPM), which for the first time enabled an accurate calculation of risk and return in stock option pricing. Prior to the publication of the BSOPM, investments in stock options were considered wildly speculative; after publication of the BSOPM, stock options trading boomed as traders were able to better quantify the risks and rewards of such trading.

In my view, this is a most elegant, eloquent, sophisticated, and concise equation. In short, BSOPM is the solution of a second-order partial differential equitation with boundary conditions and assumptions. This model was developed to price financial options. The equation is based on a delta-hedged portfolio that enables risk-free rate return. Dr. Robert Merton was awarded the Nobel Prize[5] for his contribution to the BSOPM. Merton's Variation Model-with dividend δ is as follows:

Call Option—BSOPM Merton's Revision

$$C = Se^{-\delta t}\{N(d_1)\} - Xe^{-rt}\{N(D_2)\}$$

Equation (2)

Put Option—BSOPM Merton's Revision

$$= Xe^{-rt}\{1 - N(d_2)\} - Se^{-\delta t}\{1 - N(d_2)\}$$

---

[5] In Dr. Merton's 1998 Nobel Laureate acceptance speech, he succinctly outlined the development of option pricing strategy, particularly following the breakthrough introduction of the BSOPM in 1973. Dr. Merton highlighted the many improvements made to option pricing theory and practice by a series of gifted and determined scholars during the decades following its introduction.

Equation (3)

The Put option is derived from put-call parity: that is, selling a call and buying a put.

C = Call Value

P = Put Value

S = Price of underlying Asset

X = Strike Price in Call Option or Salvage Value if aban- donment

$$d_1 = \frac{\left\{ lnln\left(\dfrac{S}{X}\right) + \left(r - \delta + \dfrac{\sigma^2}{2}\right)t \right\}}{\sigma\sqrt{t}}$$

$$d_2 = d_1 - \sigma\sqrt{t}$$

In 1984, Dr. Stewart Myers demonstrated that the rationale behind the valuation of financial options could also be applied in situations where an investor could elect to make, or decline to make, an investment in a non-financial option. He constructed the *"Real Options" (RO)* concept upon the foundation of the *BSOPM* by extending the rationale of the BSOPM beyond the valuation of financial options to the valuation of speculative real asset investment opportunities or projects.

As Real Options generated a noticeable amount of research interest in the academic field, it also caught the attention of practitioners. In particular, practitioners in many High Risk-Return industries have turned to Real Option methodology to supplement NPV in the evaluation of real asset investment opportunities. In these industries (such as speculative oil field investments) the Real Option method has demonstrated its value-added contribution to strategic and financial decision-making processes.

Similar to the definition of a financial option, a Real Option can be considered as the right but not the obligation to acquire the present value of the expected cash flows by making an investment when the opportunity is available. Unlike financial options, Real Options rarely have defined lives and are generally not tradable. This has been and still is the main limitation of Real Option[6] application in practice.[7]

How Does Real Options Concept Relate To Sportswear Industry And Nike's Flagship Stores[8]?

In today's business, successful multinational companies must have strong brand recognition to sustain and gain global market shares. The sportswear industry's dependency upon the sports business (sports events, game results, and the performance of celebrities) makes brand equity an essential part of the business success. One of the most effective venues for the promotion of brand recognition of products is flagship stores These stores require a high level of expense and the store itself may or may not directly generate financial profits from sales within the store. However, they are strategically important to the company and can broaden the brand exposure, deepen and expand the company's relationship with consumers, generate market excitement for the brand, and more.

The sportswear industry has become in some ways a high-investment/high-risk return industry. It been and presently is dominated by several key global players, namely, Nike (US), Adidas (Germany), Puma (Germany), Asics (Japan), and Lining (China). The consolidation of this industry has generated strong integration across

---

[6] These option values are: (a) the option to delay "wait-and-see"; (b) the option to expand or grow; and (c) the option to abandon the project.

[7] Myers, Stewart C. (1977) "Determinants of Corporate Borrowing", *Journal of Financial Economics 5*, 147-175. He demonstrated that real asset investment analysts could treat explicit options in real asset investments as if they were financial options (using BSOPM as one of the tools). He advocates that, even when a specific investment option is not traded, the RO methodology can still be employed, in conjunction with NPV, to improve investment decision-making process when there are embedded option values.

[8] Flagship store: a shop with a large floor area dedicated to a single brand and stocking a very wide range of the brand's products. The flagship is a principal showcase of the brand and a key tool in its promotion. It symbolized its mission, image and values and is a tangible demonstration of brand awareness. Source: Ledicodumarketing.fr. Nike "flagship store" definition varies as the company expands and evolves its marketing strategy.

the manufacturing, supply chain, marketing, and in particular, the sales functions at its retail front. Within the sportswear industry, the retail front has developed into an established sector that is different from the general retail industry.

Flagship store investments may comprise millions of dollars while, as previously described, returns oftentimes take many forms beyond immediate financial outcomes from sales within the store itself. These external value effects or economic externalities from major investment decisions of the company may be identified/ measured through Synergistic Value Options analysis complementing traditional NPV analysis.

This book will present/summarize a case-by-case analysis of investments in major flagship stores located in different countries and on different continents[9]. These mega-stores present various synergistic options applications[10]: expansion, growth, delay, and staging options. All other business-related data discussed in this work are from public sources with the exception of certain proprietary business information[11].

Broadened Primary Significance

While the original research from my dissertation explored the sportswear retail industry's invisible return from the significant investments in flagship stores, the result of the research demonstrates that this methodology is useful in analyzing any investments that generate invisible returns—returns that do not appear in the standard bookkeeping ledgers.

The concept of volatility is one of the sophisticated key factors in any investment valuation. Conventional thinking is that the lower

---

[9]   Data may be proportionally adjusted and the individual store names and locations will be concealed for business confidentiality. During this research, we interviewed business practitioners within and outside the company. The full list is in the Acknowledgement section.

[10]   Detailed reference see footnote in Literature Review and Case Studies.

[11]   Actual investment details may not be fully disclosed for reasons of business confidentiality. Details disclosed here are only for the purpose of this study.

the volatility, the safer the investment. However, lower volatility also means a lower return on financial investments. This is a very difficult "fine line" to walk. Built upon the original research, where we identified and compared the various indicators or measures of volatility, this book deepens the original study. The present study considered several candidate measures, and used an extensive proprietary database to select the best measure and demonstrate its efficacy.

The primary significance of the original research is its contribution toward improved accuracy in the investment valuation. The world has experienced and is going through unprecedented changes at a rapid pace. Valuation should no longer be just evaluating the investment project within the company or calculating the business's value based on its accounting financials.

We are evolving almost at the Moore's law[12] speed. Now with over a decade's worth of continuous research and implementation, we are ready to advance to the next stage. The Covid global pandemic is unfortunately an astonishing example of how "black swans" can and have created value. These unexpected synergistic values are associated with, or in our opinion, are derived from unexpected economic and social externalities[13]. To capture more of these synergistic values from the externalities, the Synergistic Options Model (SOM) should be used to supplement the conventional valuation methods, particularly to investments that have a High Investment-High Risk/Return profile. Below is the US Retail Yearly sales trend. It is evident that the retail industry thrives throughout the "good and bad" economies. It is more than commercial business. It is part of people's living.

---

[12] Moore's law is a term used to refer to the observation made by Gordon Moore in 1965 that the number of transistors in a dense integrated circuit (IC) doubles about every two years. https://www.synopsys.com/

[13] The Hidden Value in the "Black Swan"-Pandemic Synergistic Externalities Creates Opportunity Value Reversing Application of Black-Scholes Option Pricing Model (BSOPM), Gui, Gillpatrick, Bloom, 2022 August, ISSN: 2155-7950, Journal of Business and Economics

In this book, you will find four very compelling and actual stories of NikeTown London, NikeTown Paris, NikeTown Chicago, and NikeTown Beijing.

Figure 1: US Retail Yearly Sales Trend.

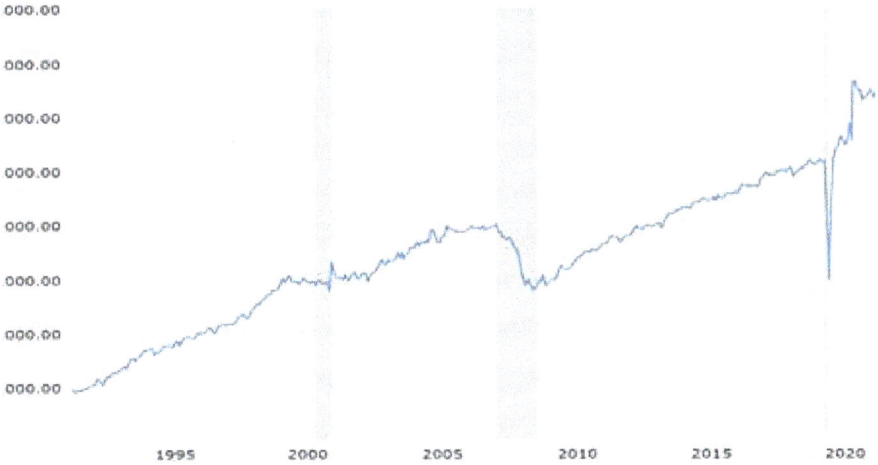

3. Sportswear Industry Development

The sportswear industry is a relatively new industry that evolved over the past few decades, particularly after the major global sportswear players emerged, consolidated, and integrated. Sportswear evolved when the sportswear industry separated from the general apparel industry and developed specialized retail capabilities. Improved living conditions over the last half century led to lifestyle changes in developed societies that contributed significantly to the development of the sportswear as a separate industry category.

3.1 Improved Living Conditions Created the Sportswear Industry

The concept of "sportswear" appeared only recently. In the past, life for most people was hard and contained enough physical activities that our ancestors did not have the time, the need, or the energy to engage in extra fitness activities. Over the years, as human society developed and technology leapt forward, people's living conditions improved due to many factors, including the following:

- industrial machinery freed people from doing many kinds of heavy physical labor;

- agricultural advances provided society with better and more dietary choices;

- technology and transportation developments combined to produce more leisure time.

The improved living conditions also had the effect of lengthening life spans. Along with this positive development new problems emerged, such as new physical ailments, many of which (such as heart disease) were related to physical inactivity. Modern society is concerned with poverty in underdeveloped countries and obesity in developed countries at the same time. The need for people in developed economies to exercise in order to combat the ill effects of sedentary lifestyles emerged. Gradually, the need for a more active lifestyle created the need for "sportswear" to be a separate sector within the general apparel industry. The sportswear industry came into being and a global sportswear market began to grow and draw attention.

3.2 Changes in Lifestyle Led to the Evolution of the Sportswear Industry

Since its emergence, the sportswear industry has been evolving rapidly. Improved living conditions and reduced physical labor made it possible and desirable for people to participate in sports activities. More leisure time not only allowed people to participate in sports events but to watch them, and modern communication tools encouraged the development of highly engaged sports fans. Sportswear has moved from the "nice-to-have" to the "should have" and eventually to the "must have" categories on many consumers' shopping lists.

As more and more people started paying attention to their overall physical wellbeing, and as sportswear became fashionable, the sportswear market continued to grow. The market size almost doubled from 2003 to 2009[14]. Fortune Business Insights™ published this information in a report titled, "Sportswear Market, 2021-2028", indicating that the overall sportswear market size was USD 160.61 billion in 2020. The report also projected that the market will grow from USD 170.94 billion in 2021 to USD 267.61 billion by 2028 at a compound annual growth rate of 6.6% during the 2021-2028 period.

This demonstrates the rapid development and expansion of the consumer base, product offerings, and distribution channels. Consequently, sportswear has also developed into an industry, and due to its inherent industry characteristics that are distinct from those of the general appeal and footwear industry. It has developed an investment profile that is difficult to predict with certainty. The following factors contribute to that profile:

---

[14] Worldwide market size (global sales of sports equipment, apparel and footwear) has grown from $143 billion in 2003 to $282 billion in 2009 (data source: NPD, Inc).

1) Business models: The companies compete across numerous dimensions, including product quality and value, logistics, customer service, and others. Sportswear competitors can rarely succeed if they excel in only one area.

2) Competition: The competitive rivalry among the major competitors is fierce and ruthless across all dimensions, featuring bidding wars for celebrity athlete and team endorsements, competition for prime sales locations, incursions into competitor's home markets, and other battles on a continual basis. Competition was intensified by a number of factors. First, retailers expanded horizontally, as retailers that previously sold only general apparel began to also carry athletic apparel or active apparel.

Second, some competitors, particularly the global companies, began opening high-profile signature retail stores, known as "flagship stores", such as Adidas' stores in Tokyo and Shanghai and Nike's own stores in London and Paris (most sportswear industry companies also sell through their own branded stores that are much less extravagant than are the flagship stores.) By expanding to the retail front, competitors can enhance their brand presence and can also directly engage with consumers drawn to such glamorous or extravagant outlets. In addition, some retailers integrated backward, developing their own private brands and selling them at cheaper prices.

Third, consolidation intensified the competition. The retail industry has been trending toward consolidation. Major retailers emerged, developing stronger buying power to drive down prices and squeezing out smaller local retailers.

3) Educated consumers: Consumers have become much more and better informed over time. They can search for the best value / price combination easily through the Internet. They can order the products even if the seller is in another country, and can order online directly from the factory. They can find information about better value bargains on a broader and

larger scale and can identify the latest new inventions much more quickly. Consumers were being "led" before; now they are "leading."

4) Shortened industry cycles. As consumers become better informed, their purchasing behavior is changing quickly. As a result, the product "shelf-life" cycles are getting shorter. The shortness of these cycles is relatively new and the industry is in the process of adapting to this change, resulting in retailers forming different types of stores (such as concept stores, store-in-store, etc.) to compete for consumers. NikeTowns and Adidas premium flagship stores are an example.

3.3 Sportswear Industry Distinguishing Characteristics

3.3.1 Sports celebrities and team endorsements.

Historically, the sportswear industry was part of the general apparel & footwear retail industry, which in the past could be counted on for steady growth. Compared to the general apparel & footwear retail industry, however, the sportswear industry today has a strong distinguishing characteristic: its major dependence on the often unpredictable outcomes of major sporting events and upon the continued success and good behavior of admired sports teams and celebrities.

Sportswear to some consumers is a declaration of their support for their team and its actual or potential achievements. This characteristic is a direct reflection of consumers' purchasing-intention. A sports celebrity or team's victory or defeat, or glory or shame, often has a direct and significant impact on the profitability of both the sportswear company and their retailers. To many other sportswear consumers, sportswear can also be the preferred means of their individual expression.

Loyalty to the team transfers to loyalty to its sportswear sponsor. For instance, Adidas is the official sponsor for the German national (soccer) football team, while Nike sponsors the French team, Umbro (a British football sportswear company) sponsors the English team and Lining (a Chinese sportswear company) has the Chinese team. German football fans will not buy Nike football sportswear, as a way of demonstrating their loyalty to their team.

3.3.2 Dependency on sports events & results & celebrities

A very distinguishing characteristic of the SPORTSWEAR is its dependency on major sporting events anticipated and/or sports celebrities admired. Wins or losses from a sports celebrity and/or sports team can have a direct impact on both the sportswear company and the retailers' profitability. Wins or losses by these teams can directly impact the sportswear companies' profits or losses.

As sales fluctuate ever more dramatically in reaction to such external events in the sports world, the industry is perceived as having become far more volatile than in the past. For example, England's unexpected early ouster from the 2008 Euro Cup for soccer had a multimillion dollar impact on sales of Umbro brand sportswear featuring that event and that team. Two weeks after the game that cost the English team its opportunity to advance, Umbro issued a profit warning to the investor community. Subsequently, major UK retailers, JJB, Sports World, and Sports Direct all followed suit. Conversely, the unexpected success of the Spanish team in winning the 2008 Euro Cup generated a boom in sales of Adidas brand sportswear associated with that team. 2022 World Cup champion Argentina's kit supplier is Adidas and France's is Nike. At the final, it felt to some as if the contest was just between Adidas vs. Nike.

Similarly, the success or failure, glory or disgrace, of individual sports stars who endorse one sportswear brand or another can make a difference in sales of associated apparel in the millions of dollars. In the U.S., NFL quarterback Michael Vick's criminal convictions for dog fighting not only destroyed the value of his sponsoring sportswear company's investment in him, it may even have harmed the value of the company's entire brand. Nike suspended the release of the Vick V Shoes while Reebok took the unprecedented step of stopping sales of his No. 7 jersey. Lance Armstrong's dishonesty and Kanye West's well-publicized antisemitic and other screeds led to significant Nike and Adidas brand damage.

To summarize, some of the notable factors of this evolution are:

1) Major national and global retailers are emerging, cannibalizing the smaller or local retailers;

2) Heavy reliance on the major sporting events and sports celebrities;

3) Glamour flagship stores are becoming one of the important venues to build brand equity, requiring a much heavier upfront investment than before;

4) Consumer spending around major sporting events is difficult to predict.

3.4 Sportswear Retail Industry Analysis

3.4.1 Retail industry increasing volatility.

Recent retail industry changes have led to a noticeable increase in the volatility in sales, earnings, and cash flow, which translates into an associated rise in standard deviation. As the standard deviations increase, Synergistic Option Model become more valuable in the retail investment valuation. As a result, in addition to the conventional valuation methodology, such as NPV, Internal Rate of Return (IRR), and/ or Payback, retailers and investors have begun to consider whether Synergistic Option Model methodology may be useful in the valuation of such store projects.

3.4.2 Sportswear Industry summation.

The sportswear industry is a relatively new industry, evolving from the general apparel and footwear industries, and emerging as a new sector in the general industry.[15] Compared to the traditional

---

[15] This study collects retail industry sales monthly data from the US Census was collected and reviewed. These data included:

apparel and footwear retail sectors, the sportswear industry has developed very distinguishing characteristics, in that brand equity is a cornerstone for success, plus heavy reliance on the sports business. The difficulties inherent in forecasting the outcomes of such dependencies have led to revenue streams that are much riskier and more volatile than those in the traditional apparel industries. Furthermore, the investment return may lie not just in financial profits, but in non-financial forms.

The particular characteristics of the sportswear industry (dependence on major sports event outcomes and on the fame or shame of sports celebrities) are unique.. In addition, there is significant institutional resistance: traditional practices have become deeply entrenched in corporate finance departments, and new paradigms can be expected to be met with resistance by incumbent practitioners. The complexity of the RO methodology itself makes it even more difficult to overcome this institutional inertia, in part due to the irreversibly of the investment. When the Synergistic Option Model result supports an investment decision in a negative-NPV scenario, if management decides to invest, the investment normally cannot be reversed or otherwise without penalty after the lease has been signed.

- Retail industry overall monthly time-series 1992-2010;

- Sporting Goods sector retail industry overall monthly time-series 1992-2010.

4. Case Studies—Why Nike and Why NikeTowns?

4.1 Overview

One of the most effective venues for the promotion of brand recognition of sportswear products is the flagship store[16]. Flagship stores define the "brand statement" (or "brand instrument" in marketing jargon) and generate "brand heat"[17]. They are primarily located in major international cities, where real estate is costly and investments often have negativeNPV[18].Their presence creates a "halo-effect"[19] that ripples vertically[20] and horizontally[21]. These external value effects or economic externalities from these major investment decisions of the company provide unique applications of synergistic value options that are complementary to NPV analysis, and in our view, are more illustrative in respect to the attributes of synergistic value options than similar analyses of investments to build smaller stores located in medium-sized cities[22].

---

[16] Flagship stores: a shop with a large floor area dedicated to a single brand and stocking a very wide range of the brand's products. The flagship is the chief outlet of the brand and a key tool in its promotion. It symbolized its mission, image and values and is a tangible demonstration of brand awareness. Source: Ledicodumarketing.fr. Nike "flagship store" definition varies as the company expands and evolves its marketing strategy. Also see footnote in Chapter 1.

[17] "Brand Heat" is a term of art in marketing terminology and refers to popularity.

[18] Tim Hershey, then-VP/North America Retail, Nike Inc. in speaking of the key criteria rely upon to make investment decision, other than financial data, such as NPV, stated: "Fact based decision making is critical in our investment decisions. However, our metrics extend well beyond the pro forma. We also consider many other key performance indicators such as traffic conversion, average basket, demographic profile and future projections."

[19] In brand marketing, a "halo effect" is one where the perceived positive features of a particular item extend to a broader brand.

[20] Vertically: "halo-effect" that benefits the local business.

[21] Horizontally: "halo-effect" that positively promotes global business through the international visitors and tourists who visit the store.

[22] In contrast to widely fluctuating buying patterns by consumers—both local residents and travelers—in flagship stores in mega cities, normal size stores located in medium size cities experience less volatility in consumer demand, and traditional NPV methodology works well for valuation purposes. Although RO can also be used to valuate store investment in mid-size stores, it is less necessary than it is in flagship stores.

In the following sections, we focus on case-by-case studies of investments in major flagship stores located in different countries and on different continents[23]. We first introduce Nike, Inc.[24] in order to understand the strategic rationale for investing in flagship stores. In our description of the company, we will use terminology and jargon that are germane to the industry.

From the Olympic Games to neighborhood tournaments, from professional athletes to sports amateurs, the Nike "Swoosh" is almost omnipresent. As one of the most recognized company logos, the Swoosh embodies a "Just do it" mantra that inspires millions of people to pursue their passions and dreams in sports and in life. This motto has in turn driven Nike, the company behind this logo, to grow from a $500 local business into a transnational company with a market capitalization of $161.82 billion today (up from $37.77 billion in 2010)[25] in less than half a century. Today Nike is the world's sportswear industry leader in the design, technological development and worldwide marketing of footwear, apparel, sports equipment and accessory products. Despite its current formidable size, Nike is still considered to be a "growth company"[26] by the investor

---

[23] Data may be proportionally adjusted and the individual store names and locations will be concealed for business confidentiality. During this research, we interviewed business practitioners within and outside the company. The full list is on the Acknowledgement section. In this section interviews conducted with: Tim Hershey (VP/GM Nike Retail North America); Trevor Vigfusson (CFO, Nike Global Retail); Eunan McLaughlin (President Nike Affiliates); Olivier Pennetier (NT Paris Former General Manager); Sean Ghouse (NTL General Manager); Orences Christian (former NT Chicago GM).

[24] NIKE, Inc. based near Beaverton, Oregon, is the world's leading designer, marketer and distributor of authentic athletic footwear, apparel, equipment and accessories for a wide variety of sports and fitness activities. Wholly-owned Nike subsidiaries include Cole Haan, which designs, markets and distributes luxury shoes, handbags, accessories and coats; Converse Inc., which designs, markets and distributes athletic footwear, apparel and accessories; Hurley International LLC, which designs, markets and distributes action sports and youth lifestyle footwear, apparel and accessories; and Umbro Ltd., a leading United Kingdom-based global football (soccer) brand.

[25] As of December 20, 2022, Nike's market capitalization value is $162 billion: common floating shares outstanding 1.26B at a price of $115.78. As of December 9, 2010, Nike's market capitalization value: common floating shares outstanding 397,462,000 at a price of $87.47.

[26] "Growth company" by definition, is an investment term that is used to define a company that has not yet matured, and that still has the markets to continue growing. From Nike's leadership point of view: "our power is quantifiable and our potential continues

community, largely due to its unique business model that includes balanced diversification, solid brand equity, the ability to learn, and the ability to apply that learning. Diversification and balance[27] are also ingrained in the company's sales force structure and distribution channels[28]. The diversification allows Nike to leverage and maximize its relationship with suppliers and customers. Nike does not rely heavily on any single account, manufacturer, supplier, and/or trading company. The resulting balance makes it possible for Nike to leverage economics of scale efficiently while proactively building local market responsiveness through its transnational strategy[29]. This diverse and balanced business model, together with its unmatchable R&D "family recipe" (that is, its innovation expertise[30]), has secured Nike's position as the foremost competitor in the industry.

Nike has built up and has been relentlessly strengthening its solid brand equity[31]. The company has never ceased refreshing its brand-

---

to grow." And, "Our performance has prompted one question that I hear more often than any other these days and that is simply, "How is NIKE, Inc. going to continue to grow?"… The short answer—we're going to continue to build, fuel, and accelerate the NIKE Inc. portfolio." Mark Parker, Nike Analyst Meeting on May 5th, 2010, New York.

[27] Commonly noted by Wall Street Investor Community Analysts—Nike has a diverse and balanced portfolio of products, geographic markets, consumer groups, and operation platforms.

[28] Nike has 18 sales offices in the United States, utilizing 4 independent sales representatives to sell specialty products for golf, and 2 for skating and outdoor products. Nike's United States distribution centers for footwear are located in Wilsonville, Oregon, and Memphis, Tennessee. Apparel and equipment products are shipped from distribution centers located in Memphis, Tennessee, Tigard, Oregon, and Foothill Ranch, California distribution centers. Cole Haan products are distributed primarily from Greenland, New Hampshire. Converse products are shipped from Ontario, California, and Hurley products are distributed from Irvine, California.

[29] The term "transnational Strategy" refers to a company that develops different capabilities and contributions from different countries, and shares them in integrated worldwide operations.

[30] Mark Parker, speaks at the Nike Analyst Meeting on May 5th, 2010, New York. "…innovative product. This will always be our top priority. There's a reason that we have the most advanced sports R&D lab in the world. There's a reason we have over 600 designers immersed in key sports cultures around the world."

[31] Brand Equity. The value from brand recognition. For consumers, brand equity is based on consumer attitudes towards positive brand attributes, awareness, and favorable consequences of brand use.

image[32], defining and refining its brand message, and evolving its brand personality[33]. Nike's celebrity-athlete endorsement[34] strategy and grassroots approach[35] has built solid brand loyalty[36]. Its world-class athletes[37] are unparalleled and constitute a powerful element of its competitive advantage[38].

Nike's most distinguishing features are its ability to learn and its agility to change and implement quickly. These features have enabled Nike to proactively adapt to rapid changes and evolvement[39] in the consumer and competitive marketplace, and to create new marketplace strategies before and during market changes. A good example of this was the company's restructuring of its operations to execute a new niche marketing strategy, a focus[40], primarily in running, basketball, sportswear, men's & women's training, soccer, and team sports. This broke down the conventional sportswear

---

[32] Brand Image—The consumer's perception of a brand; what people think about, feel about or expect from a brand.

[33] Brand Personality. The image or psychological profile the manufacturer intends to convey to the public as opposed to the "brand image," which refers to the consumer's perception and the image the consumer has of a brand.

[34] Details of Nike's Celebrity-athlete-endorsement timeline are in the Appendix section.

[35] Nike has impacted virtually every college and university athletics department in the country by investing more than $1 billion in colleges and universities through sports marketing, brand marketing, advertising and licensing royalties.

[36] Brand Loyalty. Two types, (1) The inclination of a consumer to buy the same brand of product or service repeatedly over time rather than buying from multiple manufacturers within a product category, and (2) The degree to which a consumer consistently purchases the same brand within a product class.

[37] Nike endorses athletes worldwide.

[38] Porter, Michael E. The Competitive Advantage of Nations (Macmillan, Free Press, London, 1990).

[39] Eunan McLaughlin, former President/Nike Affiliates, Nike, Inc., Analyst Meeting, May 5, 2010, in speaking of Affiliates Brands role in the Nike "family of brands". Mr. McLaughlin when speaking of Basketball, "It drifts into other areas across the sports culture continuum, into music, into rock and roll, into a great heritage story through the '70s and '80s of what basketball meant and the people who have worn it.

[40] Philip H. Knight, Nike's chairman, "Our philosophy is that we compete in a lot of different businesses, and one of them is the footwear business." In addition, "We are competing segment by segment, with specific products and advertising all aimed at a segment, and we think that makes us stronger as a company." Source: Harvard Business School case study. Source: New York Times, July 11, 1989, "Nike is Bounding Past Reebok."

industry Footwear-Apparel-Accessories silo view of looking and doing business.

A unique business strategy and superior product innovation built Nike's strong financial and brand equity. The experienced leadership and the widely respected co-founder & Chairman[41] keep motivating the employees and fostering a lively corporate culture. All these elements make Nike successful and contribute to its ability to sustain its success.

Nike makes changes in its corporate strategy as the company grows. One such change, which is most closely related to this study, concerns Nike's retail strategy, which consists of the strategic expansion from "Wholesale" to "Direct-to-Consumer"[42]. The company invests multiple millions of dollars in stores and infrastructure, to support both company-owned and external wholesale/retail productivity and performance. "Direct to Consumer" investments are reflective of and consistent with its broad array of ongoing strategic investments.

A clear and thorough understanding of Nike's retail strategy is fundamental to our study of investment valuation in mega-city flagship stores. The "retail strategy" actually started even before

---

[41]   Philip H. Knight, Nike's co-founder & Chairman, is widely respected within and outside the company for his ingenuity and generosity. Mr. Knight created "Future" wholesale selling 6-9 months in advance to Nike's retailer accounts; this is one of the examples of Knight's visionary ability. He started the shoe business representing Japan's Tiger shoes; foresaw the South East Asia's development, and stepped into the China market as early as the 1970's. Knight gave back to the two main inspirations that led to his tremendous success: intercollegiate athletics and postgraduate education. Knight and his wife Penny have given approximately $230 million to the University of Oregon, much of which has gone toward athletics development; an additional $100 million to the Oregon Athletics Legacy Fund.; $105 million to the Stanford Graduate School of Business; and $100 million to the Oregon Health & Science University Cancer Institute. Knight was inducted into the Oregon Sports Hall of Fame, and the university named its cancer institute the OHSU Knight Cancer Institute.

[42]   As of May 2010, Nike's "Direct-to-Consumer" scope is, "7 brands, 236 inline doors (Nike's owned retail stores, vs. Department Stores which sell Nike's products) serving 52 million customers, and those stores guide the 8,000 partner doors, 472 factory stores serving 225 million customers and 5 digital stores serving 150 million customers." And, "Direct-to-Consumer's role is in realizing the next phase of Nike brand growth through building capacity in the marketplace." Jeanne Jackson, President, Direct-to-Consumer, Nike, Inc., Nike Analyst Meeting, May 5, 2010.

Nike came to existence[43]. As the business expanded, Nike started recruiting in-house sales forces and targeting mass department stores, specialty stores, and general stores, while other businesses were busy developing catalogs or mail-order distribution sales channels. "Nike always changes the way and leads the way. We don't settle for the conventional"[44]. To further its competitive game and elevate its competitive advantage, Nike started selling products 6-9 months in advance[45]. A "futures" business model was created. This very ingenious move allowed the company to better plan manufacturing and distribution in advance. Not only could Nike guarantee its product orders to and with suppliers on favorable terms, it could also negotiate such favorable contract terms with its retailer accounts.

Initially Nike had only a few stores of its own, selling its products instead through existing retailers. Later, Nike's retail strategy was aimed at creating brand awareness by opening its own retail outlets and designing them to exemplify the brand. This strategy took place in the 1990's when athletic footwear and apparel was a fragmented retail market, in which the top ten sporting goods retailers represented 14% of total U.S. sales (Appendix Exhibit 1). While Nike sold products through these retailers, Nike-owned retail stores have more control of the products' flow, in-store presentation, and sales promotion[46].

---

[43] Nelson Farris, Communication Director, Nike, Inc, in speaking of Nike's early days, "At the very beginning when Nike was first established, it actually was the most 'direct' retailer: shoes were sold from Phil Knight's car trunk directly to the track runners." This changed as the business expanded. Nike started selling its product to consumers through retail intermediaries (sales representatives, distributors, retail partners, etc). Then in early '90, the company opened its first NikeTown in Portland Oregon.

[44] Lisa McKillips , (Executive Assistant to Mr. Phil Knight, Nike Inc.

[45] The foundation of this idea that created "futures sales in Nike" is the futures market in commodities. It is acknowledged that Phil Knight created the business model.

[46] Marshall McCauley, Nike North America Retail Planning Director, in speaking of inventory in retail, "Risk in Retail is inventory. If and when our retailers buy too much, they will markdown (put on sales) to keep down the inventory. This, in a long run, devalues the Brand. In our owned retail stores, we can plan & control the markdown, or transfer to our factory outlets when needed."

NikeTowns[47] were more a marketing and brand-building effort than a true sales channel. By creating the NikeTown stores, Nike created a high-end shopping experience different from traditional outlet stores[48]. At NikeTowns, Nike's objective is not to improve its revenue from product sales *per se*. Rather, NikeTowns represent a venue for Nike to present the full scope of the company's sports and fitness lines to customers and educate them on the value, quality, and benefits of Nike products[49].

While some customers might not make a purchase when visiting the NikeTowns, they would have "experienced" the brand and have seen the totality of its products. That experience may induce them to buy Nike products in the future, either in their home country, online or from retailers carrying Nike products. Although NikeTowns have long been recognized as "brand showrooms", they have also contributed to sales revenues as the company made the sensible investment decision to drive strategic values and commercial profitability at the same time" [50]. Retail spokesperson Claudine Leith once pointed out, "Nike has gone through a lot of changes as the brand evolves... Our NikeTowns were originally meant to *showcase* the brand, but we recognized they were selling merchandise."[51] This approach is again reiterated in 2010, by Jeanne Jackson, President Direct-to-Consumer, that, "The opening of the NikeTowns provided a stage where we could

---

[47] Niketown, according to the company's definition, is a Nike-owned retail store (vs. retail stores that sell Nike products) that normally features spacious store size (ranges from 35,000 square feet to 60,000 square feet), advanced store design, pinnacle products, and premium retail locations.

[48] Olivier Pennetier (NT Paris Former General Manager), Sean Ghouse (NTL General Manager), Orences Christian (former NT Chicago GM) all acknowledged—"people walk in flagship store have already set up the expectations: more 'personalized' customer service, VIP-type of in-store experience, and yes, they might not buy on the spot, but may very well make a subsequent purchase elsewhere.

[49] From Company website Nike.com.

[50] Tim Hershey, VP/North America Retail, Nike Inc. in speaking of the key criterion rely on to make investment decision, other than financial data, such as NPV—"Fact based decision making is critical in our investment decisions. However, our metrics extend well beyond the proforma. We also consider many other key performance indicators such as traffic conversion average basket, demographic profile and future projections."

[51] Nike spokeswoman Claudine Leith, spoke about Niketown investment for Outdoor Retail, September 2001.

for the first time showcase apparel and footwear collections together, setting an example for the marketplace."[52]

The first NikeTown, in Portland, Oregon, quickly earned numerous retail design and business awards after its opening. Following NikeTown Portland, Nike opened its second NikeTown, a 70,000-square-foot showcase, in Chicago. This store became a major tourist attraction for the city and is widely recognized as a one-of-a-kind destination. "This Store is a place to experience, to play, and to remember, not just to buy."[53] Back in its peak time, 7,500 visitors a day[54] came to see the two-story mural of Michael Jordan and try Nike shoes out on the store's miniature basketball court.

The NikeTowns enabled Nike to display the newest as well as the most innovative product lines, and simultaneously provide Nike the opportunity to strengthen ties with consumers—"whether it's gaining their insights or to inform new product innovation, assuring them access to our products in markets where we're going to expand our reach or take ownership or perhaps, most importantly, sharing with them our passion for sports."[55]. In addition, "Pinnacle Products," specialty items not available from typical retailers, can be found in NikeTowns. For example, the Michael Jordan Air Jordan retro-relaunch, was exclusively launched and sold in the Chicago store. Likewise, the customized Paris-Tee is only sold at NikeTown Paris.

Naturally, other retailers of Nike products worried that they would lose sales to NikeTown stores, but they eventually realized that the NikeTowns actually helped to boost their sales—an economic

---

52 Jeanne Jackson, President Direct-to-Consumer, Nike, Inc., Nike Analyst Meeting, May 5, 2010.

53 Allan Brabo, Nike Design Operations Director, the original design team lead, in speaking of the NTCH original designing theme., "NTCH's design guiding principle was as a 'Discovery Path'—various pavilions focus on different type of sports. The store had a 'soul'." In November 2009 during the four-day store visit, we interviewed over fifty in-store customers and long time staff—all remembered vividly the "old days" with great enthusiasm.

54 Peak period when the Chicago Bulls won NBA Championships in the 1990's, traffic has reduced to 3000-4000.

55 Jeanne Jackson, President Direct-to-Consumer, Nike, Inc., Nike Analyst Meeting, May 5, 2010.

externality known as the "halo effect". A good example of this is NikeTown London, located on Oxford Street. Retailers moved away when NikeTown London opened in Oxford Street but gradually moved back to the area when they began to realize the benefits of the halo effect as NikeTown London drew traffic and improved conversion rates[56]. This is one of the many facets of "intangible values" that are not reflected in the conventional NPV methods. "There are 'intrinsic values' that retail stores bring to the company, for example, growing the marketplace, 'eye-ball' impact boosting the demand for our products, enhancing our brand image."[57]

Over the next 10 years, Nike opened 14 more NikeTowns stores across the United States of America and the United Kingdom. In 1996, Nike opened NikeTown New York, its signature 'flagship' store located in midtown Manhattan. As of May 31, 2010 (Fiscal year 2010), the company operated the following retail outlets[58]: Interestingly, the total stores numbers haven't changed much between 2010—2022 (from 346 in 2010 to 344 in 2022. The major change is Nike Factory stores: from 145 to 209 and Nike in-line stores: 26 in 2010 to 48 in 2022 (replacing Cole Haan and Hurley stores)

Table 2: Summary of U.S. Nike Retail Stores as 2010.

U.S. Retail Stores	Number
NIKE Factory Stores	145
NIKE stores (including one NIKE Women store)	12
NikeTowns (designed to showcase NIKE products)	11
NIKE employee-only stores	3

---

[56] The conversion rate is a measure of the percentage of in-store visitors who actually make purchases while in the store, commonly used by the internet marketing and online retailers.

[57] Trevor Vigfusson, CFO, Nike Global Retail, when speaking of the retail stores adding value to the marketplace in speaking of Niketown advertisement effect, "Eyeball", is a marketing approach, aiming to reach as many people as possible (or in digital commerce, to reach as many touches as possible), often used to generate demands.

[58] Source: Nikebiz company information, 2010 Annual Report. Company's Investor Relation website. Affiliates Brands retail stores worldwide grows as the company plans to buy back Converse license in China & U.K.

U.S. Retail Stores	Number
Cole Haan stores (including factory and employee stores)	106
Converse stores (including factory and employee stores)	51
Hurley stores	18
Total	346

Figure 1: Summary of U.S. Nike Retail Stores 2009—2023

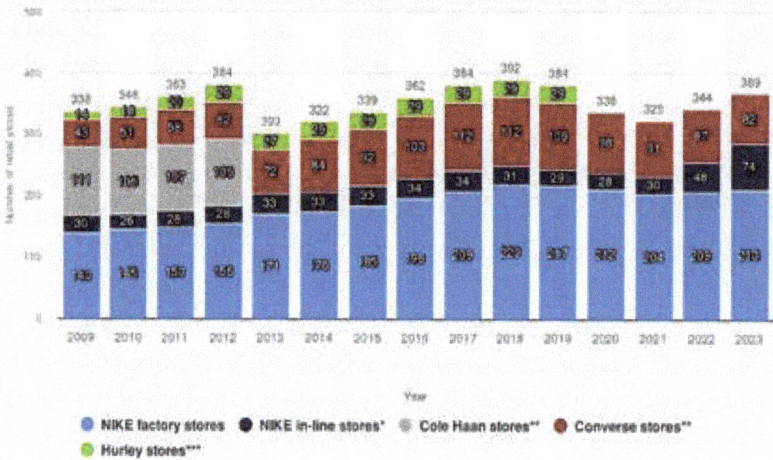

Table 3: Summary of Non-U.S. Nike Retail Stores as of Summer 2010

Non-U.S. Retail Stores	Number
NIKE factory stores	205
NIKE stores	55
NikeTowns	7
NIKE employess-only stores	12
Cole Haan stores	68
Hurley stores	1
Total	343

NikeTowns establish a dominant and compelling presence for the company in mega-cities [59] worldwide. These stores communicate the essence of Nike's spirit and energy: the "Just do it" attitude and its "If you have a body, you are an athlete" philosophy. Despite high rent in some of the key cities, the company continues opening new stores, for instance, the Tokyo flagship store opened in November 2009[60]. Further, the global presence of NikeTowns constitutes a key channel enabling full utilization of the company's "celebrity assets" in conjunction with large-scale product launches and global advertising and marketing campaigns.

Most of these flagship stores are located in the premium retail "high streets[61]" of the major cities. The stores have state-of-the-art store design and construction, well-trained and sufficient staff support, and offer pinnacle products. All these make for a superior "consumer experience[62]." NikeTown creates a self-expressive sense of belonging for consumers. Some of the self-expression examples in the store include improved personalization capabilities via NIKEiD (now called "Nike by You") and the expanded consumer ability to find and purchase product through Product Finder[63].

---

[59] A megacity is usually defined as a large city which is thickly populated region centering in a metropolis or embracing several metropolises and metropolitan areas. Source: Merriam- Webster dictionary.

[60] Tim Hershey, VP/GM North America Retail, "Tokyo is a strategic city for Nike. Its influence is certainly important on the Japan market yet extends well beyond. Additionally, to compete in Tokyo, we need to be visible, relevant and innovative. What we're bringing delivers on these expectations because of the product, the presentation, store design and overall consumer experience; like only Nike can bring."

[61] "High Street", a terminology in retail industry to distinguish from "Main Street." Jean- Philippe (Nike Director of Stores Europe), in speaking of the differences between these two: "The difference mainly resides in what composes the retailers' sales: values or volumes. sales are from luxury goods or density of traffic, accessibility or popularity.. Tokyo Ginza is an example of density of traffic drives the retail sales."

[62] A term in the retail industry denoting the experience a customer has of a product and the total service in a store or online (in digital commerce).

[63] Product Finder: one of Nike's sales tools and channels by means of which in-store customers can locate products that are not on the shelves in that Nike store. Nike stores equipped with this search tool can quickly identify whether the products are in stock and where the stock is located within Nike's stores and warehouses. Customers can place orders for the merchandise with the stores for later pick-up.

Investment in NikeTowns provides a great opportunity to apply the concept of synergy value. As in all investment analysis, when evaluating long-term investment projects, the NPV analysis is used as the basis for investment feasibility analysis and discussion. Yet, as explained earlier, although NPV may be adequate for the valuation of relatively standard retail operations with modest variability and fluctuations in performance, it is much less useful in highly volatile operations[64]. We shall analyze the company's experience in its NikeTowns investments to apply the concept of synergistic options in retail valuations.

To test the hypothesis that there are values not captured by the traditional NPV approach, we analyzed four NikeTown investments on three continents, representing various investment options[65]: expansion, delay, growth, and staging. Sensitive proprietary business information, data, and store names will be concealed in the final document[66]. All other business-related data discussed in this dissertation is from public sources.

Nike Flagship Stores—NikeTowns Analysis Synergistic Value

Values in addition to internal management projections based on traditional financial methodology have been detected by the application of the Synergistic Option Model. Can these values be

---

[64] Trevor Vigfusson, CFO, Nike Global Retail, on new retail stores "risk assessment": establishing store risk analogies and analyzing store attributes can improve risk predictability."

[65] Detailed reference see footnote in Literature Review. Here is a brief description for reference. The build option refers to most complex investments generate sequential decisions and cash outlays. The defer / delay option refers to the investments are delayed due to the internal resources limitation and/or the market (un)favorable conditions. The expansion option refers to changing operating scale, expand or contract capacity, following the evolution of the market. The option to abandon is the possibility to completely withdraw from the market and sell the facilities at their salvage value in an economically favorable environment. Divestment is considered as the Put Real Options. This application is for further research.

[66] Actual investment details may not disclose for business confidentiality. Details disclosed here is only for the purpose of this study. The final presentation of this paper may only provide partial disclosure.

explained? We propose to analyze incremental synergistic and strategic values beneficial to the company.

1) Synergistic benefits are mostly related to the brand, the company's overall global markets, and the mobility of global consumers. Such benefits constitute a form of brand enhancement value. Some consumers walk into NikeTowns and experience the "culture", almost like visiting a Nike museum. Whether they purchase anything during such visits or not, the experience reinforces their brand awareness and the memory remains, which may well trigger subsequent purchases as well as conversations with other potential customers (word of mouth advertising).

   A visitor to Nike Town London may not purchase in that store, but may purchase when at home in Frankfurt, Germany. One excellent example of the brand enhancement value attributed to these flagship stores is their impact as three-dimensional dynamic advertisements. The daily interaction of consumers in the stores that have the most modern features and the latest products and services generates an incredible impact, creating brand impression. Mostly importantly, it engages customers with a highly immersive experience. This is equivalent to Nike's engagement in, and with, a live commercial advertisement, one in which the consumer willingly and gladly participates.

2) Externality effects. These are generally associated with the upward and downward spikes or impact from the market environment or specific events. In the sportswear, this could be triggered by the results from sports events, games, or individual performances, or even the personal dramas of sports celebrities (for example, Tiger Woods' fall from grace). When sports events are occurring and/or sports celebrities are performing well, these values are positive and indeed generate a halo effect, which creates brand excitement and builds brand equity.

They are typically not included in the traditional financial valuation (NPV) because it is almost impossible to quantify their values, even though these values are widely acknowledged by management as having a significant impact the value of both the brand and the company as a whole.

The Nike flagship stores demonstrably have a halo effect that also has a positive impact on Nike's distributors. NikeTowns attract shopping traffic in and to the area and elevate the sportswear shopper conversion rate[67]. As previously mentioned, some local retailers of Nike products feared that they would lose sales to NikeTowns and moved away from the vicinity of NikeTowns, but when they recognized the benefits of the flagships stores' halo effect they moved back to the area. Halo effects are a form of synergistic value.

While managers agree that there is value beyond what is directly attributed to the project as measured by NPV, it has been difficult to measure the halo effect generated by NikeTowns. Consider the illustration mentioned above. NikeTown visitors who are tourists might be hesitant to make any purchase because of luggage space limitations. But

the experience in the NikeTown would likely to trigger a purchase later, when they return home and/or venture online. If these consumers had seen only an advertisement on TV or an Oxford street billboard instead of the in-store experience at a NikeTown, would these have the same impact as the flagship store experience? Measurement of the effect of the in-store experience on subsequent purchases elsewhere is difficult to impossible to quantify precisely.

When company-sponsored sports teams and company-sponsored sports celebrities are performing poorly during major sports events, the values generated are negative. This is considered a halo effect and it generates a negative brand image and devalues the brand. The risks associated

---

[67] A retailing term describing the percentage of walk-in customers that actually make purchases.

with teams' and/or sports celebrities' performance are unavoidable and unpredictable. In any given day, sports event results are difficult to precisely predict and, further, the conduct of individual sports celebrities is even harder to foresee.

Examples impacting sales, from disappointing game results or team performances include the University of Oregon's Rose Bowl several years ago resulted in the cancellation of the "Ducks Celebration Collection" launch and Rose Bowl-related item prices were immediately reduced. As for sports celebrities, the widely-publicized disastrous events in the personal life of Tiger Woods significantly devalued the Tiger Woods golf apparel collection and greatly damaged the brand image.

Another example of volatility and its impact on real option values can be seen in the strategic values embedded in emerging markets. In the case of NikeTown Beijing, the sportswear retail market is in a different stage of its life cycle than the sportswear retail market in megacities of more developed countries. Strategically it behooves every multinational firm to have a presence in China because of the market potential there. For sports retail multinationals like Nike, it is a highly desirable to be an early entrant in that market and to establish a showcase on the retail "high street" of China's capital city. The sportswear retail market in China is characterized as high-growth with high volatility. This volatility directly affects real option values. In our analysis of Nike Town Beijing, we adjusted the sigma variable to reflect the local market conditions in order to capture these strategic and synergistic values.

3) Contingent option values: Remodeling the NikeTown London flagship store (NTL) provided an opportunity to create and establish connections with customers in new ways. NikeiD, long available on the Web, enables consumers to custom-design their own athletic shoes. NikeiD strengthened Nike's

leading position in the personalization market[68] and enabled the company to engage directly with customers over the Internet.

Re-modeling NTL made it possible for Nike to (re) introduce NikeiD on a face-to-face basis and generate brand heat and loyalty with large numbers of global consumers, particularly during the Olympic Games in London 2008. In the NPV calculation, this strategic benefit is not reflected in the incremental revenues generated from the NikeiD studio. (NikeiD was later renamed "Nike by You".)

Three hundred meters down the road from the NikeTown London location on Oxford Street is the flagship store of one of Nike's major competitors. With three floors packed with products, it resembles a "normal" store more than a unique destination. NikeTown London, as a cultural destination, stands out among its competitors on Oxford Street.

---

[68] As of 2010, NikeiD has become one of the key features in NikeTown London. Jeanne Jackson, President Director-to-Consumer, Nike, Inc., Nike Analyst Meeting, May 5, 2010 stated, "in 1999 as consumers became enamored with e-commerce we were one of the first to recognize their desire for something personal and we launched."

London Oxford Street Scene, by the author

Contingent options create "preferential access" to the marketplace, meaning increased ease and variability of execution for the company in a market or area. The authentic store presentation and the premium consumer experience are difficult for competitors to replicate. Preferential access changes the rules of the game and raises the bar for retailers. It also helps and prompts other retailers in the area to sell Nike products. These incremental sales, driven by NikeTown London, belong to the other retailers. Although those retail partner sales generate value for Nike, that value is not captured or reflected by Net Pricing Value methodology.

4) Impact on Resource Allocation Decisions: Every company's leadership team is constantly presented with investment choices, and Nike is no exception. Resources are finite, and management must select from among competing investment alternatives. NPV is often helpful in making such resource allocation decisions, particularly for decisions about investments with little or no strategic value. For investment alternatives with perceived strategic value, NPV remains a

useful tool for evaluating direct financial returns from the investment. There are, however, some occasions in which NPV is of limited utility. For example, competing alternatives may have similar NPV's, or an investment opportunity may have a negative NPV. Without the Synergistic Option Model, management must rely on its "gut feeling" to make its decision. In both cases, however, SOM can offer management a tool that offers guidance that NPV cannot: it can provide a quantification of the strategic values associated with the competing investments, supplementing the financial returns quantified by NPV.

5) Shareholder value return. Guidance regarding how much value strategic investments can bring to the shareholders is extremely valuable to management. As we have seen, the significant investment in the NikeTown London store renovation may generate a negative NPV; however, the strategic value of having a world-class flagship store in a mega-city with recent Olympic Games engagement goes beyond the investment-specific financial returns measured by NPV. Former Nike CEO Mark Parker pointed out the company's growth strategy, saying "The third fuel for our portfolio is the amazing experiences that we create whether it's for consumers, for media, for athletes and hopefully investors. We did it in the Forbidden City when we launched our Beijing Olympics product... and with our World Cup innovation summit just recently in London."

6) Learning—The examination of the historical experience of NikeTown investments: The knowledge and expertise gained in remodeling NikeTowns can be leveraged in similar investments (such as remodeling NT Paris and/or opening a new NT in Olympics venues).

7) NikeTown investments therefore provide an excellent opportunity which allows us to examine the application of the synergistic options concept in retail valuations.

The four cases in the following section represent four types of applications:

- NikeTown London (abbreviated as NTL)—Expansion Option

- NikeTown Paris (abbreviated as NTP)—Growth Option

- NikeTown Chicago (abbreviated as NTC)—Delay Option

- NikeTown Beijing (abbreviated as NTB)—Staging investment options (in which investments generate sequential decisions)

Each of the case studies are discussed in Section 7.

5. Analysis & Analytics

Sportswear industry

We believe the Synergistic Option Model can and should be applied effectively in sportswear investment. Why? We conclude that the sportswear industry has characteristics similar to those commonly seen in high risk investments with volatility influenced by multiple sources. These sources include rapid changes in consumer consumption preferences, employment situations, and disposable income levels.

The sports industry is a multidimensional mega-business, one segment of which is sportswear. The extreme loyalty of sports fans to their teams transfers to the teams' sportswear providers, which in turn transforms into loyalty to the brand. Similarly, the success or failure, or glory or disgrace, of individual sports stars, who endorse one sportswear brand or another, can make a difference of millions of dollars in sales of associated apparel. To sports fans, sportswear has become a declaration of support for their team and its actual or potential achievements. Further, sportswear has also become casual wear and a preferred means of consumers' individual expression.

The sportswear industry is a relatively new industry that first separated from general apparel and footwear and emerged as a new sector. This industry in fact evolved as Nike grew: the company literally created a new industry and this industry, in turn, shaped Nike. Since its emergence, the sportswear industry has been evolving rapidly. Its distinguishing characteristics include a close linkage to sports events and phenomena, such as sporting events and sports celebrities. This strong connection introduces a much more volatile profitability pattern than that which is characteristic of the general apparel or footwear industry. The return fluctuates dramatically upward and downward in reaction to external events in the sports world.

From BSOPM to RO to SOM

The Black Scholes Option Pricing Model (BSOPM) was created to accurately value publicly traded financial options. Prior to the creation of this model, setting a price for the purchase and sale of stock options were a risky and uncertain endeavor; after the BSOPM became an accepted financial analytical tool, stock options became routinely traded at prices deemed by both parties to be valid and reasonable. Later, Dr. Stewart Myers extended the BSOPM to the valuation of "real assets", referring to non-tradeable, non-liquid assets that have high investment/high risk-return characteristics in the corporate finance sector. Some of the examples are to-be-developed pharmaceuticals, to-be-exploited mining spots, etc. In the previous sections, we introduced the Synergistic Options concept and its application in the high investment & high risk/return industries, such as these. In this book, we use the Black Scholes Option Pricing Model (BSOPM) to measure and capture the "Synergistic Value" of high investment & high risk/return investments in the sportswear industry. We will test the proposition that the Synergistic Options Model complements traditional NPV analysis, by examining four Nike flagship stores (called "NikeTowns") located in dispersed geographic markets. The application of synergistic options methodology to investment decision-making enables detection of value-adding aspects of a company's real investments that the NPV approach does not normally capture—Synergistic Value.

Synergistic Value cannot be not traded and thus assertions of value creation in excess of those identified by the NPV analysis cannot be directly tested. Following Jensen[69], we adopted a deductive approach to hypothesis testing to account for the difficulty in directly testing SOM.

---

[69] Jensen, M. Organization Theory and Methodology, Accounting Review, April 1983, v. LVIII, No. 2, pp. 319-339).

Why Nike Flagship Stores?

In a sophisticated business marketplace, particularly in high investment/high risk-return industries where the inter-complexities & intra-complexities in the marketplace generate a multi-dimensional risk-reward relationship, the real returns of strategic investments is comprised of multidimensional kinds of values, some of which are non-financial. Such strategic benefits may be very hard to quantify. For instance, brand equity is a key strategic value, but one that is very difficult to quantify by precise financial numbers or to detect through standard capital budgeting methods. In the sportswear industry, one of the key channels for generating and expanding brand equity is the flagship store—a primary venue and focal point for building and nurturing strong relationships with consumers. Most flagship retail stores are located in mega-cities, where store profitability is closely affected by and correlated to fluctuations in the macroeconomic environment.

The original dissertation study examined four flagship stores located in widely dispersed geographic markets where each is influenced by different global and local macro- and micro-economic conditions such as consumer preferences and local currency and capital market risks.

The case studies have common characteristics: all flagship stores are located in pre-eminent international cities and all are strategically valuable to the company's long term value appreciation: they build brand equity, enhance brand value, and deepen consumer relationships. While it is understood that these flagship stores have significant strategic value to the company and the management has felt it right to make the investments, there has not been any way to measure the accuracy of management's feeling about the rightness of the decisions or to quantify different types of strategic values. As a consequence, it has been difficult to compare the value of these entities with each other. This research suggests that SOM can be used to capture some, if not all, of these values.

These four case studies represent four types of application: expansion, growth, delays, and staging. The flagship stores in our study had negative or modest NPVs. Using the same financial data and lease term, we derive positive SOM values in all four cases[70]. This suggests that SOM captures certain embedded values not reflected by the NPV method. In each case, we compared and analyzed the NPV and SOM results. We further demonstrated that these embedded values may be intangible in financial terms, but the benefits are discernible strategically. After years of operations, these flagship stores continue to deliver "strategic values" such as increasing brand awareness during the Beijing and London Olympics, enhancing the Nike retail presentation in France and Europe, and taking the lead in creating and developing methods for deepening consumer relationships (such as NikeiD Studio[71]). These intangible contributions do increase the value of the firm, over and above the financial returns specific to each store, in improved strategic return to the firm as a whole.

These cases indicate that flagship store investments have embedded strategic values, and that the intuition of the management of Nike regarding these investments has been correct.

Further, the SOM can be used to compare the visible return and synergy value of flagship stores. This will enable decision-makers to allocate resources to the store that generates the most financial return and synergistic value (strategic value, brand value, etc.).

Using the company's internal, proprietary, and historical investment analysis data to illustrate applications, we find that the results of our study of the four cases of Nike's investments in NikeTowns London, Paris, Chicago, and Beijing are consistent with our usage of the Synergistic Option Model, and, therefore, our stated hypothesis. These case studies serve as evidence of the evolution of our understanding and application of the synergistic options concept. This is summarized in Table 19 (each of the case studies is discussed in Section 7).

---

[70] Except in NikeTown Chicago where the investment is delayed. Although both RO with and without delay are positive, we note the difference of these two scenarios SOM's indicates "opportunistic loss" to the company.

[71] NikeiD, the web-based athletic shoe customization platform, greatly strengthens Nike's leading position in the personalization market. Now renamed "Nike by you".

Table 19: NikeTown Case Study Results Summary

Store	Open Date	Type	NPV	SOM Scenario I	Scenario II	NPV 2	SOM Scenario 2
London	07/17/1990	Expansion	$4,468	$6,072	2nd Sigma	N/A	$7,220
Paris	11/25/2005	Growth	$2,320	$2,129	N/A	N/A	N/A
Chicago	07/02/1992	Delay	$2,531	$3,871	No Delay	$7,349	$19,493
Beijing	08/01/2007	Stage	$1,612	$2,062	2nd Stage	$1,254	$1,702

Investments in NikeTowns are well-suited for SOM testing. NikeTowns are not envisioned as separate profit centers by the company. Rather, the flagship stores were and still are meant to creatively showcase the best of the company's innovative products and to generate excitement and emotional ties between the brand and store visitors and area consumers. NikeTowns promote the brand and the company's array of products in dramatic and distinctive ways. In contrast to the company's other retail shops, which are envisioned as standalone profit centers that are properly evaluated in terms of sales of products on the premises, which are captured by standard accounting methods, the value that a flagship store creates for the company is more widespread.

As has been previously discussed, the halo effect and other strategic values generated by a flagship store are not reflected in or by the cash flow directly generated by the particular NikeTown being evaluated. From this perspective, the traditional incremental investment analysis of NPV is limiting, and NPV and other standard accounting measures are likely inadequate tools to evaluate NikeTown investments. The standard tools do not fully address the purpose of the investment. If used, it must be supplemented to account for the positive side effects that are not easily measured.

The Synergistic Option Model can provide, at least partially, one measurement of the value created by a flagship store above and beyond the revenues generated directly from the store premises. This is demonstrated in the sportswear industry by the results of the four case studies. Two of the four cases examined had negative NPV's, and one had a small positive NPV. However, these cases all have positive SOM (Synergistic Option Model) values. When these values are considered in the decision making process, the investments became more attractive and can be better compared with each other and with alternative investments. In the NikeTown Chicago's case, had the difference in SOM due to the delay been evaluated, the impact of delay is not only from the financial aspect, but also from the strategic value such as contingent business opportunity loss.

These results suggest that management should find it useful to utilize SOM analysis in future investment evaluations where it is intuitively obvious that the beneficial effects extend beyond the marginal investment in question, as is the case with the NikeTown flagship stores.

6. Significance of This Research

The primary significance of this research is to provide additional empirical evidence that the use of the Synergistic Options Model (SOM) to supplement traditional Net Pricing Value improves investment evaluation in High Investment/High Risk-Reward (HI/HRR) industries, in this case the sportswear industry. The research uses actual real data of four case studies of investments in NikeTowns. The result speaks for itself: while all four valuation results from the conventional net pricing method (NPV) are negative, the SOM results are positive. In the years after of the original valuations were made, when the actual results are compared to the pro forma projections, they validate SOM results. This verifies that the Synergistic Options Model (SOM) captures values that are beyond that which the traditional accounting methods could reveal. The sales from these NikeTowns in later years proved the investments were worthwhile in many ways.

This leads to the conclusion that that Synergistic Options Model (SOM) should be used together with NPV in the valuation of High Investment & High Risk-Return industry investments. Further, it seems a reasonable conclusion that SOM should become part of the standard capital budgeting analysis in corporate finance, particularly in High Investment & High Risk-Return industries.

Although SOM is still new and has not yet been widely accepted by the majority of finance academicians and practitioners, the results of the present study suggest that the Synergistic Options Model (SOM) should and will become more acceptable and necessary. This is to avoid possible missing-out opportunities and/or misallocation of resources. In part, this is due to the increasing pace of technological advancement, globalization, and competition that contributes to increased growth and volatility.

The real investments of the sports apparel industry's leading multinational corporation, Nike, Inc., in its flagship stores, upholds our hypothesis that there are real option values not captured by the application of the NPV methodology. We are pleased to make a modest contribution by demonstrating how Synergistic Options Model (SOM) complements NPV. By applying the Synergistic Options Model (SOM) methodology to the four Nike Town investment cases, we also learned about the corporate vision of its co-founder, studied a segment of the company's investment history regarding NikeTowns, and helped to demystify the growth of a dynamic company that founded the sports retail industry.

Nike's co-founder and Chairman, Mr. Philip Knight served as an external advisor to this study and supported my endeavor to pursue innovating valuation. Many Nike leaders at all levels offered their insights in this study. These demonstrates that leadership and the Company continually seeks new ways to evaluate investments in order to improve resource allocation—how to justify the "gut feeling" decision-making thought process.

Perhaps the most important contribution of this study is to reinforce with case study illustrations the counterintuitive inverse relationship between the discount rate used and the real option value. It is axiomatic that risk and reward are positively correlated in the business world. A high-return investment normally comes with correspondingly high risks. NPV values, however, are inversely related to the degree of risk posed by a potential investment because the risk is represented in the form of a higher discount rate, the weighted cost of capital (WACC), or alternatively using a form of risk-adjusted cash flow projections. In the Real Option methodology, on the other hand, the degree of investment risk and the Synergistic Options Model (SOM) values move in the same direction. The higher the risk, measured by the variance of the appropriately selected underlying asset's rate of return, the greater the value of the real option, and if this real option value is taken into account, it somewhat mitigates the risk adjustments that tend to reduce NPV.

Managers take calculated risks by undertaking investments and increased operating costs because they believe that the future rewards are worthwhile. These can be investments designed to enhance brand equity and/or actions taken to strengthen relationships with consumers. In some cases, these activities lead to short term profitability that is directly attributable to the investment. In other cases, these activities generate value in ways that are less directly traceable to these investments such as synergistic and strategic returns that add to the immediate and directly traceable financial returns. As demonstrated in this study, NPV alone cannot be expected to capture all these values.

Future Research

Complementary valuation method in corporate finance.

When academia initially introduced NPV, it was met with great resistance, because traditional analyses used accounting investment return like ROI (return on investment) or ROIC (return on invested capital). Today, the NPV method is the most common tool used by firms.

The most challenging research, however, is to develop ways to empirically validate the synergistic option value, as financial option prices are validated and real options are validating-in-process. We expect the evidence from case studies and empirical studies to eventually overcome resistance to the viability of the NPV + SOM approach.

Exploring SOM application to abandonment option

The rationale behind the abandonment option is that a firm could scale back or curtail an existing project if that project is not earning a sufficient return. Ronald Fink (2001) argues that companies may not have the built-in internal discipline to discard, abandon, or close down a project in a timely fashion when the initial investment that generated the real option values have not been realized. In terms of the options concept, there is no expiration date, and the project's potential downside risk is not zero. An interesting further study would be to test the application of Synergistic Options Model (SOM) to evaluate potential abandonment cases such as closing existing non-profitable investments. It is anticipated that the SOM "put" formula would prove to be useful in such analyses.

It is anticipated that future research will demonstrate that the method can also be applied to the retail industry in general, not only to sportswear. Synergistic Option Model can be expected to generate additional research in a number of other areas, including the determination of whether Synergistic Options Model (SOM) can be applied in situations where investments are expected to have short-term profitability but no or even negative long-term strategic benefits to the firm's value. Another potential research avenue is the determination of whether SOM value can be broken down into strategic value propositions such as brand development, consumer experience elevation, and/or customer segmentation enhancement.

Further potential areas of SOM application include the practice of paying premiums above market price—and sometimes exceedingly high premiums—to acquire controlling interests in companies. Investors, hedge funds, and raiders may use calculated real option values to calculate over-market bids. For example, SOM can assist in the benign or hostile takeover bid for investor/raider such as Carl Icahn, Another area for further research involves leases with options to buy real assets: the pricing of the lease that includes an option to buy may be an area to investigate.

The challenge in real asset investment valuation is to assess both financial and synergistic returns. NPV's primary purpose is to capture the financial returns. The SOM approach takes historical volatility measures and generates a value that investors should consider as reflecting at least part of the embedded intangible values embedded that have some probability of generating financial and/or strategic values in the future.

Dr. Robert Merton said to me, "Every model is an abstraction and simplification of complex reality and hence the result is only the approximation." I fully agree with that statement. Math is precise but the model is not. Although the model is mathematically precise, the model is only an approximation of reality. So the issue becomes how good the approximation is: whether it can generate an answer that will lead us to the right decision? How reliable is the result? That depends on various elements, including whether intelligent assumptions underlie the model, its variables, its parameters, and its sources.

The traditional valuation methods, predominately Net Pricing Value, rely on a linear relationship among inputs. It assumes that other projects are independent and irrelevant to its functioning. It uses a discount rate that in theory captures market risks. Whiles Synergistic Option Model uses BSOPM—it puts variables put into a normal distribution to derive the most appropriate probability to be "in the money" (hence to reduce the risk exposure) while using a separate variable (in addition to the discount rate used to calculate the present value of cash flows), sigma to capture the company's and the market's volatility.

In conclusion, the Synergistic Option Model effectively supplements Net Pricing Value calculation by unveiling the embedded synergistic values associated with externality effects, contingent options, and strategic values.

7.   Case Studies

Data are kept as original during the period the data was collected.
Some narratives are updated with recent changes.

Investments in NikeTowns provide a great opportunity to apply the concept of synergistic options. As in all investment analysis, when evaluating long-term investment projects, the NPV analysis normally is used as the base for investment feasibility. Yet, as explained earlier, although NPV is adequate for the valuation of relatively standard retail operations with modest variability and fluctuations in performance, it is much less useful in highly volatile operations. In highly volatile industries where investment return is closely related to both the internal and external environments on multidimensional levels, the investment uncertainty warrants the use of a higher discount rate analysis. Yet, the uncertainty increased the investment real option value requiring a complementary adjustment to the NPV.

7.1   Case—NikeTown London (NTL)

We will start with the biggest NikeTowns in the world: NTL. This is a "Expansion" Synergistic Options Model application. We begin with a brief introduction of the U.K. macroeconomic and retail environment.

NikeTown London, by the author

NikeTown London, by the author

7.1.1 The U.K. macro-economic & sportswear retail environment[72].

In 2009, U.K. retail sales rose 4.2% on a like-for-like basis from December 2008, when sales had dropped 3.3% due to turmoil in

---

[72] For the purpose of this study—NTL remodeling is during 2008-2009, we use the

financial markets that dampened consumer confidence. Retailing in the U.K. is both mature and competitive. The U.K. shoppers comprise both domestic and Continental Europeans, as well as international visitors from all parts of the world. There is more land dedicated to retail use in the U.K. than in any other European country. The total volume of annual retail sales has been increasing over many years, and despite recent declines in the rate of increase, retailers and consumers remain broadly optimistic about retailing activity in the country.

U.K. retail environments are a mix of city centre, high streets, and shopping malls. The most popular shopping regions and cities are London, Manchester, Birmingham, and Newcastle. Retail rents have seen marked growth in recent years, matched by similar growth in consumer spending. Many international brands have been keen to explore the U.K. as a new retail opportunity and have been aggressively opening stores.

7.1.2 The London macro-economic & retail demographic environment[73].

London, the capital of the U.K., is the one of the most famous cities in the world. London currently has over 40,085 retail units. It is the largest city in Europe, with a population of 7,465,100 people. Retail sales in London were estimated at around £52 billion in 2008, which was 19% of total U.K. retail sales. Over £4.5 billion is spent in the West End[74] alone, making it the U.K.'s top retail centre. London's overall Gross Value Added totaled £205 billion in 2007, 17% of the U.K.'s GVA. Seven percent of London's GVA came from retail, amounting to an estimated £13 billion in 2006. Retail and wholesale (including motor trades) was the third largest contributor to the London economy after real estate, renting and business activities,

---

2008- 2009 data for U.K. economy and retail macro economy analysis.

[73] For the purpose of this study—NTL remodeling is during 2008-2009, we use the 2008- 2009 data for London's economy and retail macro economy analysis.

[74] The West End is regarded as the "high street" retail shopping area in London and the United Kingdom.

and financial intermediation. Retail alone (excluding wholesales) is the sixth largest contributor to the London economy.

As one of the top premium shopping destinations, London is almost a mandatory location for global companies. As a leading fashion city and luxury destination, it attracts international brands such as Gucci, Cartier, Louis Vuitton, Prada, MaxMara, and Donna Karan, among others. Niketown London (herafter "NTL") thus is, and should be, the premier stage for presentation of the Nike brand. How the store represents the Nike brand is of critical importance, especially as the London 2012 Olympics is approaching.

NTL is located in Oxford Circus, one of the premium retail "high streets" in the world. It has approximately 200 million annual visitors, half of whom are single-sided walkers, while an additional 25% are cross walkers[75]. NTL is located in this premium location with great potential to grow financially and strategically[76].

7.1.3 Details of NTL remodeling investment.

Since its opening in 1998, NTL has been the premier Nike retail frontier representing the Nike brand not only to local residents and retailers but even more so to international visitors and tourists. To many, it has become Nike's showroom. After several years of operation, however, the store began to show signs of ageing and needed renovation. Moreover, in 2005 London won the right to host the largest sports event in the world—the 2012 Summer Olympics. This created a valuable opportunity for the company to remodel NTL at the constructional level[77] and to then re-launch the store as the pre-eminent retail space in London, the U.K., Europe and, indeed

---

[75] Single-sided walkers & cross-sides walkers are variables used in the calculation or estimation of retail stores' potential walk-in traffic.

[76] Stores of Nike's retailer partners and major competitors' competitors are also located on Oxford Street.

[77] The "constructional level" of renovation is a term used to describe the scope of renovation. "Floor level", or "partition level" renovation is intended to reset the floor only and could be completed in as little as a week, or even overnight, without closing the store. "Constructional level" renovation, on the other hand, would require closing the store partially or completely during portions of the construction.

the world. The space would highlight core categories, utilizing the existing space better and facilitating premium service to consumers. Nike's willingness to invest substantial resources in the remodeling reflects the Company's long-term vision, which is to deliver solid value to customers and to build brand loyalty through inspirational values that go beyond products' functionality. Nike intends that the enhancement of the store will give the brand significant exposure during the Olympics, while also generating an increase in sales.

The remodeling and refitting project was divided into working first on the ground floor and first floor, and then on the second floor and third floors. While the construction activities were being undertaken, NTL continued with its day to day business. Work on the ground floor and first floors was completed in 2008.

The reconstruction of the lowest two floors was focused on building an atrium in the center of the store from the ground floor up to the second floor. The atrium is where the NIKEiD Studio is located. This is a luxury appointment space, hosted by a Studio Concierge and situated on both the 1st and 2nd floors of a glass and steel cube suspended in the center of the store. Within this space there are four Apple Mac Stations staffed by a team of creative individuals. Consumers can set up an appointment to go in and design shoes of their liking with the assistance of Nike staff. This unique customization program enables an individual footwear statement that will stand out from the crowd. Since its opening on November 8, 2007, NIKEiD Studio has been very popular in London among both local residents and visitors from around the world.

Another major part of the renovated store is the BootRoom, which is dedicated to football (also known as soccer) gear. Since its opening on July 6, 2008, the BootRoom has generated a strong buzz in London. In its first month of operation, the BootRoom achieved 120% of its actual sales budget[78] (£X X actual sales vs £XX budgeted sales), which was a tremendous achievement given the "soft launch"[79]

---

[78] The Company's internal sales target undisclosed.

[79] Unlike a "Full Launch", which occurs during the reopening of a store to the public after closure for renovations, soft launch involves unveiling a new product or service

of the department. The BootRoom has two types of services that are unconventional—indeed, unparalleled—within the industry: ID service and Team Customization[80]. When the services were promoted effectively within the football community, sales of football related products increased—and so did sales throughout the entire store. This sales improvement is primarily from the additional in-store traffic drawn by the BootRoom and an improved conversion rate[81], which equates to success in both "brand experience" and financial return.

At the time when the NTL case was being considered as a demonstration of the synergistic options model for this dissertation, the ground floor and first floor renovations had already been completed. We then focused on the investment to build up the second and third floors. The investment required for the modern restoration and installation of state of the art store fixtures in a mega city center like London is very high[82]. We examined information taken from proprietary internal working documents regarding completion of the second and third floors of the NTL remodeling project. Based upon projected cash flows over a ten year horizon, discounted by a weighted average cost of capital (WACC) of 12%[83], we determined that the projected NPV for that part of the project was negative $4.47 million[84]. As shown in Table 4, the construction cost is estimated to

---

while construction work is still ongoing within a store.

[80] Team Customization: customers can have their favorite team names sewn on the replica tees purchased.

[81] Retail terminology, see footnotes in Section III.
(Retail Store) Traffic—the shoppers that arrive in the stores every day.
The conversion rate is derived from internet marketing and online retailers, and is a measure of the percentage of in-store visitors who actually make purchases while in the store.

[82] The investments here refer to the investment in renovating.

[83] This WACC rate is commonly used for similar investments by the company.

[84] We note that the computation does not consider adjustments in the WACC for local area investment risk including currency. We further note that there is also no adjustments for high growth as recommended by Antonio Bernardo and Bhagwan Chowdhry, "Growth Options, Beta, and the Cost of Capital", Financial Management, Summer 2007, Pg 5-17. They propose adjustment to the cost of capital for growth industries by 2-3%. However, their recommended adjustment may not cover all aspects of the external effects of an investment project.

be $17.45 million in present value terms where cash outflows are discounted by a risk free rate of 5% as these outflows are contracted and certain, and the uncertain projected cash flows is $12.98 million.

Table 4: NPV Calculation for NTL (USD Millions)

Total Investment (Construction & Fit-up Cost) PV of Projected Cash Flows	$ $	(17.45) 12.98
NPV	$	**(4.47)**[85]

Intuitively, senior management believed that there are additional strategic values associated with completing the build out or renovation that are not reflected in the NPV result, and based upon that intuitive belief it decided to go ahead with the project. *Ex post facto*, we believe that the decision to complete the renovation presents an opportunity apply the synergistic options approach to ascertain whether that approach may capture some of the intuitive values sensed by senior management but not reflected in the NPV calculation.

7.1.4 Application of Synergistic Options Model to NTL.

The table below shows the values of the six variables required to calculate the call option value of the investment in NTL. The value of the primary sigma is the standard deviation of the change in the end of quarter Nike stock closing price. On an annualized basis, the standard deviation of sigma is 33.8%. Applying these values to Equation (2), we arrive at the call option value of $6.07 million.

---

[85] As the lease term is longer than the cash flow projection, we include the last year's cash flow as a growth annuity.

Table 5: Inputs for Option Valuation Variables in NTL Calculation—Std. Dev. of Nike Stock

(S): Present value of underlying asset—the present value of cash flows expected from the investment opportunity.	$12.98	USD Millions
(X): the option strike price—The present value of total committed investment	$17.45	USD Millions
(r): risk-free rate	5%	
(t): the period for which the investment opportunity is valid	10	Lease Term
(σ): Sigma—the standard deviation of the company stock price rate of change, annualized.	33.8%	Annualized Std Dev of Nike Stock Price quarterly rate of change, 1995-2010
(δ): Dividend payouts—when applicable cost of delay—Annual cost of delay 1/n	0.00%	No delay in this re-launch model
C: Call Option Value RO_1	$6.07	USD Millions

We further include a secondary estimate of sigma by taking into consideration the quarterly sales of NTL in Table 6. The correlation between quarterly changes in NTL sales and Nike quarterly stock price changes for the period 2003-2008 is 0.61. With only 20 quarters of NTL sales data since its inception, and the comparatively small NTL sales compared to total Nike sales, we are cautious about making inferences about the results. We present this only as a secondary calculation in an attempt to use data at the source of real investment activity, and also to demonstrate the power of the variable sigma in the computation of the value of the real option. The annualized standard deviation is 43.4%.

Table 6: Inputs for Option Valuation Variables in NTL Calculation—Std. Dev. NTL Sales

(S): Present value of underlying asset—the present value of cash flows expected from the investment opportunity.	$12.98	USD Millions
(X): the option strike price—The present value of total committed investment	$17.45	USD Millions
(r): risk-free rate	5%	
(t): the period for which the investment opportunity is valid	10	Lease Term
(σ): Sigma—the standard deviation of the company stock price rate of change, annualized.	43.3%	Annualized Std_Dev NTL Qty Sales changes, 2003-2008
(δ): Dividend payouts—when applicable cost of delay—Annual cost of delay 1/n	0.00%	No delay in this re-launch model
C: Call Option Value RO_1	$7.22	USD Millions

The above results highlight the limitation of commonly used method of evaluating investment decisions. The conventional NPV is negative $4.47 million. However, that computation ignores the possibility that the investment has an embedded option, and according to our calculation, the real option value is either $6.07 million as in RO_1[86] or $7.22 million as in RO_2. In any case, the real option value is significant and positive.

---

[86] Sigma defined as the standard deviation of the Nike stock price.

7.1.5 NTL concluding remarks & actual results after the remodeling.

We have elaborated the rationale behind the SOM application in NTL. The results demonstrate that the synergistic options value increases with increased flexibility and with increased risk associated with the underlying real asset investment. The NPV methodology's stringent application of a single discount rate to capture all the dynamics and risk in the markets[87] constricts decision makers within a limited framework. This limited lens has been demonstrated as insufficient in the High Investment & High Risk-Return industries and might cause the firm to misallocate resources if the NPV is relied upon as the sole indicator of investment valuation. It is especially true when companies use one standard cost of capital for all investment projects in order to compare investment returns despite the differences in investment risk.[88]

Following completion of the renovation, NTL reopened on November 8, 2010. The store has been expanded from three to four floors with services and ground-breaking shopping experiences that distinguish NTL from other retail stores.

The following are some examples: 1. two-floor NIKEiD studio (and football boot-specific iD studio) enabling consumers to go online to design and customize their own footwear, clothing and equipment, assisted by Nike design consultants at NTL. 2. Boot fitting: allowing players the chance to steam would boots to their feet. 3. Boot embroidery service, allowing names, flags and numbers to be stitched onto football boots. 4. An online kit-builder tool for football teams to customize their own kits, along with a shirt printing and numbering service. 5. Video gait analysis and trained staff to help runners to work out exactly what type of shoe suits their running style.

Its re-launch was well received and reported by the media[89]: "NikeTown London, located in Oxford Circus, has acquired iconic

---

[87] Markets here refer to both business commodity markets and investment capital markets.

[88] Bernardo, et. al. Op. cit.

[89] Wall Street Journey, November 8,2010, Niketown London Unveiled as the World's

status with Londoners and visitors alike since it opened as one of the first brand retail experiences in 1999. NikeTown London now covers approximately 42,000 square feet over four floors. Its reopening forms part of a series of planned new store openings across the U.K. designed to provide a premium experience across the company & across key sports categories."

7.2 Case—NikeTown Paris (NTP)

We continue the case with NikeTown Paris (NTP). This is a "Growth" SOM application. We begin with a brief introduction of the France macroeconomic and retail environment.

largest Nike Store Following Striking New Redesign.

NikeTown London, by the author

7.2.1 The French macro-economic & sportswear retail environment.

France is universally known as a leader and predominant presence in the fashion industry. The country, with its well-known culture, history, heritage[90] and landscape, is one of the great tourist[91] destinations in the world. It is also one of the most popular global shopping destinations, with approximately 12 million square meters of retail space, nearly 212 square meters for every person in the country[92]. Further, France is a key economic center in Europe[93].

France has been an attractive market for sportswear retailers due to its leading position in the fashion world, its strong consumer

---

[90] France was one of the earliest countries to progress from feudalism to the nation-state. France was the dominant power in Europe. Source: US Department of State.

[91] 2010 total tourist arrival: 67,310,000. Source: United Nations World Statistics Pocketbook and Statistical Yearbook.

[92] France total country area: 551,670 sq. km. (220,668 sq. mi.); largest west European country

[93] GDP (2009): $2.66 trillion. Avg. annual growth rate (2009): -2.5%, compared with 0.1% in 2008. Per capita GDP at PPP (2009): $33,678

spending profile, and its great popularity among domestic and international tourists. The French and many international visitors to France live active life styles, and the resulting demand for sportswear is well reflected by the size of its sportswear market[94]. Nike has been one of the most dominant sportswear Brands in France; however, starting in 2003, the company's sales growth in the French market has been under significant pressure from aggressive competitors. The company identified several areas in which it had been underperforming, which included relatively low brand exposure compared to competitors' brands; limited owned distribution in shopping malls; and low distribution through chain stores.

The company's market and internal analyses led it to the decision to increase the number of its owned retail stores in order to gain market share in both its traditional footwear segment and in the rapidly growing apparel segment. It also concluded that a fully- integrated and controlled retail flagship store in France could boost brand exposure dramatically. Such a store would, in turn, boost additional sales in company-owned retail outlets while simultaneously stimulating additional demand for the company's products in chain stores.

In order to identify the best store location, the segmentation of the French sportswear market is studies. From various internal and public analysis, the main finding is that French sportswear market is concentrated primarily in high income large cities. The in-depth analysis of over thirty cities in France is conducted to determine the ideal location for its French flagship store. Some of its findings are summarized in the following table.

---

[94] NPD 2008 data: The French sportswear market size is ranked third in Europe, after the U.K. and Germany.

Table 7: City Analysis—France

City	Size, Region	Size, City	Income, City	Income, Region	Characteristics
Paris	1	2	1	1	Top European city
Paris outer	1	1	2	1	Top European city
Marseille	3	3	22	24	Large city, but lower income.
Lyon	5	4	4	3	Large city.
Toulouse	9	5	15	8	Large city, but lower income.
Nice	7	6	13	9	Large city
Nantes	11	7	6	7	Medium size city, high income
Strasbourg	13	8	9	12	Medium size city, high income
Montpellier	20	9	29	26	Medium size city
Bordeaux	10	10	8	13	Attractive income, population
Rennes	21	12	10	6	Attractive income, population
Lille	6	11	27	20	Large region, attractive population
Saint-Etienne	19	15	25	29	Working-class town
Grenoble	14	17	16	4	Outdoor city
Dijon	25	19	7	11	Attractive population
Brest	28	20	24	17	Marine city

City	Size, Region	Size, City	Income, City	Income, Region	Characteristics
Ferrand	23	22	23	15	Regional capital
Aix-En-Provence	3	23	3	24	University town
Tours	18	24	17	14	Traditional town
Metz	17	25	18	27	Commercially attractive
Orleans	22	26	12	5	Regional capital
Rouen	15	27	21	21	Attractive population
Nancy	16	28	11	16	Attractive population
Cannes/ Frejus	7	29	5	9	Small city, but Tourist center
Angers	26	18	20	19	Small region
Le Havre	24	13	28	28	Small region, unattractive
Le Mans	29	21	14	18	Small region
Reims	27	14	19	23	Small region
Toulon	12	16	26	22	Unattractive income, age, employ

Source: Deloitte Consulting, September 2008

Considering both income and influence of the cities, Paris and its outer Paris clearly stand out as the Number 1 ranking in terms of city and regional size and income. However the retail rent is significantly higher than any other cities. This factor makes other top three cities are also potential sites for store location. In order to identify the best store location, the company studied the segmentation of the French sportswear market. It found that five cities account for 22% of the

Euro 1.2 billion potential Footwear & Apparel market opportunity in France's total Footwear & Apparel market. Greater Paris alone already accounts for 14.2% of the total market. Another detailed demographic analysis is conducted to look into the spending power and retail selling price point.

According to a Deloitte Consulting demographic analysis[95], consumers at retail stores in downtown Paris spend significantly more for purchases than in any other city in France and presents a much higher selling price point[96]. Naturally, this is a real positive factor for retailers. In addition, Paris is the transportation hub of all France and is an international hot spot for fashion and a trendsetter for consumer spending around the world. For these reasons, the company chose Paris as the site for its flagship store.

7.2.2 The Paris retail environment & Champs Elysees.

Paris is one of the world's foremost retailing cities. Its shopping streets, arrondissements (districts) and shopping centers all contribute to an overall retailing mind-set. There are a number of prime retailing locations in Paris that command premium rents much higher than are charged in less prestigious areas. One of the most prestigious avenues in Paris—indeed, in the entire world—is the Avenue des Champs Elysees. The Champs Elysees consumer mix is a 50-50 split between tourists and locals (who comprise a mix of business men/women, families, urban and metro consumers) who expect to pay higher prices than anywhere else in France. Increasing numbers of sports participants shopping on the Champs Elysees, combined with high exposure in Paris to women consumers, has led to an increased number of sports retailers opening flagship or retail stores on the Champs Elysees[97].

---

95 Internal source: Deloitte Consulting, September 2008.

96 Internal source: Deloitte Consulting, September 2008Paris downtown area average Euro 55 per selling price point vs Paris Suburb Euro 43.6. Lyon ranks the second at Euro 48.9.

97 PARIS SAINT-GERMAIN FC, French elite football club, abbreviates as PSG. PSG Boutique Shop is 200m down the avenue on the same side, Lacoste, Marlboro Classics, Tara Jarmon, Ladurée/ approx. 1500 m² on 3 floors: 1100m² selling area , 400m² back

The Avenue des Champs Elysees is located in Paris's 8th arrondissement. The avenue is 1.25 miles long and connects the Place de la Concorde with the Place Charles de Gaulle (site of the Arc de Triomphe). Since 1860 it has been considered as one of the pre-eminent streets in the world for upscale shopping. It has become a veritable mass market for flagship stores[98]. Global and luxury brands, such as Adidas, Benetton, the Disney Store, Zara, Cartier, Louis Vuitton, Gap, Sephora, *et al.*, occupy major spaces; Abercrombie & Fitch has received permission to open a flagship store on the avenue in 2011, and other premium brands will surely follow.

Of approximately 2 million people per week walk along the Champs Elysees, one third walk on the left side of the street. Even with a conservative capture rate projection, a store on the left side would capture 30,000-40,000 in-store visitors. Assuming an average conversion rate of 13-16% and an average basket of $80-85, then we will reach an annual sales projection between $11-15 million. Demand for retail space is very high, while the supply is relatively limited. Rents continue to increase for the prime shopping streets such as the Champs-Elysees. Demand is such that it is a common real estate practice that key money (deposits) of Euro 1-1.8 million are required for any prime locations, even those of as small as 200 sq meters.

7.2.3 Details of the NTP Investment

Despite its sky-high rent (the highest rent per sq foot among the top retail cities / streets in the world) and build-out costs, Nike concluded that the company's strategy to increase and enhance its brand exposure warranted selection of the Champs Elysees for its flagship store in Paris. NTP occupies approximately 1500 m² on 3 floors, including 1100m² selling area and 400m² allocated to back office functions. The store

---

office.

[98] Jean-Philippe (Nike Director of Stores Europe): "The reputation of Champs Elysees is maintained well to the degree that CE Committee selects the new entrances, only limited to the premium brand and retails. In comparison to Oxford Street in London, the latter is becoming more accessible to the majority of the mass consumers."

lease was structured with duration of 12 years, with a break option in the 10 lease year (2020), with an advance notice.

7.2.4 Application of SOM to NTP

NPV was calculated, yielding a result of negative $2.28 million, as follows:

Table 8: NPV Calculation for NTP (USD Millions)

Total Investment Construction Cost plus Fit-out	$	4.34
PV of Projected Cash Flows[99]:	$	6.62
NPV:	$	(2.29)

It can be seen that the negative NPV results primarily from the very high upfront investment[100] and ongoing high rent.

According to conventional capital budgeting theory and practice, therefore, the decision suggested by NPV analysis would be to decline to make the investment. Despite the outcome of this traditional capital budgeting analytical process, as was the case in London Nike management believed the investment held strategic value not revealed by NPV analysis. Consequently, management decided to "roll the dice" and bet that the hidden strategic value was in fact present and that the investment would pay off notwithstanding the negative NPV result.

Would SOM analysis have provided useful insights to decision makers about the presence or absence of the hidden strategic value

---

[99] PV does not include a key retail partner's store sales cannibalization impact.

[100] In French Real Estate, "Key Money" is commonly paid by the new to the previous tenant at the start of a new contract. After ending the contract the new tenant will also receive key money from the subsequent tenant. Key money is generally considered being an asset, indicating the value of the contract at a certain time. IFRS has no strict rule for key money but generally it is depreciated over the lease period because of the lack of an 'active' (trading) market. But for economic analysis, key money is generally not depreciated.

that is not recognized by NPV analysis? The SOM calculation, using the BSOPM, follows[101]:

$$C = Se^{-\delta t}\{N(d_1)\} - Xe^{-rt}\{N(D_2)\}$$

Equation (2)

$$d_1 = \frac{\left\{lnln\left(\dfrac{S}{X}\right) + \left(r - \delta + \dfrac{\sigma^2}{2}\right)t\right\}}{\sigma\sqrt{t}}$$

$$d_2 = d_1 - \sigma\sqrt{t}$$

Table 9: Inputs for Option Valuation Variables in NTP Calculation—Std. Dev. Nike Stock

(S): Present value of underlying asset—the present value of cash flows expected from the investment opportunity.	$4.34	USD Millions
(X): the option strike price- The present value of total committed investment	$6.62	USD Millions
(r): risk-free rate	5%	
(t): the period for which the investment opportunity is valid	12	12 years lease
(σ): Sigma—Std_Dev Nke Qty Stock 1995-2010 annualized	33.8%	Annualized Quarterly Std_Dev Nke Qty Stock 1992-2010

---

[101] It must be emphasized that the actual decision to proceed with NTP was made on gut instinct alone, despite the project's projected negative NPV. The actual decision makers did not have access to RO analysis, which for purposes of this paper is conducted after the fact.

(δ): Dividend payouts -when applicable cost of delay— Annual cost of delay $1/n$	0.00%	No delay in this re-launch model
C: Call Option Value	$2.32	(US$ million)

The original NPV of -$2.32 million suggested that the investment will reduce the value of the firm by the amount of the negative NPV. It does not consider the possible embedded option value. As shown above, the SOM captures hidden strategic value that includes the value of growing the business and driving future growth by targeting new consumer segment (such as women consumers), by identifying and exploiting non-traditional sportswear product categories (such as sports culture and outdoor products), and establishing distribution channels in the domestic market, and future strategic initiatives.

For example, through NTP the company presents its full line of premium products on one of the busiest and most prestigious shopping streets in the world. The store's presence strengthens the company's brand image, particularly in capturing female consumers. NTP also enables the company to take full control of, experiment with, and gain new knowledge and capabilities in the product assortment, setting up a high benchmark for Nike product presentation in the marketplace.

Other examples of strategic values include the effective expansion of the business to the apparel and sports accessories business segments. Additionally, the company is able to learn new effective techniques and local practices to differentiate its product mix with attractive styles and colors. All in all, NTP enabled the company to learn to more effectively present products in a consistent way to targeted consumer groups and to gain brand market acceptance. NTP additionally provides the company with a strong position to exploit opportunities presented by the 2010 World Cup and, later, for its 2011 French Football Association sponsorship launch. Last but not least, the opening of NTP allowed Nike to address and combat strong competition generated by the presence of an Adidas flagship store on the Champs Elysees. The rival companies' head-to-head competition requires a "platform" and both flagship stores are the "stage" for the performance.

NTP achieved the original and primary goal set for it by top management: to become the pinnacle expression of the Nike brand in France, offering a premium shopping experience to consumers that is innovative and exclusive, anchored by Football and Running, while answering strategic threats posed by aggressive competitors[102].

7.2.5 NTP concluding remarks.

NTP provides, as does NTL, an example of successful strategic management by gut feeling. In NTP, NPV—the primary tool of capital budgeting—strongly indicated that the investment in the Paris flagship store should not be made, but management's belief that NTP embodied hidden strategic values not recognized by NPV led managers to "roll the dice" despite the forecast of negative NPV. Management's gut instinct has been shown to have been visionary, as NTP has recorded strong year-on-year growth.

Although NTP generated a negative NPV, we can see that SOM analysis—had it been available to management—would have demonstrated that the hidden strategic values management believed were presented by the investment opportunity were in fact present and that the investment should be made. While neither financial tool can precisely quantify the strategic values attached to an investment, in the case of NTP, SOM would have provided decision makers with more support for the decision that was made based on gut instinct.

By 2010, five years after the store opened, sales exceeded the original projections upon which the NPV analysis was based. Had NPV been calculated with more accurate sales projections[103], it still

---

[102] In 2008-2009, the global economic crisis impacted consumer behavior and spending power globally. However, Nike management firmly believes in the strategic importance and value in NTP and, in light of its 2011 French Football Association sponsorship, the company decided to invest in the NTP re-fitting in 2010. The scope of the NTP store is much smaller than NTL, primarily focusing on the ground floor to create an "initiative zone" at entrance of the store, thereby improving the consumer journey and experience.

[103] The forecasts used at the time of the NPV calculation were based on the evidence then available.

would have generated a negative—or, at best, break-even—value. Performing the SOM calculation with actual sales numbers, however, will result in a more positive outcome than when the sales projections were used, offering further validation for the utility of the SOM tool in comparison with NPV.

This offers further support for the proposition that NTP, even when first proposed with a negative NPV, did have strategic values embedded, as shown in the SOM result. These values have actualized over the years and now being reinforced by continuous investment.

7.3 Case—NikeTown Chicago (NTC)

We then study one of the oldest NikeTown and the second biggest in the U.S.: NikeTown Chicago (NTC).

NikeTown Chicago, USA, by the author

NikeTown Chicago, USA Jordan Shoe, by the author

NikeTown Chicago, USA, by the author

7.3.1 The United States macro-economic & sportswear retail environment.

The United States of America, the recognized leader of the global economy, has the highest level of output in the world, with GDP valued at US$14.1 trillion in 2009. The U.S. economy is highly developed, with the provision of services the primary industry, employing 75-85% of the labor in the country. Activities associated with this sector include retail and wholesale sales, transportation, entertainment, etc. Retail counts for more than 15% of the total trade volume of all U.S.-based businesses. The U.S. is home to many global leading brands, for example, Wal-Mart[104], Apple, The Gap, and many more. Although in recent years serious economic imbalances triggered a financial crisis that led to a deep recession in 2008-2009, the U.S. is still one of the strongest economies in the world. The downturn reduced consumer spending to sluggish levels over the past two to three years; however, retail trade alone still accounts for 7.2% of the total GDP value-added industry and 5.2% of the U.S. gross output by industry (in current dollars)[105].

The United States of America is a central hub for sports activities and sportswear. In previous sections, we have described the lifestyle and cultural changes that led to the separation of sportswear from the rest of the general apparel and footwear industry. Sports have been a growing part of the life of the American people, both for participants and spectators. Currently there are four major sportswear retailers in the country: Sports Authority, Dick's, Finish Line, and Foot Locker. All four retailers sell Nike products, as well as the products of Nike's competitors.

---

[104] Wal-Mart alone employs more than 1 million people in the US and nearly 450,000 more across the globe.

[105] The United States of America, Bureau of Economic Analysis. GDPbyInd_VA_NAICS: Value Added by Industry, Gross Output by Industry. GDPbyInd_GO_NAICS: Gross Output by Industry in Current Dollars, Quantity Indexes by Industry, Price Indexes by Industry.

7.3.2 The Chicago macro-economic & retail demographic environment.

Chicago, one of the largest cities in the U.S., is the economic and cultural capital of the Midwestern United States. It is a global city offering world-class tourist attractions and cultural events. An international destination, Chicago is one of the most vibrant and successful commercial, residential, cultural and tourist areas in the United States. It features distinctive restaurants, famous museums, luxurious hotels, landmark architecture, and prestigious educational and medical facilities. To many people around the globe, Chicago is best known as the home of the Chicago Bulls, a National Basketball Association franchise made world-famous by its iconic player, Michael Jordan.

Stable economic growth and a resilient consumer base continue to provide an attractive backdrop for retailers in Chicago, which has become a "must" location for all national and global brands. This has helped fuel demand for retail space throughout the local real estate market. In general, leasing activity in the area has been fairly strong and steady, with an average 2008 gross asking lease rate of $22.56 per sq. ft. Downtown Chicago, however, is more expensive because the area is vibrant as Chicago continues its movement toward a true 24-hour city. A surge in the convention business, continued growth of the various college campuses in the Loop (Chicago's central shopping and business core), and the attractiveness of Chicago as a premier leisure destination among both domestic and international travelers have combined to fuel the desire of retailers to move downtown.

The local economy, augmented by a large number of tourists and business visitors, has continued to expand its retail market space. Redevelopment of several inner city neighborhoods has enabled an explosion of new retail development. The Chicago metropolitan market has roughly 30 regional shopping malls, encompassing more than 30 million sq ft. The top four submarkets in the Metro area are Schaumburg (Woodfield Mall), State Street, Oak Brook Center, and Michigan Avenue. Each of these top markets is anchored by at least high performing regional mall.

Woodfield Mall, the largest mall in the state of Illinois, is located near Chicago's convention center and suburban business district. It has over 300 stores and restaurants and draws more than two million visitors annually. State Street is another major shopping destination, featuring dining and entertainment. It has Macy's and Sears as anchor tenants for two separate malls in the area. Oak Brook Center is a top shopping destination for local shoppers, with six major department stores and 160 upscale shops and restaurants.

The "Magnificent Mile"—the northern part of Michigan Avenue between the Chicago River and Lake Shore Drive—is the biggest tourist attraction in the State of Illinois. It is an unparalleled mixed-use district located in the heart of Chicago and is Chicago's version of the Champs-Elysées: a grand wide boulevard with exclusive shops, museums, restaurants and ritzy hotels. This prestigious area features more than 460 stores in eight blocks, mostly upscale boutiques and larger national tenants such as Apple, Ralph Lauren, Nordstrom, and Saks, among others.

An estimated 50,000-60,000 people walk along the Magnificent Mile each day. These passers-by include domestic tourists and shoppers (business traffic on Michigan Avenues and Midwestern regional travelers) and those traveling internationally (tourists and international travelers passing through O'Hare Airport, one of the busiest airports in the world, and laying over in Chicago).

7.3.3 NikeTown Chicago.

NTC opened in 1991 with a sizable 49,792 sq ft. It was a great fanfare. At its peak in the 1990's, this store was a major tourist attraction in Chicago, with over 7,500 visitors daily. This peak coincided with the peak of Chicago's winning NBA basketball team whose most flamboyant and talented player was Michael Jordan, a Nike-sponsored celebrity. The store generated huge enthusiasm among loyal Nike fans whenever new products were launched. On several occasions, such launches were greeted by long waiting lines outside the store in the early morning or even overnight before the launch date.

However, during the first decade of the 21st Century, NTC found its daily traffic gradually diminishing from its former peak. Part of this decrease can be attributed to aggressive action on the part of the company's competitors, who opened newer state-of-the-art flagship and concept stores on the Avenue. Meanwhile, NTC received no more than modest upgrades following its opening. Leadership at Nike Inc. began to ask if it would be worthwhile to conduct a major remodel of NTC in order to improve the store's commercial profitability and strategic presence. Would the results be likely to justify the substantial investment required to completely upgrade and remodel the store?

To understand why a thorough remodel has strategic implications, it is necessary to understand the drivers of retail sales at a flagship— or, for that matter, at any—retail store. There are three store-specific factors that influence sales in a given store. The first is the capture rate. It is the percentage of passers-by that decide to enter the store. The second is the conversion rate, which is the percent of persons entering the store who actually make a purchase. The third is the average dollars per transaction.

Clearly, an exciting, modern and intriguing store exterior design will impact the capture rate. Potential shoppers are more likely to be drawn into an exciting retail establishment than to one that is unremarkable or uninviting. The company's competitors have flashy, exciting designs that draw potential customers from NTC to the competitors' stores. A dramatic remodel can reverse that trend.

The conversion rate[106] and average dollars per transaction are strongly influenced both by overall store design and by merchandizing. These two factors interact. The store design limits or enhances what can be merchandised. For example, if significant prime space is dedicated to the display of historical sports artifacts instead of the latest merchandise it is likely that both the conversion rate and the average dollars per transaction will be reduced.

---

[106] It has been estimated that a one percent improvement in the conversion rate will generate approximately $1.2 million annual net sales. (Proprietary data only for academic research, approval to release the data pending.)

It is obvious, based on the foregoing, that a major redesign and remodel intended to increase the capture rate and to boost the conversion rate and average dollars per transaction should have a positive effect on sales. These effects can be predicted with some accuracy. The increased sales and associated cash flows can be evaluated using traditional NPV analysis to determine whether or not the investment will add value to the company.

But what about the hidden strategic value involved in the decision? If the company's NPV analysis were to generate a positive result, then additional strategic values often would not need to be examined closely. But if the company's NPV analysis were to generate a negative result, then strategic values must be addressed. If the company were to decline to remodel the store, not only would it lose possible sales but it could also lose brand heat if potential customers were to pass by NTC to shop at competitors' flagship and concept stores. A company historically on the cutting edge of design and merchandising cannot afford to let itself be seen as a "has-been" or wallflower. Once that perception takes hold in the mind of the consumer, it is hard to reverse.

NTC merchandises first-launch or hard-to-find products. Some specialty items are exclusively offered at NTC, such as Michael Jordan Air Jordan retro style or other paraphernalia not available from typical retailers. Despite such new product launches and the specialty product offerings, it was observed that the NTC floor plans permit less efficient and effective merchandizing configurations than other NikeTowns, or even stores of industry peers.

The existing store configuration does not maximize effective merchandising efficiency[107]. This is because the store's original (and still) existing configuration was aligned with the original NikeTown concept, which was that the flagship stores would provide a showcase to present Nike's newest or most innovative product

---

[107] The percentage of selling sq ft / total store sq ft is usually used as one of the measurement for store space efficiency. The store's actual selling space is relatively low. This is our view drawn from the actual store visit and survey conversation with the in-store customers. NTC's percentage is low. Detail merchandizing percentage is proprietary information, available only for academic commit of this paper. Not disclosed here.

lines to consumers. NikeTowns were not originally intended to be independently profitable, or even to be major selling channels. Rather, the concept was thought of as an opportunity to strengthen ties with consumers, enabling otherwise hard-to-obtain consumer feedback about the Nike brand and products, and to provide an extraordinary brand advertising opportunity[108]. The conclusion is that NTC underperforms its commercial potential[109] and its strategic importance.

In order to improve the store performance both in terms of representing the brand and regaining its attractiveness to "Magnificent Mile" shoppers, the NTC remodeling project was proposed. The main goal is to deliver the pinnacle category retail experience in all floors of NTC by investing in an interior remodel with a focus on creating a premium consumer and brand experience for the consumers from the city, the Midwest region, and the world.

7.3.4 Details of the NTC remodeling investment[110].

The investment is planned as follows: the remodeling will be over multiyear project and the total investment will amount to up to $24 million over 10 years, consisting of an upfront investment of $10 million followed by a $14 million investment to complete the remodel. During the remodel NTC will remain open for business, with closure only of the floor being remodeled. It is estimated that the store will sustain a significant loss of sales due to the partial closure during the first year. It is anticipated that the store will resume normal sales figures during the second year. Upon completion of the remodeling, the store is expected to achieve up to 40% growth, compared to sales prior to the remodeling. The increased sales will be generated primarily from incremental increased selling space and

---

[108] Source: Harvard Business Review, "Conflict of Interest", EC-9B.

[109] Internal analysis. The underperformance is measured in both conversion rate and average dollars per transaction.

[110] Actual investment details concealed for business confidentiality. Details disclosed here is only for the purpose of this study. The final presentation of this paper may only provide partial disclosure.

effective improvements to the shopping experience that will result in improvement in the conversion rate).

The remodeling aims to create more selling space and to rearrange the current configuration to enhance the consumer experience and ignite Nike brand energy. The objective is the optimization of store space usage by allowing the store to hold a greater depth and breadth of inventory in the front of the store while at the same time enhancing back room processing. These benefits if achieved as projected will deliver a significant lift to NTC's sales and enable it to regain its popularity by, for example, attracting more passers-by to enter the store and to make purchases once inside the store. However, the investments are significant, as are the depreciation & rent expenses that will follow. These are constraints that could hold back this remodeling project at a time when the resources are limited and other investment opportunities are competing for priority within the company. It is difficult but necessary for the company to go beyond the traditional financial context to evaluate the project in a much deeper and broader magnitude.

The NTC remodel investment represents another opportunity to examine the application of traditional NPV analysis complemented by the SOM methodology. The SOM methodology in this case examines the delay option.

7.3.5 Application of SOM to NTC.

The calculated NPV (including termination value) shown in Table 10, is a positive $7.4 million. The buoyant cash flow projections are based on the increasing selling space, improved conversion rate and capture rate.

In sum, the optimization of the store configuration generates improved efficiencies in recapturing more selling space (remodeling the current store configuration will add more selling space that will generate incremental sales), enabling broader assortments of merchandise on the floor and improving store operations. This will improve product presentation and availability, service levels, and the overall in-store shopping experience. And hence improve conversion rate. The table below shows the values of the NPV of the investment in NTC.

Table 10: NPV Calculation for NTC (USD Millions)

Total Investment Construction Cost plus Fit-out	$	(30.9)
PV of Projected Cash Flows:	$	23.60
NPV (Lease Term: 12 year with renewal option) [111]	$	7.4

Table 11 and Table 12 incorporate the values of the six variables required to calculate the call option value of the investment in NTC. The variables, $S, X, r, t,$ and δ are as explained in the last column of the tables. The value of the primary sigma is the standard deviation of the change in the end of quarter Nike stock price closing price from 1992-2010. On an annualized basis, the standard deviation of sigma is 33.8%. Applying these values to Equation 2, the call option value is $19.49 million, assuming no delay in investment).

Table 11: Inputs for Option Valuation Variables in NTC Calculation—No Delay

(S): Present value of underlying asset—the present value of cash flows expected from the investment opportunity.	$30.95	
(X): the option strike price- The present value of total committed investment	$23.60	
(r): risk-free rate	5%	
(t): the period for which the investment opportunity is valid	10	Lease Term

---

[111] The NPV calculation assumes on the last year all "working capital" will be fully liquidated.

(σ): Sigma—Std_Dev Nke Qty Stock 1995-2010 annualized	33.8%	Annualized Quarterly Std_Dev Nke Qty Stock 1992-2010
(δ): Dividend payouts -when applicable cost of delay— Annual cost of delay 1/n	0.00%	Delay translates into opportunity cost
C: Call Option Value	$19.49	

The decision to invest, however, was delayed by management for a variety of reasons. The increased rent expense would significantly outpace revenue growth at NTC.; limited resource availability, particularly during the U.S. recession, may also have contributed to the decision to delay the investment. This delay provides us with an opportunity to apply SOM in a formulation that uses the variable δ, which is the dividend payment in the financial optional application, to capture the loss attributable to the delay. The holder of the financial option foregoes the dividend payment of the underlying stock, which reduces in value after the payment. Likewise in the real option application, the holder of the real option also experiences a loss in the value of the underlying asset, or opportunity cost, through the delaying of the investment. We assume that the opportunity cost is equivalent to 1/n where n is the term of the lease. The numerator identifies the number of periods of delay. Table 12 applies the concept of delay in the real asset investment.

Table 12: Inputs for Option Valuation Variables in NTP Calculation—With Delay

(S): Present value of underlying asset—the present value of cash flows expected from the investment opportunity.	$30.95	PV of cash flows after the remodeling is completed.

85

(X): the option strike price- The present value of total committed investment	$23.60	
(r): risk-free rate	5%	
(t): the period for which the investment opportunity is valid	10	Lease Term
(σ): Sigma—Std_Dev Nke Qty Stock 1995-2010 annualized	33.8%	Annualized Quarterly Std_Dev Nke Qty Stock 1995-2010
(δ): Dividend payouts -when appli- cable cost of delay— Annual cost of delay 1/n	0.00%	Delay translates into opportunity cost
C: Call Option Value	$19.49	If no delay would be $19.5 million
	$(15.62)	Opportunity cost due to delay

The real option value without any delay of the investment is $19.49 million as in RO_1 [112] or with the delay is $3.87 million as in RO_2. The difference between the two SOM results is considerable: $15.62 million. This figure reflects how much values could have been generated had the investment been made when originally proposed. It is worthwhile noting that the difference in two SOM results is significant, when considering the total store sales per year[113]. The SOM results indicate the "opportunity cost" is more than just the financial sales loss. The financial loss from the delay is only reflected in sales lost due to the delay (the remodeled NTC has more selling space and hence contributes incremental sales, by estimate will achieve approximately $** million by adding a selling floor). The opportunity

---

[112] Assuming the project had no delay.

[113] Average sales per square footage in Michigan Avenues is estimated between $250-$500. NTC is 69,000 Sq. Ft.

cost can also be measured using KPI (Key Performance Indicators), such as conversion rate (assuming a better store presentation will promote a higher percentage of buying when consumers are in the store), in-store traffic (assuming a better store presentation will attract more passers-by to enter the store); and Average Dollars Per Basket (assuming a better product presentation assortment will encourage consumers to spend more per visit).

The SOM results, in both delay and no delay cases, the real option values are positive, and provide solid support to the investment decision (particularly in the no-delay scenario). The results further strengthen our hypothesis that the traditional NPV method is insufficient to capture all investment return values. NTC's investment delays leads to two SOM results while NPV remains the same (using same sets of cash flows projections). This demonstrate that the real option value increases (or decreases) with increased flexibility (or inflexibility) and with increased risk (decreased risk, such as delay investment) associated with the underlying real asset investment. As mentioned in the NTL case, NPV's stringent application of a single discount rate to capture all the dynamics and risk in the markets[114] constricts the decision makers to a limited framework. This limitation is particularly apparent in a few high-risk high-return industries and has been demonstrated in the NTL and NTP cases. In the NTC case, this limitation is exemplified by NPV's inability to capture the "opportunity loss" associated with the delay. Using the same sets of cash flow projection, we derive two significantly different SOM results, but the same NPV (all other factors assumed to be the same).[115] In addition to the tangible financial benefits (from adding

more selling space, improving the capture rate, the conversion rate, and average basket size, for instance), SOM demonstrates there are more unaccounted values, tangible and intangible, associated with this investment. There are both offensive and defensive intangible strategic values associated with a remodeled NTC. Offensive strategic values are associated with the revitalized projection of the Nike

---

[114] Markets here refer to both business commodity markets and investment capital markets.

[115] WACC remains the same at **%, reinvestment rate stays at **%; same sets of cash flows projection. Same depreciation methodology.

brand in a state-of-the-art store featuring unique and dramatic brand-specific in-store consumer experience; this creates brand heat and stimulates consumer loyalty and increased sales not only at NTC but throughout the region. In addition, staff morale and productivity can be expected to improve, further enhancing both sales and brand heat. Defensive strategic values include neutralizing and regaining the competitive advantage ceded to the company's rivals who had installed more modern and eye-catching flagship stores on the Magnificent Mile.

7.3.6 NTC concluding remarks.

NTC demonstrates how SOM captures strategic values, including the value (in this case, a decreased value) resulting from the delay in the investment. The NTC remodeling investment was proposed twice. If we use the same set of cash flow projections, merely delaying their onset for a year or two, we would have derived the same NPV. However, using the very same set of projections, we derive two different SOM values, the difference between them signifying the NTC embedded hidden strategic values not recognized by NPV.

When we examine NTC's values through a broader lens, there is a greater significance beyond the computed value contributing to NTC and to the Nike brand, for instance, growing the sportswear market overall. As one of the anchor Nike Towns in the U.S., its radiance ripples throughout the Midwest region, particularly in the Chicago area. NTC is deeply connected to sports, reflecting the region's long and rich sports legacy[116]. NTC maintains a highly visible Nike presence in the Midwest region of the US market. It presents products that are locally relevant to the City and the region; examples include the Jordan basketball product collection. NTC's location is a retail hot spot in Chicago, competing directly with key competitors' flagship stores[117].

---

[116] For example, Michael Jordan (Chicago Bulls), Sammy Sosa (Chicago Cubs), Charles Comiskey (Chicago White Sox).

[117] Adidas Originals / Heritage Store, Puma Concept Store, Crate & Barrel, and North Face Concept / Flagship Store.

SOM results indicate the "opportunity cost" is more than these losses. It also reflects the embedded strategic and synergistic values. One of the examples, as mentioned in previous section, is the billboard advertisement impact. The exposure of the Nike brand creates a wide- ranging commercial advertisement impact in generating demand for Nike products. Approximately 15 million people walk by the NTC block annually, and assuming a double digit capture rate, millions of these people will walk into the store[118]. NTC enables Nike to reach out to this broad population as a live billboard, reaching key consumer demographics and delivering premium products, consumer experiences and brand impressions[119]. They might or might not make any purchases, but the strong and positive impression of the Nike brand stays with the consumer. This is, again, the synergistic value.

7.4   Case—NikeTown Beijing (NTB)

We now turn to the final application of the real option model for this study. We will examine the investment of NikeTown Beijing, which will be a "staged" investment. While the Nike-Town Beijing investment is still an "Expansion" application, it differs in that the first stage of the investment allows the corporation to hold an option to commit further investments, and more importantly, the early option allows the company to be able to select highly sought after location in a city that has just shown the world the excitement of the city through the opening ceremony of the Olympics. We begin with a brief introduction of China's macroeconomic and retail environment.

---

[118] These people are local residents, domestic visitors, and international tourists.

[119] While the local shoppers are more time sensitive and have a high expectation on the products (product-seekers), the tourists and visitors are more into store experience and less prices sensitive. For most European visitors, the products are cheaper compared to home country.

NikeTown Beijing, China by Donghua Ma, 2024

7.4.1 The Chinese macro-economic & sportswear retail environment.

The Chinese economy has experienced phenomenal growth over the past few decades, making solid strides in economic development on almost all fronts. One of the key economic measurements, year-over-year change in Gross Domestic Product (GDP YoY), has been in the high single digits over the past decades. From 1989 through 2010, China's average annual GDP growth was 9.30 percent, ranging from a record low of 3.80 percent in December of 1990 to a historical high of 14.20 percent in December of 1992. According to the World Bank, China's 2010 Gross Domestic Product is approximately $4,909 billion, or 7.92% of the world economy, and China is focused on catching up with the West. If growth continues at its current pace, China will eventually emerge as a leading player in all major industries. By 2024 China's nominal GDP will have overtaken the US, becoming the largest economy in the world. China has the largest population and is the second largest geographic area in the world. It is one of the most active global retail markets. In 2004, China opened the country's retail sector to foreign investments. By the end of 2005, the total retail and wholesale sector reached $28.5 billion (year-on-year growth of 22.3%). China has emerged not just as a manufacturing base but as a massive consumer market to many foreign companies.

Nike is among the early foreign entrants to China. In 1980, Phil Knight made his first trip to China. The following year, Nike opened its first factory in China and sponsored the Chinese national basketball team. Nike's shoes were first sold in China in 1982 at the state-owned Beijing Friendship Store, where they were enthusiastically received. In 1994-1995, Nike helped establish China's first professional sports leagues for soccer and basketball.

In 1998, Nike discovered a 17-year-old basketball player, Yao Ming, who became a world-class NBA star. Then in 2002, Nike signed hurdler Liu Xiang, who won a gold medal in the 2004 Athens Olympics. In 1994, Nike China was an $8 million enterprise; by 2002, sales had reached $100 million. Nike's strategy for building that market was and remains focused on the Chinese consumers of the future;

to serve them the company opened hundreds of new retail outlets within the country. In 2008, Nike hit the benchmark of $1 billion in revenues from China, and it is clearly established as the leading global sportswear company in China.

China's development is unique. The country transformed from a "centrally planned economy" in early 1980's to a more market oriented and entrepreneurial economy while retaining a strong centrally controlled politically socialist organization. It has been growing at a phenomenal pace. China has been one of the main contract manufacturer for many global apparel and footwear companies as well as a contract manufacturer for many other products for multinational companies. As Chinese companies learn modern manufacturing and other business skills, they began to manufacture and market their own products domestically and compete internationally in addition to being contract manufacturers to multinationals. Furthermore, domestic development raises standards of living, and therefore, raises domestic demand for products. Today China has become one of the most attractive consumer markets for many companies in the world. Our application of the real option model for Nike Town Beijing must integrate the dynamism, risk, and the pace of growth of the Chinese economy.

7.4.2 (Branded) sportswear industry in China.

Sportswear is a newly established industry in China. It is well observed that the increasing wealth in the general public and enhanced quality of life are changing the people's lifestyle. Sports are no longer just the speculators' TV time, but more so becoming participants' pastime. China's winning the bid to hold the 2008 Olympic Games is a defining moment for Chinese sportswear industry and greatly accelerated industry acceptance and popularity among Chinese consumers.

There are limited industry statistics available. Based on internal and external industry analysis, sales of branded sporting goods were mainly channeled through shopping centers in first-tier cities, and through specialized retail stores in second-tier and third-tier cities.

Consumers in first-tier cities and high-end consumers tend to focus on product functionality and performance because of their more mature consumption behavior, greater participation in sports, and greater propensity to spend. As a result, product diversification offers significant opportunities in these markets.

The sportswear industry in China is highly competitive. In addition to foreign competitors like Adidas, leading domestic brands have emerged and grown at a rapid pace. There are many local and international sports brands competing in the China market. The principal competitors are Nike, Adidas, LiNing, Anta, Doublestar and Kangwei. Generally international brands perform better in 1st-tier cities and some coastal cities where consumer spending is higher on a per capita basis. Domestic brands are more competitive in 2nd-tier and 3rd-tier cities. LiNing has competitive advantages given its strong heritage as the "national" hero brand. Its early entry has secured a long-term relationship with the Chinese sports community. Furthermore, LiNing's sponsorship of major sports teams, sporting events and key athletes have created public confidence and passion and have achieved significant advertising and promotional impact. In addition, it has an extensive sales network, well-defined market positioning and comprehensive product offerings.

Li Ning Company Limited[120] is a well developed company which has established an extensive supply chain management system, distribution channels, and retail network in the PRC, primarily through outsourcing of manufacturing operations and distribution via franchised agents. The company has been growing at a rapid pace since its public offering on June 4, 2004. As of 31 May, 2004, Li Ning had already over 200 distributors operating over 2,200 franchised retail outlets for the LI-NING and KAPPA brands in China. It also operated 110 retail stores and 199 concessions for the LI-NING and KAPPA brands. The company keeps expanding its retail section. As of

---

[120] Li Ning Company Limited is one of the leading sports brand enterprises in the PRC, possessing brand marketing, research and development, design, manufacturing, distribution and retail capabilities. The Group's products mainly include footwear, apparel, accessories and equipment for sport and leisure uses under its own LI-NING brand.

2009, it has already owned more than 7,200 branded retail stores in the country, just in 2008-2009 alone, it opened additional 1,000 more stores, focusing on smaller markets priced at affordability for the majority of Chinese who might not be inclined to spend over US $100 on a pair of sneakers. The company has been taking marketshare from the global brands, such as Adidas and Nike, which are dominant in the Tier one cities.

As of 2008, Nike had the highest market share (12.7%) among sportswear brands in China based on fiscal year 2008 sales data[121], Adidas was in second place (11.0%), and LiNing was the largest domestic sportswear brand (9.5%).

The following exhibit demonstrates the sportswear brands' market shares in China, for the fiscal year of 2008.

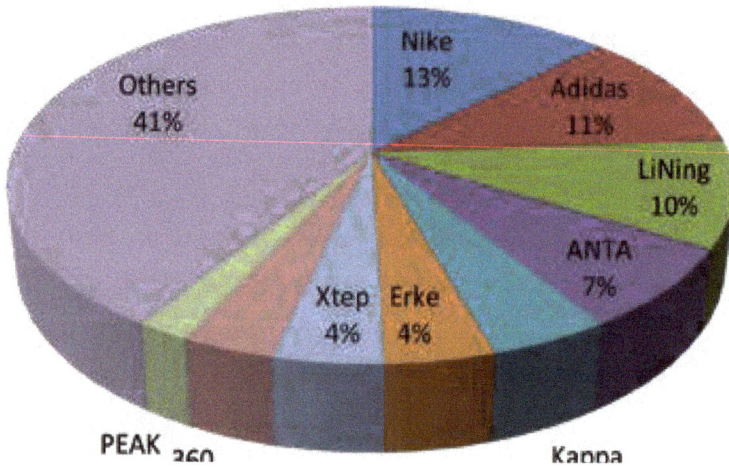

[121] Source: Euromonitor, Flyke International, complied by Daiwa, in July 10 2010 Analysis report.

Figure 2: China Sportswear Industry Key Players

Top 5 sportswear brands in China by market share

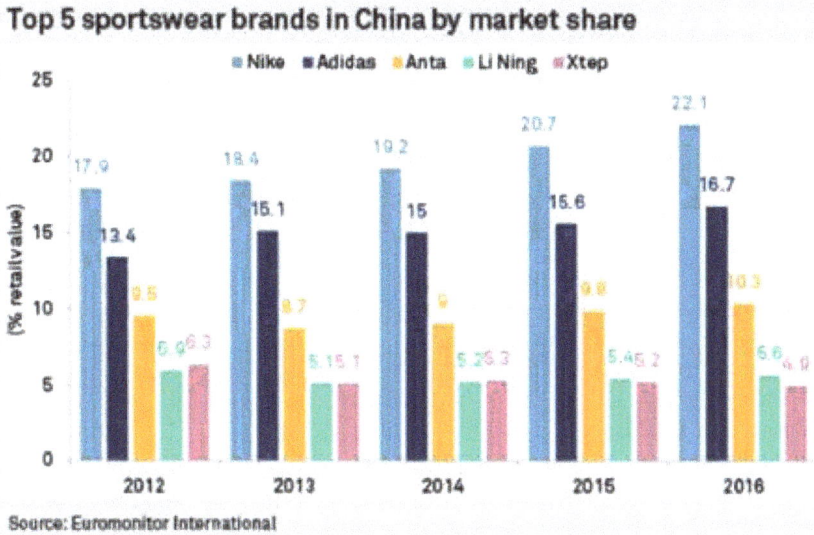

Source: Euromonitor International

7.4.3 Sigma in SOM Application in NTB.

In the synergistic options applications of NikeTown investments in London, Paris, and Chicago, we have used the stock price return of Nike Corporation (Nike B stock) as the underlying asset for our analyses. We are comfortable with using Nike's stock return as we assumed that stock markets in United States and Europe are closely correlated in movements and, more importantly, in the timely and generally accurate disclosure of financial information. Would Nike stock price return still be the appropriate underlying asset for the real option analysis of Nike Town Beijing in China, an emerging economy that has maintained surging real rates of growth? If the securities market in China are "not in sync" with securities markets in the U.S. and Europe, we may need to find a comparable company in China, sometimes called a "pure play" local company, whose stock price return variance, and risk-return profile reflect more closely approximate the (real) investments in its dynamic high growth economy.

We will first examine the correlations of securities markets of the U.S. with two European securities market indices and two stock market indices in China. These are the Standard and Poor 500 Index (S&P)which is a capitalization weighted index of 500 of the largest companies in the U.S.; the FTSE 100 (Financial Times-London Stock Exchange) which is an index of 100 most highly capitalized stocks in the London Stock Exchange and a benchmark index of the stock market in England; the CAC (Contation Assistee Continu), a benchmark French Stock Market Index which is a capitalization weighted measure of 40 of the most significant values among the 100 highest market capitalization companies in the Paris Bourse (now Euronext Paris); the Hang Seng Index (HSI), a benchmark stock market index in Hong Kong which is a market capitalization weighted measure of 40 of the largest companies that trade in Hong Kong; and the Shanghai Stock Exchange (SSE), a composite stock market index that is capitalization weighted consisting of all A and B shares listed on the Shanghai Stock Exchange. The correlation matrix is based on the monthly index values between January 1, 2005 and December 31, 2010.

Table 13: Correlation Matrix

	S&P	HSI	CAC	FTSE	SSE
S&P	1.0	0.52	0.954	0.956	0.411
HSI		1.0	0.391	0.611	0.890
CAC			1.0	0.92	0.353
FTSE				1.0	0.475
SSE					1.0

From the correlations shown above, it is clear that the S&P 500 Index of the U.S. is very closely correlated with the European stock market indices and not very closely correlated with the Hong Kong or Shanghai stock market indices. The London index is slightly more correlated with the Hong Kong index. On the other hand, the Shanghai and Hong Kong Indexes are closely correlated. With these correlations, we are comfortable that we have appropriately used the Nike stock price return as the underlying asset for analyzing Nike Town London, Paris, and Chicago. For Nike Town Beijing, we are hesitant to use the Nike stock price return due to the lack of correlation with the local securities markets. Instead, we will use a pure play company in China, the Li Ning Company Limited, whose stock is traded in the Hong Kong Stock Exchange. Our rationale is that Li Ning is operating mainly in the China markets and its stock price return should more properly reflect the risk-return characteristics of investors' expectations in that region.

Along the lines of the Capital Asset Price Model to capture the systematic risk (beta from the regression) and return of the stock, we ran regressions of monthly Li Ning stock returns against the monthly Hang Sheng Index returns from January 2005 through December 2010. As a comparison, we ran similar regressions of monthly returns of Nike stock against the monthly returns of the S&P over the same period. Regression results are as follows:

$$\text{Li Ning} = 0.019 + 1.30 R_{HSI} \qquad R^2 = 0.4$$

$$Nike = 0.012 + 0.90 R_{S\&P} \qquad R^2 = 0.$$

The variable R represents the rate of return of the stock and respective market return index. The first term is the intercept, and the coefficient of the market index is the beta (β) of the stock. The values in parenthesis are the standard error of the estimates. The β coefficients for both Li Ning and Nike have reasonably small standard errors (t-statistics are 7.31 and 6.94 for Li Ning and Nike respectively) and significant at the 95% level. These beta estimates and their range of estimates within the 95% significance level, indicate that to investors Li Ning operating in the Chinese market has much higher systematic risk than Nike operating in the U.S. market. We expect a company operating in the fast growing China would experience higher variances in operating cash flows than a company operating in the

U.S. Likewise, a younger company operating in a high growth region would experience higher variances in operating cash flows than a more mature company operating in a more stable growth region. With these considerations, we believe that it is more appropriate to use Li Ning stock returns as the underlying asset for our application of synergistic options to NikeTown Beijing.

7.4.4 Beijing macro-economic & retail demographic environment.

On July 13, 2001, Beijing won the bid to host the 2008 Summer Olympics. It was a day of triumph for China. It also represented a tremendous opportunity for Nike, which has a track record of delivering stunning investment return performance during the Olympics years. Before 2007, however, Nike had no premium owned retail space on the high street in China. Rather, it relied on a network of distributors (department stores and partner stores) to distribute its products in the country. The company felt that this retail network would simply be insufficient to maximize the brand-building opportunity presented by the Beijing Olympics. Not only would the company be unable to rely on these distributors to provide ample space for Nike products, but Nike lacked control of the brand presentation in third party stores. The company concluded that the Beijing Olympics warranted the creation of a new flagship store in China, not only to maximize sales through the store itself (and, via the brand heat created, through its distribution partners) but, also, through increased brand visibility to deepen the brand's relationship with the younger generation. A further advantage is that the new store would steal the thunder of its competitors' stores and cool their own brand heat.

From among the top tier cities in China, the company selected Beijing to build the new store. Not only would Beijing be the host city for China's first Olympic Games, it is also the capital of China and has a long and well-established history and culture. It is the leading city in the country. Its nominal GDP has experienced tremendous growth over the years. In 2007, a year before the Olympics, Beijing GDP was USD$138 billion (935 RMB billion)—a remarkable 229%

increase from USD$42 billion (285 RMB billion) in 2001. Further, it is anticipated that Beijing will continue to experience accelerated urbanization and globalization.

The primary focus of opening a flagship store in BJ is to secure solid brand presentation at the premier location in China, ahead of the Olympic Games. This flagship store was planned to be the best of Nike in China and to be the archetype for the other retailers that sell Nike products. It is therefore much more than a store; it is a venue intended to elevate the Nike brand image in this fast growing market. "It's extremely exciting to open a flagship Nike retail presence in one of the world's great cities. China is one of Nike's biggest growth opportunities, and one of the most dynamic retail markets in the world. Our Beijing flagship store creates a strong brand statement with a compelling world-class shopping experience. "[122]

The strategic move to build a flagship store in Beijing was shared and followed by competitors. A year after the opening of NTB, Adidas opened its flagship store, the "Adidas brand center", in Sanlitun, the capital's main entertainment district[123]. Their 34,100 square foot store is about 1½ times the size of Adidas's previous largest outlet on the Champs-Elysées in Paris. The company invested heavily in China in the near term to promote Adidas's role as the official sportswear provider for the Beijing Games. In the longer term, Adidas is planning to grow its business in China significantly[124].

In order to find the best location for NTB, Nike conducted an in-depth analysis that compared different prominent retail districts— Wanfujing Aveneue, Xidan, Jingoumen, Donzhimen, and ChaoYang

---

[122] Charlie Denson, Brand President, Nike, Inc, at Beijing store opening, August 7, 2007. Source: Company site.

[123] The fact that Adidas opened its megastore in Beijing's entertainment district may signify the company's intention to present its flagship store experience as a form of entertainment rather than as a pure retailing experience.

[124] Christophe Bezu, GM Adidas Asia, "China is already Adidas's second-largest market by the end of this year, overtaking Japan and coming after the U.S. China is already Adidas's most profitable market, having passed Japan and some other European markets at the end of 2007." Chief Executive Herbert Hainer has said that Adidas's China sales will surpass $1.58 billion by 2010.

- within the Chinese capital. The districts were categorized by the demographic characteristics deemed significant by Nike for store location (membership in the 16-24 age group, student or non-student population, and amount of tourist and local foot traffic)[125]. A matrix, Table 14, was created in 20** that matched the demographics of each district, weighted by expected revenue[126], that the company estimated would be generate sales. The results show that Wangfujing Avenue ranked the highest in student and tourist populations and was in a virtual tie with Xidan for youth as a percentage of the population. Wanfujing Avenue had the highest estimated retail revenue potential among the five districts and, in addition, it was the most popular of the districts among the local population.

Table 14: Beijing Major Retail District Demographic Comparison

Matrix	Wangfujing	Xidan	Jingoumen	Dongzhi-men	ChaoYang	Total
Youth	34.0%	34.7%	12.3%	11.2%	7.9%	100.0%
Students	41.2%	27.9%	9.9%	17.4%	3.6%	100.0%
Tourist	56.9%	26.9%	0.0%	10.1%	6.1%	100.0%

Wanfujing Avenue has become one of the world's most famous shopping areas in recent decades, and is sometimes called Beijing's "Golden Mile." It is the most well known and popular shopping district in China. Seven hundred thousand pedestrians walk along the Avenue each day, comprising a highly desirable demographic mix. Many major consumer brands seek locations on Wanfujing Avenue for their flagship stores. The Avenue has two major plazas: the Oriental Plaza and the Sun Dong An Plaza. The Oriental Plaza has very high-end retail shops that maximize the overall spending habits and profile of the consumers attracted to that area. Sun Dong An Plaza[127], however,

---

[125] Data derived from census and from several governmental agencies. Details are available only for academic study.

[126] Dollar amount of estimated revenue data is confidential, and therefore only percentage breakdowns may be used in this study.

[127] Occupying an area of 120,000 sq. meters spread over seven levels, the Plaza's balanced

presents the ultimate address for a flagship store. It features excellent access to a main subway line and other transportation resources. Because of this accessibility, Sun Dong An Plaza has higher foot traffic. Research estimates that Sun Dong An Plaza will have over a million visitors a day after the opening of the new subway extension.

7.4.5 Application of SOM to NTB

On August 3, 2007, Nike opened its first flagship store in Beijing. The calculated NPV[128], as shown in the table below, was $1.6 million. The total present value of the cash flow projection was $3.7 million over a period of 5 years, with $2.1 million upfront investment. This investment is only for the construction and fixture costs to set the store[129].

Table 15: NPV Calculation for NTB

Total Investment Construction Cost plus Fit-out	$	3.7
PV of Projected Cash Flows[130]	$	2.7
Lease Term: 5 year with renew option		5
NPV[131]	$	1.61

Viewed from the standpoint of financial return, this investment would be considered acceptable as project acceptance would provide an expected present value of $1.61 million. The measurement of

---

mix of retailers will attract a large and diverse range of consumers. The retail mix includes two department stores of around 30,000 and 10,000 sq. meters, an eight-screen Cineplex, food court, F&B outlets and an entertainment center, etc. In addition, parking for 500 cars and 3,500 bicycles, cargo loading and unloading and E&M facilities offer supreme convenience for tenants and visitors alike.

[128] The NPV here calculated is based on a five-year lease term, using the liquidation of the inventory at the end of the lease term to represent (partially) the termination values.

[129] Much of the other R&D investments are already occurred as "sunk costs."

[130] The NPV is calculated to include the final year's working capital liquidation.

[131] NPV is calculated including the last year cash flow as "growth annuity."

return nevertheless does not consider the value associated with externalities, or the embedded option value in the investment.

In the SOM methodology we use the same data for the present value of the underlying asset (S) and the present value of the committed investment (X) which is also the strike price as in the NPV calculation. The tables below show the values of the six variables required to calculate the call option value of the investment in NTB.

As in previous NikeTown investment cases, the Nike Town Beijing is expected not only to generate commercial profits, but also to generate external benefits. These benefits may include the synergistic effects NTB will have on general sales in the region and the strategic values arising from Nike's major presence in the regional and national retail segment of China. We have further proposed that using the standard deviation of the monthly rate of change of LiNing closing stock price from 2004-2011 is more appropriate for the analysis than using Nike's stock price return. On an annualized basis, the standard deviation of sigma is 45.1%, compared to sigma of 33.8% used in previous three cases.

Table 16: Inputs for Option Valuation Variables in NTB Calculation—5 Year

(S): Present value of underlying asset—the present value of cash flows expected from the investment opportunity.	$2.7	
(X): the option strike price—The present value of total committed investment	$3.7	
(r): risk-free rate	5%	
(t): the period for which the investment opportunity is valid	5	Lease term
(σ): Sigma—Std_Dev Nke Qty Stock 1995-2010 annulized	45.1%	Annualized LiNing Monthly Std_Dev LiNing Mthly Stock 2004-2011
(δ): Dividend payouts -when applicable cost of delay—Annual cost of delay 1/n	0.00%	Annual cost of delay = 1/n
C: Call Option Value	$2.06	

Table 16 above lists the values of the six variables in the call option equation and the resulting call option value of $2.06 million. The positive value indicates that there is some additional embedded option value in the investment project, which reinforces the result from the NPV analysis. The primary contribution of the use of SOM in the NTB case is to be found in the evaluation of the staging opportunity, as described next.

As an aside, we note that some analysts may argue that investment in the rapidly growing economy of China may introduce considerably more risk and uncertainty than are typically present in developed countries. Thus, they might want to adjust upward the hurdle rate to accommodate the higher risk and uncertainty. These risks could also include currency and political risks in addition to the risk associated with higher growth of an emerging economy. On the other hand, one might also argue that the low correlation of China's securities markets with the more developed securities markets of the Western industrialized economies may be indicative of diversification possibilities that can decrease systematic risk as well as provide better diversification of unsystematic risk. This latter argument could result in a lower the cost of capital of the multinational firm[132].

In normal practice, a retail store of such size and scale would expect to remain in operation between 10-30 years. This is particularly the case in China, where the market is seen as a strategically important market for the company in the long term. It is very likely that the company will exercise its option to extend the lease for an addition ** years at the termination of the initial ** year lease term. The reasons why the company only entered a **-year lease have not been publicly disclosed. Although it is possible that the **-year lease term could simply be due to local real estate regulations or have been unilaterally imposed by the landlord, we believe one of the key reasons could be the unique market risk posed by China at the beginning of the 21st Century.

As 2012 is a year of major political leadership change for China[133], the decision by the company to sign a **-year lease with an option to renew for an additional ** year term appears to be a very shrewd way to hedge its bet in China. The short-term renewable lease provides an example of a "staging investment" experiment conducive to the application and understanding of embedded option value. In other words, by holding the short-term renewable lease, the lessee has the option to plan a second stage of investment based upon uncertain events unfolding. That option has value and is embedded in the initial renewable lease.

---

[132] See for example, Rene M. Stulz, "Globalization of Capital Markets and the Cost of Capital: the case of Nestle", Journal of Applied Corporate Finance, Fall 1995, pp 30-38, and Ali Fatemi, "Shareholder Benefits from Corporate International Diversification, Journal of Finance, Dec. 1984, pp. 1325-1344.

[133] Year 2012 is the Chinese "Central Political Committee" election year.

7.4.6 NTB 2nd stage investment.

In the previous discussion, we assumed the company would exercise the option to renew the lease upon the expiration of the initial lease term. We observed that the company may have used the short initial lease term as a way of testing the NTB investment while minimizing its exposure to risks presented by political uncertainty. Both propositions still hold true. However, the company did not wait the entire testing period before deciding to make a subsequent investment, a reaction consistent with the real option concept that there is embedded call option value in the initial stage investment.

Since NTB opened in August 2007, the store has attracted many visitors and has become a "must-visit" landmark on Wangfujing Street. The amount of consumer inflow and market demand ahead of the Olympics was unprecedented. The initial store square footage became inadequate to stock and to display the company's pinnacle products. One of the options available to the company was to increase the store size with the anticipation that the increased space would attract more customers, and generate significant associated incremental revenue. The company estimated both costs and resulting incremental revenues in making its decision.

Including these calculations in our NPV and SOM analyses enable us to derive another set of NPV and SOM values. The NPV of the Stage II is smaller than the NPV of the Stage I investment as expected. The smaller Stage II investment is primarily to extend the lease area by adding an additional floor, and the present value of the cash flows relates only to the revenues generated by and from that additional floor space. The NPV as shown in Table 17 is $1.25 million.

Table 17: NTB Second Stage Investment NPV Calculation

PV of Projected Cash Flows:	$	2.7
Total Investment Construction Cost plus Fit-out	$	1.6
Lease Term: ** year with renewed ** years		
NPV	$	1.25

Table 18: Inputs for Option Valuation Variables in NTB
Calculation—Second Stage Investment

(S): Present value of underlying asset—the present value of cash flows expected from the investment opportunity.	$2.7	Incremental CF from Stage II Investment
(X): the option strike price— The present value of total committed investment	$1.6	Stage II Investment
(r): risk-free rate	5%	
(t): the period for which the investment opportunity is valid	5	Lease Term
(σ): Sigma—Std_Dev Nke Qty Stock 1995-2010 annualized	45.1%	Annualized LiNing Monthly Std_Dev 2004-2011
(δ): Dividend payouts -when applicable cost of delay— Annual cost of delay 1/n	0.00%	Annual cost of delay = 1/n
C: Call Option Value	$1.70	

Using the incremental cash flow projections for Stage II, we derive another call option value, $1.70 million. Note that the four other input variables in the SOM calculation, r, t, σ, and δ are similar to the Stage I investment. Only the S and X variables are from the new estimates of NPV for Stage II.

We note from the results that the option values $2.06 million for Stage I, and $1.70 million for Stage II are both larger than the corresponding NPV values. These results indicate that option values embedded in the store are greater than the financial values reflected in their NPVs. Had this analysis had been done before the investment decisions were made, management might well have resolved to increase the size of the investment in each stage.

7.4.7 NTB concluding remarks.

As previously stated, the primary goal behind the opening of NTB is not merely to deliver financial profits from store operations. It is part of a long-term strategic objective to create and amplify the brand heat, driving the entire business of Nike China before, during, and after the Olympic Games. The close and direct connection between NTB and the company's business goal in China was clearly articulated by Charlie Denson, Brand President, Nike, Inc, at the Beijing store opening on August 7, 2007. Mr. Denson said, "As we head toward the Olympics, we're extending our brand leadership, deepening our consumer relationships and building what we expect soon to be a $1 billion[134] business and Nike's second-largest market in the world"[135]. The leadership strategically envisioned and specifically connected the business goal in China to the NTB.

Given that China in 2007 was an emerging market, the company initially invested cautiously, with initial store size and investment that was smaller than that of other NikeTowns. The lease term was only five years, reflecting the intention to "test" the market. We assumed that at the end of the "testing" period, the option to renew would be exercised and another **-year lease term. However, Nike actually took action to increase its Stage I investment prior to the expiration of the initial lease term. Rather than wait for the end of the "testing period", the company invested in Stage II by committing additional investment to increase the store size within the year after the NTB opened.

The decision to invest in Stage II prior to the expiration of the first lease term can be explained from the NPV (and SOM) analysis. Unlike the other Nike Town investments examined in this study, the initial NPV analysis of Nike Town Beijing was positive, indicating that the investment will add value to the company as a "stand alone"

---

[134] Nike China has grown at a phenomenal face: in 1994 Nike China was an $8 million en- terprise; by 2002 sales had reached $100 million. In 2008, achieved $1 billion revenues in 2008. Source: the company's website.

[135] Charlie Denson, Brand President, Nike, Inc, at Beijing store opening, August 7, 2007. Source: Company site.

entity. After Stage I was implemented, the result was better than expected by the initial cash flow projections, leading to the early Stage II investment commitment with more confidence of success. Our SOM application, if applied to the initial internal NPV estimates would have enhanced the confidence of making the Stage I and Stage II investment as it would have accounted for more than the "stand alone" value added from the NPV analyses.

The Beijing case also demonstrates the implementation of an alternative sigma from a local comparative company. In the previous three cases, we use the standard deviation of Nike stock to as sigma in the three markets (UK, France, and US) that have similar market characteristics and high market correlation. China, at the moment is a distinctive market compared to the other Western markets. Its ample labor resources have invited many foreigner investments and its gigantic market demand has attracted global brands. As analyzed in the previous section, a company operating in the fast growing China would experience higher variances in operating cash flows than a company operating in the U.S. In our judgment, it is more appropriate to use an alternative sigma for our application of synergistic options to NikeTown Beijing. We selected Li Ning stock returns as the underlying asset. Li Ning stock returns reflect the Chinese sportswear industry more than the global brands (Nike and/ or Addidas) operating in China. The company's aggressive growth and expansion are reflective of its life cycle that also coincides with the growth spurt of the Chinese economy. We are fairly confident that the result embedded option values generally mirrors the external benefits of the Nike Town investment.

Since its opening on August 3, 2007, NTB has been performing well, better than the initial estimates.[136] The store has been well received[137] and has been utilized in many ways other than selling Nike products such as hosting running events and world famous sports celebrities' visits. Nike Town Beijing signals that Nike is committed long term to not only producing in China, but distributing through

---

[136] For business confidentiality, the actual results cannot be disclosed in this paper.

[137] Source: from industry general observation and media response.

retail channels that are typical of the companies present operations in the U.S. and European countries.

* WACC **% used in this study is for all investment projects, regardless of country risk, currency risk, variations of general retail sales, and sports retail sales in particular, different economic cycles compared to home country. This figure may have to be re-examined since it is project risk that dominates the risk measurement in the investment evaluation rather than home country financing cost.

7.5   Skepticism to Synergistic Option Model Validity Potential Residence from academia

The resistance to, or at least the current failure to embrace, the use of Synergistic Options Model (SOM) in general corporate finance is understandable, and is similar to the resistance to NPV methodology, the current gold standard in corporate financial valuation, when it was initially introduced as a capital investment valuation method. The pioneering work of Professor Ezra Solomon, introducing concepts of modern financial management (including the controversial topics of market-based cost of capital and net present worth) in the late 1950s and early 1960s, was also met with initial skepticism.

The integration of SOM methodology to supplement NPV can be expected to have a similar gestation period. Meanwhile, more evidence of successful implementation and other direct or indirect empirical evidence is needed to allay the concerns of skeptics. Skeptics of the Synergistic Value approach may argue that the SOM approach can be easily manipulated to support the desired outcomes or conclusions of the real investment decision-maker involved. Reasons given by these skeptics would be based on (a) the conceptual application of financial option pricing theory to real asset investment, and, (b) the potential limitations of obtaining and accurately measuring the input variables. Thus, even if one skirts the conceptual limitation, it may be suggested Grounding all calculations firmly in the data, and ensuring that rigorous quantitative methods of regression and correlation are followed by financial analysts is the best insurance against such manipulation, which, is done in this study and recommended in any of the SOM application.

Further limitations may be associated with the six input variables. The S and X variables are the present value estimates of cash inflows and outflows from the real investment project, respectively. If there are estimation errors for S and X, these errors will also appear in the associated NPV calculation, so the estimation errors are not unique or endemic to Invisible Value Model. There is not as much of a concern regarding the variables r, the risk free rate, and t, the time period of the investment. The dividend payout variable delta, which we have made equivalent to the cost of delay, $1/n$, in the Synergistic Options Model application, also seems plausible.

The variable sigma, however, is the variable of greatest concern and interest. Sigma in the financial option application is the standard deviation of the rate of return of the underlying financial asset. In our application, we used the standard deviation of rate of return of Nike stock price as the proxy for the non-traded asset investment in NikeTowns for three of the four cases, and the standard deviation of the rate of return of the stock price of the local Chinese competitor, Li Ning, as the proxy. The resulting call option values are very sensitive to the size of sigma. One can rationalize the use of specific proxies to justify larger or smaller embedded real option values in investment projects. This introduces subjectivity.

In this study, we addressed this subjectivity by running sets of regression and correlation to test the company's stock price and the local investment markets. The risk exposure and opportunity potential are different in mature markets such as Chicago, London and Paris than in expanding markets such as Beijing. Our regression and correlation testing supports our use of two different sigmas, one in London, Paris and Chicago and one in Beijing. This minimizes the bias introduced by the use of a sigma value appropriate to mature markets that is less suitable for developing markets.

BSOPM was originally created to derive a theoretical value for financial options. Traders armed with the theoretical option value could exercise arbitrage in the market, purchasing options that the market undervalues and selling options that the market overvalues. However, when we apply this model to real assets, the underlying asset is not tradable, unlike listed common stock, and the option is also not tradable unlike listed financial options.[138] Arbitrage is therefore not possible. It could be argued that tradable assets cannot be appropriately used as proxies for the non-tradable real asset investment in real option applications. However, the widespread acceptance of the real options method in a number of high investment & high risk-return industries, and the publication of numerous studies exploring and expanding Synergistic Options Model (SOM) methodology, indicates that the method has validity and utility.

Potential Residence from Practitioners

Given the above conceptual limitations and the risk of possible misuse of the SO concept, management might consider implementing a process requiring investment proposals to satisfy several essential parameters or tests when using Synergistic Option Model addition to the traditional NPV. In our view, any well-reasoned attempt to quantitatively estimate the value of embedded options is preferable to having no estimates. Qualitative judgments, though a necessary part of the analytical process, are insufficient on their own. For instance, to add internal discipline to the investment review process, when strategic and/or synergistic values are given as rationale to invest in a project that has a negative net pricing value (NPV result), the proposal could be required to demonstrate that there is embedded option value in the project. Requiring quantitative justification in addition to qualitative reasoning would mean that internal analysts would have to personally learn the synergistic option concept and be able to provide reasons for selecting appropriate proxies for the variables to determine the synergistic option value. As previously mentioned, institutional resistance to any new methodology can be expected, and management must be diligent advocates to ensure that synergistic value options is ultimately accepted by financial analysts.

---

[138] Damodaran, Aswath, *Damodaran on Valuation: Security Analysis for Investment and Corporate Finance*, 2nd Edition (NY, Wiley, 2006), especially Chapter 12. Also see, Ronald Fink, "Reality Check for Real Options", *CFO Magazine*, September 13, 2001.

Management may further require qualitative and quantitative information to determine if the strategic advantages advocated are temporary competitive advantages or sustaining competitive advantages. An attempt to secure a first-mover advantage in a retail market for a limited time would be likely to generate only a temporary competitive advantage and a modest synergistic value options value, whereas an initiative aimed at not only securing first-mover advantage but also leveraging that advantage into sustained market share leadership would generate a much larger synergistic value options.

8. "Technical" Stuff

8.1 Overview—Research Methodology

This study aims to demonstrate that the use of the Synergistic Option Model (SOM) methodology in sportswear investment valuation to supplement NPV methods will improve sportswear investment valuation quality and assist managerial decision-making in investment decisions that have embedded option value, including the following: (a) expand (changing operating scale, expand or contract capacity); (b) grow (enter new markets or open new stores); (c) defer/delay option (the investments are delayed due to internal resource limitations and/or (un)favorable market conditions the option to delay investment—"wait-and-see" till the uncertainties are removed); and (d) stage investment (the investments are spread out into stages). This study examines the evolution of the sportswear industry.

The industry demonstrates characteristics similar to those of the High Investment & High Risk-Return industries. The sportswear industry thus presents opportunities for SOM analysis, particularly when 1) the investment has a embedded strategic value that is not captured by the traditional NPV; and 2) the anticipated return depends largely on market information that does not yet exist. No competitors in the sportswear, or in any other retail industry, have yet used the BSOPM to analyze such synergistic options. SOM methodology has also not yet been used by firms in the sportswear industry, although there is no theoretical reason why it could not be used. This study is the first to examine and propose the use of SOM methodology in the sportswear industry.

Furthermore, this study aims to demonstrate a rationale for applying SOM methodology to supplement the NPV method in sportswear industry investment valuation. This is an innovative and much-needed extension of SOM application. This paper illustrates that the SOM analysis can successfully capture some if not all of the non-financial values embedded within investments in sportswear industry flagship store investments[139].

This extension of the SOM approach to sportswear investments is new. While future research may broaden and generalize this application to other industries, the dynamics of the sportswear industry cannot be assumed to be exactly the same as those of traditional High Investment & High Risk-Return industries. In this study, therefore, the application of SOM methodology is appropriately examined on a case by case basis.

Due to the shortcomings in the NPV financial valuation model in such High Investment & High Risk-Return industries, financial analysts in these industries began searching for alternative or supplemental methods of valuing investments. The SOM concept proved successful in overcoming the weaknesses of the NPV model and has proven to be a useful alternative and supplement to that model when applied to such industries. NPV still has its merits when it is used in the right way. However, using the NPV method alone has become less useful in valuing investment opportunities in HRR industries, and SOM methodology has therefore come to be employed in capital budgeting in these industries as a supplement to NPV.

The study describes the model to be tested in this study: the BSOPM formula, as applied to synergistic options. It elaborates how to estimate each of the components in the BSOPM equations in the real asset valuation process. In addition, it integrated the case study with the testing analyses; and concludes its generalizability of this application.

- BSOPM variables applied in other HRR industries are not directly transferable to the sportswear industry in most cases:

---

[139] This study focuses on the investments RO application in capturing the embedded non-financial values in sportswear industry investments. It is our view that it is possible that the reversal of the SOM application may also enable the divestment decision making, such as abandoning an investment opportunity when there is little or none long-term strategic value. In this "abandonment" divestment scenario, the Put BSOPM formula will be used.

a) *Strike Price (X):* One of the variables utilized in the BSOPM is the Option Strike price. In financial options, the strike price is the specified value of the underlying asset. In the oil exploration industry, a traditional High Investment & High Risk-Return industry that has adopted SOM analysis, the strike price would be the present value of the exploration development cost. This development cost is normally millions of dollars. In the sportswear industry, the total investments in the store need to be fully included, such as the initial build-out capital investment along with subsequent investments for refits or store upgrades.

b) *Dividend Payout (ä):* Sportswear investment does not possess the characteristics of payouts that are seen in some of the HRR industries, such as the oil extraction industry. In such industries, it is not unusual for parties to development agreements to have the right to withdraw from the agreement prior to the expiration of the development term. In addition, sportswear industry leases are generally for a fixed term and, once signed. neither party may withdraw from it prior to its expiration date without suffering severe penalties. Thus, oil industry development agreements (like real options in many other HRR industries) are similar to American financial options[140], whereas synergistic options in the sportswear industry is more likely characterized as European financial options[141]. However, when considering a "growth option" or "wait-and-see" option scenarios, the cost of delay of a sportswear investment could be characterized as the potential "opportunity cost." Each year of delay translates into one less year of value- creating cash flows from the life of the project. Hence, it is possible to derive an applicable equivalent to the dividend payout ratio by using 1/n as the

---

[140] American Financial Options: a style of options contract that allows holders to exercise their rights at any time before and including the expiration date.

[141] European Financial Options: a version of an options contract that limits execution to its expiration date.

proxy. In this paper, the application will be using the original BSOPM with Merton's revision when applicable.

c) *Sigma (ó):* Sigma is a measure of the uncertainty associated with a long term investment return. It can be defined in different ways, depending on industry structures as discussed in the previous section[142]. Sigma varies according to the characteristics of the product, industry, or firm. It would not be accurately transferable among industries. Indeed, the return on a sportswear investment by the same entity could be different among regions (as will be demonstrated in the case studies).

8.2 The SOM Models to be Tested

As discussed in the previous chapter, the sportswear industry has evolved from a relatively steady and low risk phenomenon requiring only modest investments to a highly competitive and volatile multinational phenomenon characterized by high risks. The traditional valuation tools used in industry generally—principally the NPV model—are inadequate for sportswear investment valuation decision-making. NPV can no longer adequately capture the embedded strategic value or market risks presented in the highly volatile phase of the industry that exists today. This study proposes that by using SOM methodology, the store's investment return value can be more accurately captured.

The BSOPM Equations are reproduced here for reference.

$$C = Se^{-\delta t}\{N(d_1)\} - Xe^{-rt}\{N(D_2)\}$$

Equation (2)

$$= Xe^{-rt}\{1 - N(d_2)\} - Se^{-\delta t}\{1 - N(d_2)\}$$

---

[142] See Literature Review, RO Application in Industries with Volatility.

Equation (3)

$$d_1 = \frac{\left\{ lnln\left(\dfrac{S}{X}\right) + \left(r - \delta + \dfrac{\sigma^2}{2}\right)t \right\}}{\sigma\sqrt{t}}$$

$$d_2 = d_1 - \sigma\sqrt{t}$$

C: Call Option Value

P: Put Option Value

(S):   Present value of underlying asset—the present value of cash flows expected from the investment opportunity.

(X):   the option strike price- The present value of total committed investment

(σ):   Sigma—the standard deviation of the sales growth rate

(t):   the period for which the investment opportunity is valid

(r):   risk-free rate

(δ):   Dividend payouts -when applicable cost of delay—Annual cost of delay 1/n

N(d) = cumulative normal probability

The application of this model determines the "option value" of an investment or divestment. In the investment valuation, C is added to the NPV value when valuing existing investments (option value is embedded), and either reduces the negative NPV or increases the already-positive NPV. The final SOM-adjusted NPV value represents the asset's investment value. When NPV is positive, but the cash flows are accompanied by great uncertainty, utilizing SOM in addition to NPV allows the analyst to place a "value" appropriate for that risk. In the divestment valuation, P is compared to the Net Liquidation. Value to determine if the investment should be terminated or remain in operation.

To utilize the BSOPM (Merton Revised) formula, sources for various components in the formula must be identified and estimated. Table 1 summarizes how this study proposes to implement / estimate the BSOPM variables in the valuation of call options in the sportswear industry. (Note: The "dividend" variable in the table only applies when the scenario might involve a delay of the investment, where some fraction of true value-creating cash flows during the life of the investment might be "lost.")

Table 19: Inputs for Option Valuation in General in the Sportswear Retail Industry

Components	Description	Estimators in Sportswear
S	Value of the Underlying Asset	Present Value of Expected Cash Inflows (discounted by the company-wide cost of capital rate)
σ	Std Dev of rate of the return of Underlying Asset (sigma)	Std_Dev of company's stock price Std_Dev of the store's sales (store specific) Std_Dev of the major local competitor stock prices (store specific)
X	Exercise / Strike Price on Option	Present Value of the cost of making the full investment on the project: upfront construction costs, fit-out costs, etc. (discounted by the risk-free rate if cost is known with certainty. If uncertain, discount rate is company-wide cost of capital).
t	Expiration of the Option	Life of the store investment duration

δ	Dividend Yield—which is forgone as an option holder—(if appropriate)	Proxy: Annual cost of delay = 1/n (Each year of delay translates into one less year of value-creating cash flows from the life of the projects)

8.3   Determining Sigma in the Sportswear Industry

Sigma (σ) in BSOPM is an important variable to determine in the Synergistic Options Model application. In the Literature Review Section of this paper, the three main applications of sigma were discussed. As the sportswear industry has its own distinguishing characteristics, sigma for the industry needs to be determined to reflect its industry characteristics. Historically, the following sigma application has been used in the industries that applied Synergistic Options Model.

1) *Historical volatility of the underlying asset:* When the price of a natural resource determines the future cash flow of the investment, the historical volatility of that resource can be utilized as sigma.

2) *Historical volatility of the company's stock price:* This estimation of sigma can be utilized when project volatility correlates with the stock price movement of the company.

3) *Historical volatility of the industry index:* The historical volatility of the industrial group index has also been used to estimate the volatility of the project value.

In searching and testing the appropriate sigma for the sportswear industry, we have examined each of the above. The detailed analysis is in Chapter 5, Case Studies Overview.

8.4 Data Sources / Cases

8.4.1 Data Sources.

This research is based on case-by-case studies of investments in major stores located in different countries and on different continents. Data used in calculating NPV and SOM are the same sets of historical data at the time when the stores were under consideration of investments. We would not have any indication of how these stores were to perform against the original projections and/or expectation. Certain criteria to conduct the blindfolded selection include geographic diversity, size of the stores, investments required, and strategic influence. Although the data may be proportionally adjusted and the individual store names and locations will be concealed for business confidentiality, this proprietary database[143] is a significant contribution toward development of the SOM methodology proposed in this study, since it enables verification of the model by allowing "back-testing" to compare the results of SOM-augmented valuation versus NPV-only valuation, particularly in capturing the "non-financial" strategic substance.

The present study focuses on four flagship[144] retail stores with the following general considerations:

4) Stores are selected based on magnitude in their store size, sales, investments involved.

5) Data may need to be "flushed" of identifiers relating to place, store name, and investors.

6) The original sets of data used for the initial NPV analysis will be extracted for each store and will be inserted into the SOM formula where appropriate.

---

[143] The company examined in this study, Nike, is a global leader in the sportswear industry and its operations should provide a reasonably good foundation for this research. Data may be proportionally adjusted and the individual store names and locations will be concealed for business confidentiality.

[144] Flagship stores: mega-stores featuring enhanced product presentation, normally located in key cities around the world.

7) All additional data required for the SOM will be extracted from the same database.

8.5 Testing Procedure / Analyses for Investment Decisions

Before stores were built, NPV analyses were performed to support the store-opening decisions. When NPV was negative, no store was built (unless other strategic reasons mandated building the store). When NPV was positive, normally the decision was made to build the store. Most of the original NPV calculations remain accessible for examination in connection with this study.

First, we identify the variables in BSOPM in Sportswear Industry and their appropriate applications; second, we use the same data that were available at the time the original NPV calculation to calculate the SOM. Third, we compare the NPV and SOM results and rationalize the embedded "non-financial" values. Finally, the NPV and SOM results will together be examined to determine whether and how supplementing NPV with SOM would have added value to real investment valuation.

8.6 Inputs required in the application of the Synergistic Options Model

We have stated in previous sections that the traditional valuation tools used in industry, principally the NPV methodology and variations thereof, are insufficient and incomplete for major investment valuation decisions in the sportswear industry. NPV uses a "discount" rate that in theory is capable of capturing the market risk. This approach may be suited for stable growth companies in mature industries; however, in highly volatile high growth industries with multidimensional variables contributing to uncertainty, and therefore, to market risk, the NPV method must be supplemented by other tools to adequately value investment feasibility.

While research questions raised in finance are normally resolved empirically, the current literature on synergistic options is lacking in robust econometrically modeled research. The primary reason for this is that unlike financial options, synergistic options as well as the assets underlying these synergistic options are not traded, and thus, cannot be directly tested against the theoretical attributes. With this in mind, we will use the case study method to examine theoretical attributes of BSOPM, based on the data taken from actual investment decisions within a large multinational company.

Undoubtedly, the case study approach will be unsettling to financial economists who are accustomed to conducting quantitative empirical studies. Nevertheless, it is instructive to follow the arguments of Jensen (1983), particularly Section VII on Methodology and subsection C on the "Nature of Evidence"[145]. Jensen's discussion is based on his development of a Positive Theory of Organizations via his proposed General Theory of Contracts where he refers to the organization as a nexus for a complex set of contracts. Our study proposes to apply the deductive approach, testing the predictions of synergistic value options against the actual data of a firm's investment projects. If the results from our application of the Synergistic Options Model to the data are substantially inconsistent with the predictions—the hypothesis that synergistic options have value not captured by commonly investment evaluation tool, NPV—then according to Jensen the "positive theory" should be modified or replaced with an alternative. Otherwise, the theory is not invalidated by our application to the case examples and serves as evidence in the continuing test of the theory[146].

We have discussed earlier the evolution of the sportswear industry from a relatively steady to a highly competitive industry sector and from a low risk phenomenon requiring only modest investments to a volatile multinational phenomenon characterized by high growth and high risk. It is our view that this evolution has primarily been driven by the nature and dimensions of the impact that sport has on the lives

---

[145] Jensen, M. Organization Theory and Methodology, Accounting Review, April 1983, v. LVIII, No. 2, pp. 319-339).

[146] Unlike financial options, almost no real options can be detached from the underlying real assets—options to real estate may be argued to be an exception. We cannot predict future innovations that detach part or all of the "real" option value arising from a real asset investment, and thus, present observable market prices for quantitative studies.

of people today, making the sports retail industry one that can be fairly characterized as dynamic, highly competitive, and uncertain. In today's sportswear industry, successful multinational companies must have strong brand recognition to sustain and gain global market shares. To build and maintain that brand image, multinational sports retail companies have focused intensely on inducing major sports "icons" to use their products, and in doing so, they have vaulted these sports "superstars" to celebrity status. This strategy was pioneered in the global sports industry by the company that we examine in this study, Nike Inc.

As discussed in the previous sections, the SOM approach utilizes the Black Scholes Option Pricing Model (the "BSOPM"). The BSOPM[147] is a valuation model with a built-in capability to replicate a non-arbitrage (risk-neutral) portfolio.

Equation 2 indicates that the value of the call option in real assets depends on six variables. S is the present value of the underlying asset which is determined from discounting and summing the expected cash flows from the investment. In our case studies, it is the management's estimations of net cash inflows discounted by the corporate Weighted Average Cost of Capital (WACC). X is the option strike price. It is the cost in present value terms of the investment calculated by discounting and summing the estimated cash outflows using the risk free rate. Note that S minus X is the NPV.

The third variable is sigma (σ), which measures the volatility of the underlying asset value. We note here the counterintuitive implication of volatility and call value when compared to NPV. For example, if there is significant uncertainty or variance in the value of the underlying asset, sigma will have a higher value. And the call option value will increase. This is counterintuitive because in the NPV approach, increased uncertainty is compensated by increasing the discount rate to account for the increased risk which should then lower the sum of the present value of the cash inflows, resulting a

---

[147] Black Scholes, op. cit. Black and Scholes (1973) stated, "it is possible to create a fully hedged position, consisting of a long position in the stock and a short position in the option, whose value will not depend on the price of the stock, but will depend only on time and the values of known constants."

lower NPV. In short, higher volatility increases the real option value of the investment, but higher volatility decreases computed NPV. Reliance on NPV alone becomes problematic if synergistic options, as hypothesized, are shown to have value. As stated before, neither the remodeling project nor the real assets are tradable; thus, the value of sigma cannot be observed from the market and must be estimated.

The fourth variable is "t", the time period for which the investment opportunity is valid. The fifth variable is "r", risk-free rate, assuming that the investment outlay in present value terms is known with certainty. The final variable is delta, δ. In the financial option application of the Black Scholes model, δ is the dividend yield that is foregone as an option holder and it is in the model to take into consideration that the payment of dividend reduces the underlying stock price. For the real option application, we will use a proxy to reflect the annual cost of delay, $1/n$, if applicable, for the reason that each year of delay translates into one less year of value-creating cash inflows from the life of the projects—equivalent to the foregone dividend yield. Of the six input variables, sigma requires further explanation since the estimated value of the variance of the underlying asset has a significant influence on the value of the option. In the literature review section, we have identified extensively, and summarized in Table 26, what prior studies have used to estimate the variance in the return of underlying asset.

Earlier in the methodology section we had proposed that the variance of the rate of change of sales be used as the basis for estimating sigma. Regression analysis documents the relationship of 64 quarters of Nike sales and Nike stock prices[148]. Other financial variables, including cash flows and return on invested capital, were

---

[148] When businesses are "publicly traded," their equity can be purchased and sold by investors in stock markets available to the general public. Stock prices are recognized and perceived by investors as one of the key valuation indicators when assessing the return of an investment. They also reflect market volatility and the industry's specific risks and opportunities. The stock price has therefore been widely considered as one of the key performance indicators representing the company's value. It is a perceptible manifestation of the company's value, comprised of both current operational performance and future growth potential. It, the stock price, is considered as the primary proxy for a (public-traded) company's valuation.

also tested against the Nike stock price. However, results of the regression of sales and Nike stock price are the most robust. This provides us with confidence to propose the variance of the return on historical Nike stock price be used as the primary estimate for sigma.

8.7   Regressions and Correlations

When a company uses the word "growth", it invariably means the growth of sales. Companies with a history of high growth, the so- called "high growth" companies, inevitably find investment analysts and all current and potential investors in the company's stock closely track sales levels over time. Investors will buy or sell the stock depending on whether they believe the company is meeting the sales growth expectations. Nike Inc. has been known in the investment community as a growth company. In our view, growth companies like Nike will find their stock prices are significantly driven by their sales levels. This is not uncommon in industry-leading companies. These companies have established economies of scale in sourcing, manufacturing, supply chains, and distribution. These competitive advantages enable these companies to retain a greater proportion of its top line sales revenue, enhancing its EBIT [149] efficiently and effectively in comparison to smaller companies[150]. Nike is known for investing in marketing campaigns[151] and sports

---

[149] Bodie, Z., Kane, A. and Marcus, A. J. *Essentials of Investments*, McGraw Hill Irwin, 2004, p. 452. Defined as an accounting and finance term, earnings before interest and taxes (EBIT) or operating income is a measure of a firm's profitability that excludes interest and income tax expenses.

[150] In addition to the foregoing, the changes in accounting methods and treatments also make sales performance a more direct valuation measure of return on investment than some of the traditional accounting measurements, such as ROIC (Return On Invested Capital). Different methods (including depreciation choices, inventory valuation methods, write-offs, asset-mix definitions, goodwill valuations, and/or tax treatments) will generate differences in earnings and cash flow. Although all these methods are consistent with and comply with GAAP (the US standard General Accepted Accounting Principles), these differences introduce factors other than the business performance itself. For these reasons, investors and financial analysts consider sales performance and the ability to generate future sales as the key indictors representing return on investments, rather than alternative accounting or financial measures.

[151] For instance, June 24th, 2010, Nike Fiscal Year and 4th Quarter Earnings Release, "Demand creation expenses were higher last year due to expenses incurred to support

celebrity endorsements[152]. Nevertheless, it also has the reputation for effectively managing operating expenses by saving expenses in other areas[153].

To test the relationship of sales and stock price, we ran a regression in which stock price (P) is the dependent variable, and Sales (S) is the independent variable. The 64 quarters of data from 1995 to 2008 is taken from publicly available sources. We further note that the stock price data are adjusted for stock splits. Regression results are as follows where the figures in parenthesis are the t-values.

$$\text{Stock Price } (P) = -4.67 + 1.31(S) \quad R^2 = 0.83$$

$$(-1.88) \; (17.34)$$

The regression fit is robust and the coefficients are significant at the 5% level. The correlation of sales and stock prices is 0.91. Given these results, we are more confident in using the variance of stock price as the proxy for the variance of the underlying investment made in the flagship stores.

8.7.1 The Key Variable in the Model: Sigma

Sigma is a measure of volatility that helps to capture or represent strategic value. This study evaluated the use of SOM analysis to supplement NPV in evaluating sportswear retail store investments' total benefits in terms of both financial returns and strategic values. To determine the SOM equation variable sigma, we explored three major alternative proxies: the company's stock price performance, the retail industry index performance, and store sales performances.

---

the Olympic Games in Beijing and the European Championships."

[152] Some examples are: Nike signed Michael Jordan first 5-year contract for $2.5 million in 1984; Nike signed Tiger Woods a five-year contract for $40 million in 1996; signed LeBron James a seven-year endorsement contract worth more than $90 million in 2003 and resigned in 2010.

[153] For instance, June 24th, 2010, Nike Fiscal Year and 4th Quarter Earnings Release, "The effective tax rate for the first quarter was 24.7 percent compared to 28.5 percent for the same period last year. The first quarter tax rate benefitted from our lower on-going tax rate on operations outside the United States."

We ran regressions to document the relationship between 64 quarters of Nike sales and Nike stock prices. We ran regressions of other financial variables such as cash flows and return on invested capital against the Nike stock price. The regression and correlation analysis conducted using multiple observations in different time periods generates a strong correlation. The results of the Nike stock price regression are the most robust of the variables tested, providing us with confidence in our proposal that the variance of the return on historical Nike stock price is an appropriate estimate for sigma. Nike's recent emphasis on "Direct to Consumer" investments[154] is reflective of, and consistent with, its broad array of ongoing strategic investments. The company's major capital investment projects, such as opening new or renovating existing NikeTowns, should correlate to the company's overall stock performance.

---

[154] According to Jeanne Jackson, President of Direct-to-Consumers, Nike, Inc., the "Direct-to-Consumer" program proposes to achieve the next phase of Nike brand growth through building capacity in the retail marketplace. The company plans to invest between $500 million and $600 million in the next few years until 2015, in stores and in infrastructure to support both company-owned and external wholesale/retail productivity and performance.

9. Literature Review

9.1 Theoretical Foundation Overview

9.1.1 Financial Foundation Overview.

In 1973, Fischer Black and Myron Scholes devised a formula to value financial options[155], known as the Black Scholes Option Pricing Model. The original formula calculates the theoretical option value—the present value of the expected option payoff—under the assumption that no dividends, taxes, or transaction costs were paid. This model was based on the proposition that options are not correctly priced in the market. If they could be more accurately priced through use of a financial model, it would become possible to capture riskless profits by creating portfolios of long and short positions in options and stocks.[156]

Later modified by Robert Merton, the formula incorporates dividends. This dividend variable reduces the value of the share to the option holder by the present value of the forgone dividend and reduces the cost of holding a share by the dividend stream that would be received[157]. Since then, the Black Scholes Option Pricing Model with Merton's modification has been widely used to value options in the financial investment sector because the theory proved to be quite accurate. In 1997, Myron Scholes and Robert Merton were awarded the Nobel Prize in Economics.

---

[155] Financial options: for the payment of a specific price, a financial option provide the right (but not the obligation) to buy or sell a specific amount of a stock or other financial asset during a specified time window, for a specified price (the "strike" price). Financial options are generally freely tradable. The underlying financial asset might be common stock, bonds or other financial instruments.

[156] Black, F. and Scholes, M. (1973) "The Pricing of Options and Corporate Liabilities", Journal of Political Economy, (May-June), 637-659.

[157] Merton, R.C. (1973) "Theory of Rational Option Pricing", *Bell Journal of Economics and Management Science* vol. 4 (Spring).

In 1984, Stewart Myers extended the option pricing analysis of financial options to the valuation of real asset[158] investments in the corporate finance sector. This review will provide an overall summary of the literature and will then concentrate on the most significant research addressing the application of the BSOPM to real asset valuation in corporate financial planning.

In their 1973 article, "The Pricing of Options and Corporate Liabilities", Black and Scholes started with a general introduction to options and demonstrated the relationship between option price and stock price. In general, the higher the stock price, the higher will be its call option price; in a simple call option scenario, a given percentage change in stock price (given the maturity constant) will result in a larger percentage change in the corresponding option value. "The relative volatility of the option is not constant, however: it depends on both the stock price and maturity."[159] Before proceeding to use the relationship to derive the BSOPM, they analyzed the previous work on the valuation of options[160].

In 1969, Merton, together with Scholes, recognized that "discounting the expected value of the distribution of possible values of the warrant when it is exercised is not an appropriate procedure. ... But they do not make use of the fact that investors must hold other assets as well, so that the risk of an option or stock that affects its discount rate is only that part of the risk that cannot be diversified away."[161]

The last developed concept is expressed by Thorp and Kassouf (1967), who "obtain[ed] an empirical valuation formula for warrants

---

[158] Real assets: Actual, tangible asset (such as valuable antique or art, buildings, coins, commodity, machinery and equipment, stamp collection) as opposed to financial assets (such as bonds, debentures, shares).

[159] Black, F. and Scholes, M. (1973) "The Pricing of Options and Corporate Liabilities", Journal of Political Economy, (May-June).

[160] Starting from Sprenkle's 1961 formula for valuing warrants. In this expression, however, Black & Scholes commented that Sprenkle was not able to identify two variables: k and k^*.

[161] Ibid. Direct source: Samuelson, Paul A., and Merton, Robert C. "A Complete Model of Warrant Pricing that Maximizes Utility.", Indus. Management Rev. 10, (Winter 1969): 17-46.

by fitting a curve to actual warrant prices. ... What they fail to pursue is the fact that in equilibrium, the expected return on such a hedged position must be equal to the return on a riskless asset."[162]

Quite interestingly, in his 1973 paper, Merton argues BSOPM is "to express the expected return on the option in terms of the option price function and its partial derivatives."[163] Merton's bold statement is based on the distributional assumptions of BSOPM and on the proposition that the option price is a function of the common stock price.

Black and Scholes went through their model's rationale in a step-by-step fashion, beginning with the assumed "Ideal Conditions" in the stock and options market:

1) The short-term interest rate is known and constant;

2) The stock price follows a random walk in continuous time with a variance rate proportional to the square of the stock price.

3) The stock pays no dividends during the option's life.[164]

4) Inflexible European option exercise terms exist, i.e., the option can only be exercised on its expiration date.[165]

5) No commissions are charged

Black and Scholes proposed that under those assumptions, "it is possible to create a fully hedged position, consisting of a long position in the stock and a short position in the option, whose value will not

---

[162] Black, F. and Scholes, M. (1973) "The Pricing of Options and Corporate Liabilities", *Journal of Political Economy*, (May-June).

[163] Merton, R.C. (1973) "Theory of Rational Option pricing", *Bell Journal of Economics and Management Science* vol. 4 (Spring).

[164] This limitation was later eliminated by Merton (1973).

[165] American exercise terms allow the option to be exercised at any time during the life of the option, making American options more valuable due to their greater flexibility. European options only permit the option to be exercised at the expiration date. By way of illustration, in the case of an American-style call option for common stock, the fixed amount might be 100 shares, offered for a fixed price (the exercise price), payable on or before a fixed date (the expiration date).

depend on the price of the stock, but will depend only on time and the values of known constants."[166]

The authors observed that, "The ratio of the change in the option value to the change in the stock price, when the change in the stock price is small, is $w_1(x,t)$ ... Thus, the change in the value of a long position in the stock will be approximately offset by the change in value of a short position in 1/w1 options."[167]

They further noted that, "The ratio of the decline in the equity value to the magnitude of the change in the stock price becomes smaller as the magnitude of the change in the stock price becomes smaller."[168] A third discovery was that "the stock price follows a continuous random walk[169] and that the return has a constant variance rate, the covariance between the return on the equity and the return on the stock will be zero. If the stock price and the value of the 'market portfolio' follow a joint continuous random walk with constant covariance rate it means that the covariance between the return on the equity and the return on the market will be zero." They conclude, "the risk in the hedged position is zero."[170]

This brilliant consequential deterministic thinking gave birth to the major contribution in the history of option valuation: a valuation model with a built-in capability to replicate a non-arbitrage portfolio (risk-neutral)[171]. The option value model is a function of the stock

---

[166] Black, F. and Scholes, M. (1973) "The Pricing of Options and Corporate Liabilities", *Journal of Political Economy*, (May-June).

[167] Ibid.

[168] Ibid.

[169] There are non-linear practitioners who do not believe in the continuous random walk. Keith Fitz-Gerald, licensed CTA, Investment Director Money Map Press, says, "stock prices and options prices can and do sometimes move outside model pricing parameters or into contagion which again actually introduces an element of risk that, according to the BSOPM, is not theoretically possible."

[170] Black, F. and Scholes, M. (1973) "The Pricing of Options and Corporate Liabilities", *Journal of Political Economy*, (May-June).

[171] In real trading, practitioners could urge caution on a "truly risk free portfolio": "there is no such thing as a truly riskless position except under extremely specialized circumstances usually associated with mispricing that occurs at the money when puts and calls may be disproportionately priced.", Keith Fitz-Gerald, licensed CTA, Investment Director Money Map Press.

price (which is obtainable in the trading market) and is independent of the expected return on the stock.

The introduction of the BSOPM as a valid and reliable option pricing mechanism led to the increasing popularity of financial options and to the subsequent introduction and widespread trading of financial options, including currency and stock options, on organized exchanges. Thanks to the BSOPM, the valuation of such investments is well understood by investors and financial analysts.

The Original BSOPM formula is as follows:

$$BSOPM = S\left\{N\left(d_1\right)\right\} - Xe^{-rt}\left\{N\left(d_2\right)\right\}$$

Equation (1)

(S): Present value of underlying stock

(X): the option strike price

(σ): Sigma uncertainty

(t): the period for which the investment opportunity is valid

(r): the yield of a risk-less security with the same maturity as the duration of the option.

N(d) = cumulative normal probability

$$d_1 = \frac{\left\{lnln\left(\dfrac{S}{X}\right) + \left(r - \delta + \dfrac{\sigma^2}{2}\right)t\right\}}{\sigma\sqrt{t}}$$

$$d_2 = d_1 - \sigma\sqrt{t}$$

S{N(d₁)} is the present value of the expected terminal stock price based on the assumption that the call option[172] will be profitable (in

---

[172] A *call option* is a contract giving its owner the right to buy, and a *put option* is a contract giving its owner the right to sell, a fixed amount of a specified underlying asset at a fixed

the money) at expiration multiplied by the probability that the call will be in the money at expiration. $Xe^{-rt}\{N(d_2)\}$ is the present value of the cost of exercising the option at expiration multiplied by the probability that the call will be in the money at expiration. The difference of these two expressions is equal to the market value of the option.

Table 20 shows the effect of increase in equation (1) variables on the call and put option prices as the respective variables changes. Overall, all five of the variables in the original BSOPM are increasing the options values.

Table 20: Effect of Increase in BSOPM Variable on Call and Put Option Prices

Increase in:	Call Price	Put Price
1. Current Stock Price	Increase	Decrease
2. Exercise Price	Decrease	Increase
3. Volatility	Increase	Increase
4. Interest Rates	Increase	Decrease
5. Time to Expiration	Increase	Increase

Using US Treasury bonds as an illustration, consider an option to buy a US Treasury bond (with a coupon rate of 8%, and with maturity in 30 years) at a price of $87. This American option[173] can be exercised at any time between the date of its purchase and its expiration date. Assume that the expiration date is September 30th. For the purpose of demonstration, let's assume the cost of the call (that is, the option premium) is $1.50. Based on these assumptions, the next table can be readily derived:

---

price (known as the "strike price" or "exercise price") at any time prior to the expiration date (American Option) or on a fixed date (European Option).

[173] American Option is a *financial option* that can be exercised at any time prior to the expiration date.

Table 21: Black Scholes Option Valuation Model Example—US Treasury Bond

T-bond Price on Sept. 30	Gross Payoff	Net Payoff
$86	0	-1.5
$87	0	-1.5
$88	1	-0.5
$89	2	0.5
$90	3	1.5
$91	4	2.5
$100	13	12.5
$110	23	22.5

From the table, it can be seen that only when the T-Bond price exceeds $88.5 ($87 +$1.50) will an investor be making money (in the money). If the T-Bond price is lower than $87, then the investor will lost only the option premium of $1.5. This seems rather obvious; however, in reality, we don't know if the price of the T-Bond on September 30th (when the option expires) will be higher or lower than $87, nor do we know if the option premium is reasonably priced. This is why a valuation model or formula was needed to evaluate the price of the option when financial options emerged as investment derivatives.

9.1.1.1 *Black-Scholes Model Assumptions.*[174]

1) It is possible to borrow and lend cash at a known constant risk- free interest rate.

2) There is no arbitrage opportunity.

3) The underlying security does not pay a dividend—although later revised by Merton. Most companies pay dividends to their shareholders. A common way of adjusting the model for

---

[174] Black, F. and Scholes, M. (1973) "The Pricing of Options and Corporate Liabilities", *Journal of Political Economy*, (May-June).

this situation is to subtract the discounted value of a future dividend from the stock price.

4) The stock price follows a geometric Brownian motion with constant drift and volatility.

5) All securities are infinitely divisible (i.e., it is possible to buy any fraction of a share).

6) There are no restrictions on short selling not transaction costs, taxes or bid-ask spread.

9.1.1.2 Theory building Blocks—Black & Scholes & Merton.

In Merton's 1973 article[175], he introduced continuous changes in the option prices as the underlying asset value changes. In so doing, he extended the BSOPM to apply to the American Options. Furthermore, he incorporated the dividend element into the BSOPM. Because option holders are not receiving the stock prices, they would be reduced by the dividend yield. Merton's Variation Model-with dividend δ is as follows:

Call Option—BSOPM Merton's Revision

$$C = Se^{-\delta t}\{N(d_1)\} - Xe^{-rt}\{N(D_2)\}$$

Equation (2)

Put Option—BSOPM Merton's Revision

$$P = Xe^{-rt}\left\{1 - N\left(d_2\right)\right\} - Se^{\delta t}\left\{1 - N\left(d_1\right)\right\}$$

Equation (3)

The Put option is derived from put-call parity: that is, selling a call and buying a put.

---

[175] Merton, R.C. (1973) "Theory of Rational Option pricing", *Bell Journal of Economics and Management Science* vol. 4 (Spring).

$$C - P = S - Xe^{-rt}$$

C = Call Value

P = Put Value

S = Price of underlying Asset

X = Strike Price in Call Option or Salvage Value if abandonment

$$d_1 = \frac{\left\{ lnln\left(\dfrac{S}{X}\right) + \left(r - \delta + \dfrac{\sigma^2}{2} \right)t \right\}}{\sigma\sqrt{t}}$$

$$d_2 = d_1 - \sigma\sqrt{t}$$

Table 22: Put-Call Option Parity

	Pay off when S > X	Pay off at t when S < X
Sell Call	$-(Se^{-\delta t} - X)$	0
Buy Put	0	$X - Se^{-\delta t}$
Buying Stock outright	$Se^{-\delta t}$	$Se^{-\delta t}$
Total	X	X

Put call parity yields X with certainty , cost of creating parity with certainly is PV of X at riskless rate, Xe^{-rt}

$$S + P - C = Xe^{-rt}$$

$$C - P = S = e^{-rt}$$

Substitute into BSOPM:

Value of

$$P = Xe^{-rt}\{1 - N(d_2)\} - Se^{-\delta t}\{1 - N(d_2)\}$$

Essentially, same type of the information required for the Call Option model calculation. S, X, T may be different from the ones used to estimate call value, but it is probably the same.

Dividends payout (δ): the value that drains away over the duration of the option. In this revised version, the dividend value changes the d_1 value and the first expression value (). Another way to explain this modified model is: 1) discount both S and X to PV; 2) adjust X by the interest yield an investor can get by depositing the money instead of buying the underlying stock outright 3) reduce the S by the dividend yield that one wouldn't receive as a call option holder (δt) here is the continuously compounded dividend yield. The d_1 and d_2 are formulas in which variables are used to look up the N values in the probability distribution table.

A simple example[176] will demonstrate the workings of this model. Suppose a stock is trading at $57 on October 16, 2008, and after passage of one year, on October 16th, 2009, it will trade for either $75 or $55. The stock will pay a dividend of $1.15 if the stock price is $75. If the strike price is $63, what is an appropriate option price? The option value can be found by directly plugging all the variables into the BSOPM formula, as follows:

    (S)   Stock price: $57 (as of October 16, 2008)

    (X)   The option strike price: $63

    (σ)   Sigma: 37% (the firm's 1-year historic volatility)

    (t)   1 Year

    (r)   10% (assuming risk-free rate)

Utilizing these values, the BSOPM formula yields an option value of $7.72. This means that a buyer, using the formula, would spend $7.72 to buy the right to buy the stock at $63 at the end of

---

[176] This example is extracted from MorningStar Option Trading Platform on a real-time market priced existing option as of October 16, 2008, adjusted using 1-year expiry time period for the sake of simplicity. This option pays a dividend and therefore the calculation is based on BSOPM (Merton's 1973 adjusted version), Merton, R.C. (1973) "Theory of Rational Option pricing", *Bell Journal of Economics and Management Science* vol. 4 (Spring), 160.

the year (or, possibly, before the end of the year if the buyer decides to exercise the option prior to its expiration date). This option price will be fully covered if the stock price reaches above "Strike Price + Option Premium + Dividend Loss as an option holder"—that is, $71.87 ($63+$7.72+$1.15) or if the stock is below $70 when the option terminates. To calculate the option value, it is first necessary to construct the value of a portfolio of this stock with exactly the same payoffs as the option. Secondly, the number of shares of stock in the portfolio must be found by generating a portfolio by holding the stock and selling the option. According to the logic of Black and Scholes, the portfolio is of the non-arbitrage variety and, hence, should be independent of the change in the stock price[177].

This manually calculated result of $7.32 is very close to the result of $7.8 from spreadsheet calculation. Black and Scholes used the same logic: the value of the option can be tracked by holding a combination of the stock and risk-free securities, which creates a leveraged position in the stock. If the portfolio is continuously being updated with the number of shares to hold, whenever the value of the stock changes, (in financial jargon, "rebalancing the portfolio") the portfolio will change with both the stock price and time.[178] Merton, in his own research, described the B-S hedging portfolio as such: "A hedged portfolio containing the common stock, the option, and

---

[177] The calculation is as follows:

$75Δ—$1.15= $55—$0

$Δ = 0.75$

Therefore, the portfolio will consist of holding 0.75 shares of stock and selling the option. Next, the value of the portfolio in one year must be calculated. The portfolio consists of holding 0.75 shares of stock and the option. There are 0.75 shares in the portfolio, the value of the portfolio is $75*0.75, from which we must delete the value of the dividend paid at the end of the year:

$75*0.75—1.15 = $55

This value must then be discounted back to present (using a 10% discount rate as an example):

$55-($55*10%) = $50

The portfolio value consists of holding long stock and selling the option, and so the value of the option will be the difference between the portfolio value ($50) and the value of the long stock position ($57 * 0.75 shares) = $42.6

$50- $42.6=$7.32

[178] Black, F. and Scholes, M. (1973) "The Pricing of Options and Corporate Liabilities", *Journal of Political Economy*, (May-June).

short- term, riskless security, is constructed where the portfolio weights are chosen to eliminate all 'market risk.'" [179]

Merton's first contribution to option pricing modeling consisted of his recognition that "discounting the expected value of the distribution of possible values of the warrant when it is exercised is not an appropriate procedure.[180]" More importantly, he pointed out to Black & Scholes while they were developing the model that, "if the hedged portfolio is maintained continuously, the approximations become exact, and the return on the hedged position is completely independent of the change in the value of the stock."[181]

"To derive the formula, they assume that the option price is a function of the stock price and time to expiration, and note that, over "short" time intervals, the stochastic part of the change in the option price will be perfectly correlated with changes in the stock price."[182]

Merton in his own research has shown that "the value of the option is always greater than the value it would have if it were exercised immediately."[183] He demonstrated that "the value of an American put option will be greater than the value of a European put option... [Merton] was the first to point out that the current adjustment for dividends is not adequate."[184]

Merton's earlier work on valuing financial options built upon the pioneering work of Fischer Black and Myron Scholes.[185] Later, he advanced BSOPM further by incorporating dividends into the model[186]. He demonstrated that financial options could be valued by

---

[179] Merton, R.C. (1973) "Theory of Rational Option pricing", *Bell Journal of Economics and Management Science* vol. 4 (Spring), 160.

[180] Ibid.

[181] Ibid.

[182] Merton, R.C. (1973) "Theory of Rational Option pricing", *Bell Journal of Economics and Management Science* vol. 4 (Spring), 160.

[183] Ibid.

[184] Black, F. and Scholes, M. (1973) "The Pricing of Options and Corporate Liabilities", *Journal of Political Economy*, (May-June) (3).

[185] Ibid.

[186] Merton, R.C. (1973) "Theory of Rational Option pricing", *Bell Journal of Economics and Management Science* vol. 4 (Spring).

constructing portfolios that perfectly replicate all of the potential payoffs of options and that the value of this replicated portfolio could be the fair market price of the option; and the BSOPM could be used to yield this result. Any difference between the market price of this option and the BSOPM result would, at least in theory, constitute an opportunity to earn a riskless profit.

In his 1998 paper, *"Application of Option-Pricing Theory: Twenty-Five Years Later"*, Merton reviewed the history of financial innovations over the preceding twenty-five years. He then covered the application of option pricing methods; and concluded with a forecast of the future direction of options research.

As Merton pointed out, "As we shall see, the underlying conceptual framework originally used to derive the option-pricing formula can be used to price and evaluate the risk in a wide array of application, both financial and non-financial." He further stated that "Option-pricing technology has played a fundamental role in supporting the creation of new financial products and markets around the globe."[187]

Merton pointed out that in the BSOPM, the market values of options are calculated using "risk-adjusted" or "risk-neutral" probabilities. However, corporate finance has not yet fully embraced the "no-arbitrage concept"[188]. The most widely used model is still the traditional DCF approach. The DCF uses a risk-adjusted discount rate to discount cash flows of an investment. In this paper, Merton addresses this point. He thinks the use of financial options valuation methodology to value is a breakthrough in option-pricing methodology. He argues that it is important to recognize the existence of these hedging opportunities; then modify or adjust the probabilities associated with these risks. One example cited by Merton is the application of real option methodology within the natural resources exploration industry; the probability can be determined by the price of these natural resources in the commodity futures markets. However there are many industries that have no relevant markets.

---

[187] Merton, R.C. (1998) "Applications of Option-Pricing Theory: Twenty-Five Years Later", *The American Economic Review*, June.

[188] Page 33, per discussion of efficient financial market.

Merton uses an example of assessing production systems. "They exemplify their central theme with several industrial examples which include computer and automobile production...in assessing the value of modularity for production; they employ an option-pricing type of methodology, where complexity in the production system is comparable to uncertainty in the financial one."[189] He gives credits to the recent development, "much financial research and broad-based practitioner experience developed over that period have led to vast improvements in our understanding of how to apply the new financial technologies to manage risk."[190] Moreover, he stated, "we have seen how wide ranging are the applications of our technology for pricing and measuring the risk of derivatives." But he also recognizes that, "there still remains an intense uneasiness among managers, regulators, politicians, the press, and the public over these new derivative security activities and their perceived risks to financial institutions."[191]

Pointing out "further research," Merton suggests that there are two essentially different frames of reference for analyzing and understanding changes in the financial systems. "One perspective takes as given the existing institutional structure of financial service providers, whether governmental or private-sector, and examines what can be done to make those institutions perform their particular financial services more efficiently and profitably. On the other hand, "An alternative to this traditional institutional perspective is the functional perspective, which takes as given the economic functions served by the financial system and examines what is the best institutional structure to perform those functions."[192]

Merton observes that in the past, "applications of mathematical models had only limited and side-stream effects on finance practice."

---

[189] Merton, R.C. (1998) "Applications of Option-Pricing Theory: Twenty-Five Years Later", *The American Economic Review*, June.

[190] Ibid. Part III.

[191] Ibid. Part III.

[192] Ibid. Part III, also for elaboration on the functional perspective, see Merton (1993, 1995).

But, he notes, over the twenty-five years preceding his 1998 article, mathematical modeling has become mainstream—and the BSOPM has played a significant role in accelerating the acceptance of such models in financial institutions around the world. His conclusion is that, "It is safe to say that mathematical models will play an indispensable role in the functioning of the global financial systems."[193]

This influential article provides an insightful reflection on financial theory (particularly in regard to the option-pricing model) over the last quarter of the 20th Century. Merton also points out the future direction of the global financial systems; in particular, he warned that, "At times, we can lose sight of the ultimate purpose of the models when their mathematics become too interesting. The mathematics of financial models can be applied precisely, but the models are not at all precise in their application to the complex real world. Their accuracy as a useful approximation to that world varies significantly across time and place. The models should be applied in practice only tentatively, with careful assessment of their limitations in each application.[194]" Merton's vision strategically offered illumination for both academic research (which generates practical applications) and corporate practitioners.

9.1.2 Real Options.

Similar to financial option's definition, a Real Option can be considered as a right but not the obligation to acquire the present value of the expected cash flows by making an investment when the opportunity is available. Unlike financial options, Synergy Value rarely have defined lives and are generally not tradable. This has been and still is the main limitation of real option application in practice. Myers[195] constructed the "Real Option" concept for the valuation of financial options but extended the use of the concept beyond to

---

[193] Ibid, Pg. 349.

[194] Ibid, Pg. 349.

[195] Myers, Stewart C. (1977) "Determinants of Corporate Borrowing", *Journal of Financial Economics 5*, 147-175.

the valuation of opportunities embedded in long-term investment projects.

Dr. Stewart C. Myers in his research (1977) [196], he predicts "corporate borrowing is inversely related to the proportion of market value accounted for by synergistic options." He starts with a discussion of a "gap in modern finance theory", that is, "on the issue of corporate debt policy."[197] Myers suggested that, "The firm financed with risky debt will, in some states of nature, pass up valuable investment opportunities—opportunities which could make a positive net contribution to the market value of the firm."[198]

He then uses an example to demonstrate how the existence of corporate debt can reduce the present market value of the firm by weakening the corporation's incentive to undertake good future investments. He gears the discussion towards the essential characteristics of the "growth opportunities," stating that "[growth opportunities] flow from the fact that they can be regarded as a call option on a real asset."[199] He then makes a pioneering statement, "The option's exercise price is the future investment needed to acquire the asset. Whether the option has any value when it expires depends on the asset's future value, and also on whether the firm chooses to exercise. The decision to exercise is not trivial and automatic, as it is for options written on securities, because it depends on the magnitude of promised payments to bondholders."[200] This important conclusion is derived from his observation that, "The market value of almost all real assets can be partly attributed to associated call options...the ultimate payoff of almost all assets depends on future discretionary investment by the firm."

Later, in his 1984 research paper[201], Myers coined the term "Real Option" and stated for the first time that Synergistic Option

---

[196] Ibid.

[197] Ibid.

[198] Ibid.

[199] Myers, Stewart C. (1973) "Determinants of Corporate Borrowing", *Journal of Financial Economics 5*, 1977, 155.

[200] Ibid.

[201] Myers, S.C. (1984), "Financial theory and financial strategy", Interfaces, Vol. 14 No.1,

Modeltheory has the potential to close the wide gap between strategic planning and finance. "Strategic planning needs finance. Present value calculations are needed as a check on strategic analysis and vice versa.... Corporate finance theory requires extension to deal with real options."[202]

9.1.2.1 *Real Options Theory Development Building Blocks— Other Contributors.*

Dr. Stewart Myers in his 1984[203] paper indicated that traditional Discounted Cash Flow (DCF) methods have both merits and limitations in the valuation of investments. He described various misapplications of the DCF method in corporate finance, and proposed that the use of the BSOPM, previously used in the valuation of financial options, would avoid or compensate for such DCF misapplications in the valuation of real assets. He argued that option pricing holds the most promise in the valuation of such investments. Myers went on to "close the wide gap between strategic planning and finance."[204] This was recognized by some critics, among them, Hayes and Abernathy, who stated: "The traditional investments evaluation methods are not enough to catch the value associated with the real options." [205] Hodder and Riggs pointed out that the problem is not the DCF method itself, but the corporate finance practices that have misused the DCF techniques.

Trigeorgis, one of the key contributors to real option methodology development, has been a primary leader in real option modeling and

---

pp.126-37.

[202] Ibid.

[203] Myers, S.C. (1984), "Financial theory and financial strategy", Interfaces, Vol. 14 No.1, pp.126-37.

[204] See earlier section per Myers' article review.

[205] Hayes, R.H., Abernathy, William, (1980), "Managing Our Way to Economic Decline", Harvard Business Review, July-August, Pg 67-77.
This article intends to demonstrate that the flexibility effect in the investment decision. Hayes and Abernathy argue the traditional investments evaluation methods are not enough to catch the value associated with the real options and they appeal to the options valuation theory and in analogy with that catch the true value of investments with real options.

research efforts over the last decade. He has advanced the treatment of real options (in a way similar to the treatment of financial options)[206]; and he has also made positive contributions to the ongoing debate over the risk-neutral rate[207]. Further, in one of his most significant publications[208], Trigeorgis synergizes a "scattered knowledge and research" on the REAL OPTION concept and applications and provided excellent illustrations of ways and opportunities to apply the real option model to investment valuation; these illustrations included options to defer, to expand and to contract. Trigeorgis's 'growth options' research laid the foundation for subsequent conceptual discussion of the strategic and competitive aspects of gReal Optionwth opportunities[209]. The general real options frameworks presented by Merton[210] drew upon this decision.

The studies of Amram & Kulatilaka and Copeland & Keenan have also advanced real option research, making the Synergistic Options Model (SOM) concept applicable to more industries. As a result of this research advancement, the energy sector, for example, has reported that a number of strong performers[211] within the industry view their investment opportunities intuitively or instinctively as Real Options,

---

[206] "Real options in principle may be valued similar to financial options, even though real options may not be traded, since in capital budgeting we are interested in determining what the projected cash flows would be worth if they were traded in the market" (Trigeorgis, L. (1996), "Real Options: Managerial Flexibility and Strategy in Resource Allocation, MIT Press, Cambridge, MA, 1996).

[207] "For traded assets in equilibrium or for real assets with no systematic risk (e.g., R&D and exploration or drilling for certain precious metals or natural resources), the certainty-equivalent or risk-neutral growth rate just equals the risk-free interest rate (minus 'dividends')" (Trigeorgis, 1996).

[208] Trigeorgis, L. (1996), "Real Options: Managerial Flexibility and Strategy in Resource Allocation", MIT Press, Cambridge, MA, 1996.

[209] Mason, Pindyck, Kasanen, and Sick, have also contributed to the RO research through their analysis.

[210] Merton, R.C. (1998) "Applications of Option-Pricing Theory: Twenty-Five Years Later", *The American Economic Review*, June.

[211] Industry Survey: The De Jong & Koedjik, the Netherlands conducted a survey on "corporate management in the financial decision making." This process sample consists of a cross-section of 6,500 companies, represents the second largest survey sample in financial literature. The main purpose is to provide a general guidance for the main methodology currently being used by corporate management in the financial decision making process. While the Real Option comes not on the top, the result shows a positive trend of acceptance. (More details are in the Literature Review last sub-section).

positioning themselves to tap possible future cash flows without making a final decision to invest until the potential is confirmed. To sum up, since Myers' 1984 REAL OPTION introduction, Mason and Merton (1985), Dixit & Pindyck (1994), Trigeorgis (1995), Amram & Kulatilak (1999), Leslie & Michaels (2000), Gordon Sick (2001), Moel & Tufano (2002), Cassimon (2004), Lemley & Shapiro (2005), McDonald (2006), Moon & Yao & et al. (2007), surveyed the role of real options in the investment strategies of various industries[212]. The development of the REAL OPTION concept and its application to industry is summarized by the chronological milestones the table below.

Table 23: Real Option Evolution Building Blocks

YEAR	Papers	Contribution	Key Theory
1973	Black, Scholes, Merton	Pricing model	BS Option Pricing Model BS Option Pricing Model— Dividend modified
1973	Cox, Ross, Rubinstein	Binomial	Options can be replicated from an equivalent portfolio
1976	Rubinstein	Furthered studies of Cox and Ross	Risk aversion
1979	Geske	Compound option	
1984	Myers		Introducing RO to capital budgeting
1985	Brennan, Schwarts	Futures prices of contracts with different maturities	

---

[212] Detailed Literature review is in the 2nd section.

YEAR	Papers	Contribution	Key Theory
1985	Mason & Merton	Real options may be valued similar to financial options	
1984	McDonald & Siegel	Dividend-like adjustment	
1985	McDonald & Siegel	Market-equilibrium model	Address the return shortfall
1986	McDonald & Siegel	Defer investment option	
1987	Trigeorgis & Mason	Staged investment / growth option	
1988	Kulatilaka	Switch option	
1994	Trigeorgis & Kulatilaka	Switch use (input and output)	Synergizing
1996	Trigeorgis	Option based capital budgeting and strategic decisions	Resource allocation or project appraisal under uncertainty
1996	Myers		RO applied in capital budgeting
1996	Faulkner	R&D investments valuation using RO in the capital budgeting	
1998	Copeland & Keenan		Compound options
1998	Merton	Option Pricing Application from 1973-1998	
1998	Luehrman		NPV intrinsic value in the defer- investment option

YEAR	Papers	Contribution	Key Theory
1999	Amram & Kulatilak	Applicability of RO to various industries	RO methodology milestone
1999	Benaroch & Kauffman	Point-of-scale transaction	
2000	Copeland & Antikarov	Real options practitioners' guide: how to do	Risk –neutral growth rate equals the risk-free interest rate
2000	Copeland & Antikarov	R&D Investment	compound option
2002	Herath & Park	R&D investment	Compound option
2001	Schwaratz	R&D investment	Compound option
2001	Sick	PUD—Pre-served land	

Some research indicates that the real option valuation methodology is the most useful in the investment-intensive industries. These are industries such as oil or mineral extraction[213], pharmaceutical product development[214], high technology start-ups, and R&D investment, and any other High-investment/High

---

[213] Actual Application Case— British Petroleum Corporation. UK-based British Petroleum Corporation is known to have been benefiting through its use of the RO approach in its investment valuation since 1990. The company exercises options to extend the life of its existing infrastructure to defer new investment and to save the cost of removing redundant facilities; it uses options to continue committing incremental investments while insuring that plants maximize potential profits. *Unleashing the power of learning: An interview with British Petroleum's John Browne,"Harvard Business Review, September– October 1997, for BP's own account of its value-creating strategy since 1992.*

[214] New product development in pharmaceutical companies has also begun using RO. This industry requires huge R&D investments and sometimes involves investing in stages, depending on whether the new drug is progressing in the right direction and/ or whether the Federal Drug Association (FDA) approves the continuation of the drug research. The R&D effort cannot produce a positive net cash flow until the new drug is successfully developed and approved by FDA, but may yield a very high return if successfully launched in the market. However, this application is still in debate as the industry's volatility is difficult to determine.

Risk-Return (HI/HRR) industries. A detailed literature review, by year and by application industry, is summarized in the following table.

Table 24: Chronological Real Option Development (Empirical Testing, Case Studies, and Theory Contribution)

YEAR	Papers	Application (Empirical studies)	Synergized Theory Contribution
1979	Tourinho	Natural resources	
1984	Myers		Introducing RO to capital budgeting
1985	Brennan, Schwarts	Copper	
1985	Brenna, Schwarts	Natural resources	
1985	Titman	Land	
1986	McDonald & Siegel	Project management	
1991	Trigeorgis	Impact of competition on the optimal timing of project initiation using option methodology	RO types
1993	Quigg	Real Estate	
1993	Kemna	Oil	
1993	Pindyck	Uncertain completion costs to capture a "leaning effect"	
1994	Dixit & Pindyck		Synergizing the empirical applications in various industries
1996	Trigeorgis		RO types

YEAR	Papers	Application (Empirical studies)	Synergized Theory Contribution
1996	Trigeorgis		Risk –neutral growth rate equals the risk-free interest rate
1998	Simth & McCardle	Oil	
1996	Myers		RO applied in capital budgeting
1996	Faulkner	R&D investments valuation using RO in the capital budgeting	
1998	Copeland & Keenan		Compound options
1998	Luehrman		NPV intrinsic value in defer option
1998	McAllister & O'Rarty	Break clauses in real estate	
1998	Cortazar & Casassus	Copper	
1998	Davis	Precious metal	
1999	Chils & Triantis	R&D investment policies and RO valuation with multiple interaction	
1999	Amram & Kulatilak	Various industries application	RO methodology milestone
1999	Benaroch & Kauffman	Point-of-scale transaction	
2000	Schwarts & Moon	Includes project revenues uncertainty and catastrophic events	

YEAR	Papers	Application (Empirical studies)	Synergized Theory Contribution
2000	Copeland & Antikarov	R&D investment	compound option
2002	Herath & Park	R&D investment	Compound option
2000	Schartz & Moon	High-growth firms	
2001	Schwaratz	R&D investment	
2001	Sick	PUD—Preserved Underdeveloped land	
2002	Moel & Turfano	Gold	
1996	Faulkner	R&D investments valuation using RO in the capital budgeting	
1998	Copeland & Keenan		Compound options
1998	Luehrman		NPV intrinsic value in defer option
1998	McAllister & O'Rarty	Break clauses in real estate	
1998	Cortazar & Casassus	Copper	
1998	Davis	Precious metal	
1999	Chils & Triantis	R&D investment policies and RO valuation with multiple interaction	
1999	Amram & Kulatilak	Various industries application	RO methodology milestone
1999	Benaroch & Kauffman	Point-of-scale transaction	

YEAR	Papers	Application (Empirical studies)	Synergized Theory Contribution
2000	Schwarts & Moon	Includes project revenues uncertainty and catastrophic events	
2000	Copeland & Antikarov	R&D investment	compound option
2002	Herath & Park	R&D investment	Compound option
2000	Schartz & Moon	High-growth firms	
2001	Schwaratz	R&D investment	
2001	Sick	PUD—Preserved Underdeveloped land	
2002	Moel & Turfano	Gold	
2002	McMillan & McGroath	R&D Project Mgt	
2003	Smit	Flight Demand	
2004	Armstrong	Oil exploration	
2004	Cassimon	Pharmaceutical industry	
2005	Tanguturi & Harmantzis	IT—2nd Wireless transition to 3rd Wireless	
2006	Laate	New biotechnology development and commercialization	
2006	Rubio, Lamoth	Empirical Evidence European Biotech firms	

YEAR	Papers	Application (Empirical studies)	Synergized Theory Contribution
2006	Power & Reid	OR logic by entrepreneurs	Firm performance improvement related to RO counts
2006	Chen, Longm, & Wang	Firms' default risk in different competition markets	Default risk similar; empirical evidence supports hypothesis
2006	Cho	retail-shopping center	retail lease contract
2007	Hoe & Diltz	Optimal investment policies in R&D projects	
2007	Dikos & Thomakos	Tanker Markets	
2008	Leung	Real Estate	valuation model for acquisition of a property

During the years 2000 to 2008, RO application has drawn noticeable attention from both academic researchers and corporate practitioners. In the academic arena, numerous dissertations on RO applications have been published recently. The following is a brief summary from those dissertations.

2001: Haylett demonstrated how the real option value of a petroleum exploration mineral rights lease could be calculated (using Monte Carlo simulation), while Vladimir applied real options methodology to sales of power plants by U.S. electric utilities.

2002: Lee presented the Real options theory: Implications on entrepreneurship development and options value under uncertainty. Maya proposed a Creative Destruction-Real Options Approach (CD-ROA) to value start-ups in the midst of technological uncertainty.

2006: Pagaza & Gabriela (2006) advanced the "Partnership model" introduced by Kulatilaka and Patel (2002), supporting the results of Grenadier and Wang (2005), that argued that incentives may induce a manager to raise firm value by exercising the appropriate real options.

2006: Cho provided a general formulation for valuing a retail-shopping center under conditions of uncertainty. Cho's study integrated two lines of research, one of which consisted of the valuation of embedded options in a retail lease contract. He examined whether the use of capital budgeting methods can reduce decision makers' tendency to escalate commitment to a failing course of action.

2007: RO research during this year expanded to address a broader arena of issues. Scucci developed a continuous time general equilibrium model involving embedded options in the physical health environment, identifying stochastic intertemporal dynamics of the underlying health process and the disruptions in the underlying process resulting from illness.

Wang compared NPV, decision trees, and real option methods in valuating technology innovation and adoption projects. In her dissertation, she studied the feasibility, advantages, and discrepancies of each method in technology investment valuation at various phases of innovation.

Bryan introduced a flexible system using real options as a method of managing uncertainty, which is composed of interconnected technological, organizational, and process components, creating a "Life-Cycle Flexibility (LCF) Framework." This study uses two cases:

(1) a large body aircraft in a commercial aircraft manufacturing enterprise, and (2) Intelligent Transportation System (ITS) capabilities in an urban region with multiple public and private stakeholders. This research found that without the proposed LCF framework, existing processes for evaluating real options were not adequate to account for the interacting technical, organizational, and process components of "complex" real options.

Also in 2007, Qin suggested that RO should be chosen as the approach most suitable for exploiting Knowledge Workforce Agility (KWA), because RO can capture the essence of KWA embedded options in manipulating knowledge capacity, a human asset, or a self-cultivated organizational capability for pursuing interests associated with change. He suggested that the real options valuation process provides a methodology to measure the inherent value of flexibility, and can therefore assist decision makers in making the optimal investment decision.

Alimov developed and tested a hypotheses about the impact of growth options, embedded in innovative investments, on the risk and the expected return of a firm's equity, based on recently developed real options models, such as described in Berk, Green and Naik (1999, 2004).

Leung focused on a niche field: a valuation model for acquisition of a property with excessive land that can potentially be converted into a new development. He proposed the Real Estate with Real Options (RERO) model as a framework; the model combines DCF, ROA, and DTA analyses to specifically value real estate acquisition with excessive infill land.

Dissertation research continued in 2008. Miao discussed when a firm, whose investment cost depends on economic situations, faces a future real investment opportunity. Investment timing can be treated as a perpetual American option when the strike price switches between two possible values depending on the economic situations.

Also in 2008, Zhang argued that the application of RO enables manufacturing systems to capture the strategic value of management and operational flexibility for capital investments in the automotive industry. The research findings of this study are built on four criteria: coping with uncertainty, adaptability, information cost, and overall utility. These are developed to measure the application values of the methods. Zhang concludes that Real Options and Decision Trees are superior to NPV in coping with uncertainties. The advantages of RO and DT are better reflected in sequential technology investments and product portfolio.

9.1.3 RO Application in Industries Summary.

In the original BSOPM, the only unknown variable that needs to be identified is sigma, representing volatility. In using BSOPM to value real assets, the quality of the option valuation depends on the ability to track the underlying asset volatility. Merton's 1977 & 1998 articles on option pricing strategy established a framework that identified what "private risk" is; he demonstrated that it can be objectively defined and measured using the data available in the market place, and that it can be made easier to quantify as more underlying assets are securitized.

Since RO's application in various industries, the question has been whether RO can be supported with sufficient empirical evidence, testing, and verification. In Henri's research[215], he argues that a case study is a more feasible process for providing such evidence, testing and verification than is empirical evidence. One of the primary reasons for his belief is the lack of a broad, consistent, and generally accessible database, which may allow researcher subjectivity to contaminate research efforts.[216] RO's growing acceptance in a variety of industries can be seen in the following table.

Table 25: RO Application Development (Empirical Testing, Case Studies, and Contribution, sorted by Application Area)

Authors / Researchers	Application (Empirical / Case studies)	Key Focus / Contribution	YEAR
Rubio, Lamoth	Biotech	Empirical Evidence European Biotech firms	2006
Laate	Biotech	New biotechnology development and commercialization	2006
Brennan, Schwarts	Natural resources	Copper	1985
Cortazar & Casassus	Natural resources	Copper	1998

---

[215] See Literature Review 2.9.

[216] This proposal suggests that volatility is the primary limiting factor in the use of RO for real asset valuation.

Authors / Researchers	Application (Empirical / Case studies)	Key Focus / Contribution	YEAR
Moel & Turfano	Natural resources	Gold	2002
Kemna	Natural resources	Oil	1993
Simth & McCardle	Natural resources	Oil	1998
Armstrong	Natural resources	Oil	2004
Cassimon	Pharmaceutical industry	Drug R&D	2004
Trigeorgis	Project Management	Impact of competition on the optimal timing of project initiation using option methodology	1991
Schwarts & Moon	Project Management	Project revenues uncertainty and catastrophic events	2000
McDonald & Siegel	Project Management	Various projects application	1986
Childs & Triantis	R&D	Investment policies and RO valuation with multiple interaction	1999
Faulkner	R&D	Investments valuation using RO in the capital budgeting	1996
Copeland & Antikarov	R&D investment	Compound option	2000
Herath & Park	R&D investment	Compound option	2002
Quigg	Real Estate	Real estate market prices	1993

Authors / Researchers	Application (Empirical / Case studies)	Key Focus / Contribution	YEAR
Leung	Real Estate	valuation model for acquisition of a property	2008
McAllister & O'Rarty	Real estate	Break clauses	1998
Titman	Real Estate	Land	1985
Sick	Real Estate	PUD—Preserved Underdeveloped land	2001
Cho	retail-shopping center	Retail lease contract	2006
Tanguturi & Harmantzis	Startup	IT—2nd Wireless transition to 3rd Wireless	2005
Power & Reid	Starup—entrepreneurs	Firm performance improvement related to RO counts	2006
Pindyck	Various industries application	Uncertain completion costs to capture a "leaning effect"	1993
Amram & Kulatilak	Various industries application	RO methodology milestone	1999
Dixit & Pindyck		Synergizing the empirical applications in various industries	1994
Trigeorgis		Risk –neutral growth rate equals the risk-free interest rate	1996
Myers		RO applied in capital budgeting	1996

Authors / Researchers	Application (Empirical / Case studies)	Key Focus / Contribution	YEAR
Copeland & Keenan		Compound options	1998

From the table, we see that RO applications reflected in the literature to date are primarily concentrated in the areas of 1) natural resources; 2) R&D; 3) real estate; 4) start-up or technology venture capital); and 5) project valuation. These industries / sectors, which have adapted and successfully used RO to value investment, have heavy investment and high risk/reward (HI/HRR) profiles. A key reason for RO application in these industries is that sigma can either be determined or supported by actual historic volatility data. The price of commodities tradable in liquid and well-functioning international markets[217] can be readily ascertained and tracked. For instance, one of the earliest applications of real options was in the petroleum leasing sector[218], in which Paddock, Siegel and Smith used data based on historical oil prices as the standard deviation of the rate of change of the value of the reserves[219].

9.1.3.1 *Applicable Valuation Situations*

In summary, the RO methodology is particularly applicable in the following situations[220]:

a) when there is a high degree of uncertainty involved in the course of the investment;

---

[217] Such prices and markets include spot, futures, and spark spread (the price of electricity minus the price of natural gas adjusted for burner efficiency) in the futures or commodities financial markets or derivative instruments financial markets.

[218] Paddock, Siegel, and Smith, "Option Valuation of Claims on Real Assets: The Case of Offshore Petroleum Leases," *Quarterly Journal of Economics*, 1988.

[219] For more detail see 2.4, Henri Philippe, "Real Options: Still Looking for Evidence", Real Options Conference Paper, 2005.

[220] Not all industry valuation can use BSOPM due to its limitations & assumptions outlined.

b) when the investment environment (macro-, local-, and/or political environment) is highly volatile;

c) when there is a strategic value attached with the investment;

d) when there is critical information that can affect the investment return but only will be known at a later point in time.

9.1.3.2 *RO Types*

There are several ways to view RO types, commonly Grow, Wait-and-See, and Abandonment. Trigeorgis proposed detailed alternative investment and divestment decision making choices in 1998: 1) deferment; 2) building; 3) abandonment; 4) switching; 5) growth.

Deferment is the ability of the company to wait until the market conditions improve to a favorable stage (e.g. the commodity price reaches an economically acceptable level). For example, if the price of oil was very low (as opposed to the current reality), some oil fields could not be exploited; but they would have a value if it were anticipated that the market price of the commodity may later exceed the extraction cost.

The option to build takes into account the fact that most complex investments generate sequential decisions and cash outlays. If, during the construction, the environment moves favorably or unfavorably, it is possible to abandon the project and/or design new objectives.

The option to alter operating scale is the ability to expand or contract capacity, following the evolution of the market. This is of crucial importance when the reaction of the market is quite uncertain,

e.g. when the product changes the consumers' habits dramatically or when the competition has the possibility to react promptly and introduce rival products. This category also includes the option to shut down current plant and/or restart operations in another venue—operational strategic practice commonly seen in the mining industry. Another way to classified RO is: simple, compounded, expansion, abandonment, etc. A simple option is the ability to buy or sell the option at a defined price on one occasion at or before the expiration of the option. Compound options are options that, when exercised, generate another option. They are commonly used for staggered investment involving multiple decisions through the lifecycle of a project. Expansion options are the right, but not the obligation, to expand the investment of a project. Abandonment options are the right to stop or postpone the project if the expected cash flows are below the salvage value.

9.1.3.2.1 *RO Advantage*

When comparing RO to NPV in these situations which RO are applicable[221]:

a) when there is a high degree of uncertainty involved in the course of the investment

   ~ NPV is static decision making approach;

b) when the investment environment (macro-, local-, and/or political environment) is highly volatile

   ~ NPV's discount rate theoretically reflects the underlying asset (investment)'s market risk, but in HIGH INVESTMENT & HIGH RISK-RETURN industry, this discount rate is not sufficient to capture the risks.

c) when there is a strategic value attached with the investment;

   ~ NPV reflects only tangible financial benefits;

d) when there is critical information that affects the investment return but not available at the time of making decision.

   ~ NPV will use scenario analysis but the decision is still "accept" or "reject."

---

[221] Not all industry valuation can use BSOPM due to its limitations & assumptions outlined.

9.1.3.2.2 RO Limitation

Primary limitations: its un-tradability and difficulty to identify volatility. More discussion is in Section 2.1.3.3.

9.1.3.3 RO Application Modification Overview—Industries Volatility

As discussed, the volatility (sigma) is the only unknown variable that must be identified in the B-S model. How to determine sigma in RO application in various industries has been the major challenge. Various empirical research works (more precisely, case studies) have been conducted in searching, modeling, and testing volatility.

Methods discussed here are the primary approached proposed and testing by various studies. They can be categorized as the following per specific industry characteristics.

- Historical volatility of the underlying asset: When the price of a natural resource determines the future cash flow of the investment, the historical volatility of commodity price can be utilized as sigma. In addition to the oil lease example in which Paddock et al. used historical oil prices as sigma, Moel & Turfano used return on gold price as the estimate of volatility in gold mine closures[222], while Quigg used land price fluctuations as sigma to analyze land development[223]

- Historical volatility of the company's stock price: This estimation of sigma can be utilized only when the project volatility correlates with the stock price movement of the company. Herath and Park (1999) demonstrated that the stock price of a typical R&D company is perfectly correlated to the company's R&D project.

- Historical volatility of the industry index: The historical volatility of the industrial group index of equity prices has

---

[222] Ibid.
[223] Ibid.

also been used to estimate the volatility of the project value. For example, R&D of pharmaceutical companies, using the pharmaceutical industry's standard deviation of equity, can serve as sigma.

- Historical sales growth rate volatility of the local market or SportswearRetail Store[224]: to be further investigated and tested in this research.

Table 26 summarizes recent applications of RO by volatility[225]. In this table, the following symbols are utilized to demonstrate the volatility estimation methods and correspond to the categories specified[226]:

a) V-UA: Volatility of price of underlying asset;

b) V-SP: Volatility of historic stock price;

c) V-Index: Volatility of underlying industry index

Table 26: Real Option Development—Volatility Modification

Authors / Researchers	Application (Empirical studies)	Modification / Synergized Contribution	Modification: Volatility Estimation	YEAR
Tourinho*	Natural resources		V-UA	1979
Brenna, Schwarts	Natural resources		V-UA	1985
Davis*	Natural resources	Precious metal	V-UA	1998
Brennan, Schwarts	Natural resources	Copper	V-UA	1985

---

[224] Sportswear Retail Store Types include (owned) mono-brand, factory outlet stores (discount), and mega-stores (flagship stores).

[225] * indicates the original source is from Han, "Estimating Project Volatility and Developing Decision Support System n Real Options Analysis", Dissertation 2007

[226] Other methods include Monte Carlo simulation and Bayesian Revision Process.

Authors / Researchers	Application (Empirical studies)	Modification / Synergized Contribution	Modification: Volatility Estimation	YEAR
Cortazar & Casassus*	Natural resources	Copper	V-UA	1998
Moel & Turfano	Natural resources	Gold	V-UA	2002
Kemna*	Natural resources	Oil	V-UA	1993
Simth & McCardle	Natural resources	Oil	V-UA	1998
Armstrong*	Natural resources	Oil	V-UA	2004
Cassimon*	Pharmaceutical industry	Application	V-SP	2004
Trigeorgis	Project—Impact of competition on the optimal timing of project initiation using option methodology	RO types	V-Various	1991
Chils & Triantis	R&D	investment policies and RO valuation with multiple interaction	V-Index	1999
Faulkner*	R&D	investments valuation using RO in the capital budgeting	V-Index	1996
McMillan & McGroath*	R&D	Project Mgt		2002

Authors / Researchers	Application (Empirical studies)	Modification / Synergized Contribution	Modification: Volatility Estimation	YEAR
Hoe & Diltz	R&D—Optimal investment policies in R&D projects	Optimal investment policies in R&D projects	V-Index	2007
Copeland & Antikarov	R&D investment	Compound option	V-Index	2000
Herath & Park	R&D investment	Compound option	V-Index	2002
Schwaratz	R&D investment		V-Index	2001
Quigg	Real Estate	Application	V-UA	1993
Leung	Real Estate	valuation model for acquisition of a property	V-UA	2008
McAllister & O'Rarty	Real estate	Break clauses	V-UA	1998
Titman	Real Estate	Land	V-UA	1985
Sick	Real Estate	PUD—Pre-served Under-developed land	V-UA	2001

9.1.3.4   Limitation in RO Application.

One of the primary limitations of RO is its un-tradability. In addition, the analysis requires sufficient data input and variables. The lack of data to support is application in industries limits its generability. As earlier discussed,[227] most of the empirical studies primarily covered the natural resources sector due to its "tradability." Other limitation in RO applications are:

1) The difficulty in obtaining a tractable dataset;

2) Lack of sufficient databases;

3) The subjectivity of the data validation[228]

In addition, RO's complexity and a lack of understanding of its applications also cause its limitation. The Real Options model approach requires more time to obtain all the elements needed for its calculation and this makes it less appealing. As a result of this, it takes much longer to complete the analysis when using the RO methodology.

In the following section, books, research papers and articles that synergize and broaden the application of RO application are presented and reviewed in detail. They respond to the business challenges today[229]. These works challenged the conventional wisdom, and successfully moved the RO concept forward, laying the foundation for further study and, primarily, for practical application.

---

[227] Literature Review 2.4, Henri Philippe, "RO: Still Looking for Evidence?

[228] See Section 4 for a more thorough discussion of this literature's influence on this proposal.

[229] Businesses today are challenged by with consumers who are savvier in their expectations and purchasing behaviors and challenged by competitors who are more aggressive in the marketplace and more sophisticated in their execution. In addition, more types of investment possibilities are provided and offered in the financial markets, which in turn challenging better returns on the investments on real assets.

9.2 Real Option: Managing Strategic Investment in an Uncertain World

Martha Amram & Nalin Kulatilaka, 1999

In their first book, Amram and Kulatilaka propose: "The current set of valuation and decision-making tools aren't sufficient for the new business realities." This was bold statement back in 1999. They go on to state: "Real options are an important way of thinking about valuation and strategic decision-making, and the power of this approach is starting to change the economic 'equation' of many industries."[230] They challenged companies to adapt to changes in the evolving marketplace in order to maximize investment return while managing risk, particularly with regard to strategic investments that require huge capital requirements and involves a lot of uncertainty.

In this book, Amram and Kulatilaka differentiated "real options" from financial options. They argued that the traditional discounted cash flow methods (NPV and IRR) do not accurately value investments with contingencies and options, whereas a real options approach to capital budgeting does incorporate these alternatives. Further, they proposed that Real Option methodology reflects actual managerial flexibility by providing for the analysis of the application of real options to phases in investment—expansion, extension, and abandonment.

In each of these RO types, Amram and Kulatilaka propose that in the RO application (specifically using BSOPM), the risk is captured in the value of the traded security. For example, in natural resources exploration, the price of the resources is captured in "futures contracts" in the financial market. In the situation where there is no traded security, the authors suggest that this private risk is "naturally diversified away at the portfolio level", as in pharmaceutical companies where individual drug development risks would be diversified throughout the whole portfolio of products. In the scenario of a particular project, the authors argue that the private

---

[230] Amram, M. and N. Kulatilaka, Real Options: Managing Strategic Investment in an Uncertain World, Harvard Business School Press, Boston, 1999.

risk of each project should be investigated and used, and that "there is an enormous amount of private risk that affects decisions in all stages of development."[231]

- If an initial investment is successful, then the management can exercise the option to expand its commitment to the strategy. By way of example, a company entering a new geographic market may consider building a distribution center if the market demand reaches a certain level. While waiting for the demand to materialize, the company may outsource its distribution function to a local warehouse instead of committing to own an in-house warehouse.[232] This approach retains managerial and investment flexibility if the market demand gets weaker or unstable and a new warehouse proves to be unnecessary.

- An initial investment can serve as a platform to extend a company's scope into related market opportunities. As an example, a substantial investment to develop a sportswear company's customer base, brand name, and regional distribution infrastructure for its core footwear business might lead to the development of a portfolio of sports-related business, such as sports & fitness accessories.

- Management may begin with a relatively small trial investment, retaining or creating an option to abandon the project if results are unsatisfactory. Research and development spending decisions provide a good example. A company's future investment in product development often depends on specific performance targets achieved in the lab. Whether it is Nike's Shoe Kitchen in the US or Adidas' Apparel Laboratory in Germany, the option to abandon a prototype is valuable because the company can retain the option or

---

[231] Amram, M. and N. Kulatilaka, Real Options: Managing Strategic Investment in an Uncertain World, Harvard Business School Press, Boston, 1999.

[232] In emerging markets, local third party warehouse carriers (also called "satellite distribution centers) are oftentimes contracted to handle the goods.

flexibility to make investments in stages rather than all up-front.

Each of these options—expansion, extension and abandonment—offers additional flexibility to management, in comparison to the simple GO/NO-GO decision based on a positive or negative NPV. Amram and Kulatilaka argue that flexibility adds value in at least two ways: first, deferral of an investment preserves the time value of money, and, second, it allows management to take action based on a change in the value of the project before the option expires. If the value of the project increases, the investment is good; on the other hand, if the value decreases only the costs of the option itself are incurred, as the company will decline to invest in the project further. Amram and Kulatilaka summarize the management position reflected by Real Options as: "If things go well, then we'll add some capital."

To sum up, in today's ever-changing and rapidly developing world, businesses recognize how risky and uncertain costly investment opportunities are, and how quickly they must divest themselves of unprofitable projects to free up cash for other valuable investment opportunities. To best capitalize on future uncertainties, Amram and Kulatilaka argue that Real Options methodology should be used in strategic investment decision-making as a supplement to the traditional conventional methods, such as NPV.

9.3 Strategic Flexibility in the Financial Services Industry

Michael E. Raynor, Deloitte Research, 2001

In this research paper, Raynor, together with his Research Consulting team at Deloitte, developed a "four-phase framework: Anticipate, Operate, Formulate, Accumulate. The goal is to reflect a "Strategic Flexibility" mindset in corporate planning. Raynor regards NPV as one of the well-understood and widely-used tools for comparing investment opportunities. This method "requires predicting the cash flows associated with a given project and then discounting the associated cash flows into present day currency using an appropriate risk-adjusted rate." For example, opening a new retail store might have negative cashflows in early years because of the opening-fixture investment; later on a potential high cash flows coming in as the store starts generating sales and profits (all costs and expenses are stabilizing as the store assumes normal operation after the investment.

NPV norm is that if the discounted cash flows have a value that is more than zero, the Store investment is regarded as a "profitable investment." However when a market changes rapidly, many factors could and would change the profit prospective of this store. In order to deal with these situations, companies normally use numerous scenario analyses, one of which is expected NPV (eNPV). This more complex NPV reflects a simple triangle probability: high, medium, and low investment-return possibility to a store. And the eNPV is actually the weighted average of the three NPV calculations with respective probabilities assigned.

However, Raynor suggests that, "highly uncertain investment environments reveal the many weaknesses of this approach." He uses an example of NPV's common practice: "increasing the discount rate applied to highly uncertain cash flows, thereby reducing their value." In the financial market, however, uncertainty raises both upside sales' possibility and downside risk. As a result, just as Raynor comments, "arbitrarily increasing the discount rate serves only to penalize uncertainty when in fact, as with financial options, higher levels of uncertainty surrounding an investment's outcome might actually make that investment more attractive."

If the project or investment can occur in stages, or can be made to have stages (full investment can be divided in phases) the company is in the position operationally to invest money to "learn something about how best to pursue an opportunity." In such instances, Raynor thinks "even NPV approaches are inadequate, because they penalize potentially valuable flexibility in implementation."

9.4 Real Options: Still Looking for Evidence?

Henri Philippe, Real Options Conference, 2005

In this working paper, Philippe argues that despite a large body of literature on the RO application, empirical tests of real options models remain limited, primarily due to the lack of the empirical data. In addition, there are other intrinsic reasons. The author analyzes four traditionally cited as the "empirical studies" to build his argument that case studies are still more feasible to the solution to RO application.

- Paddock et al. (1998) empirically tested a RO model to value undeveloped oil reserves. The model was tested on a limited number of contracts for offshore oil leases in the US, using data provided by an anonymous company. The authors conclude that a strategy based on option value could be more cost effective than one based on NPV.

- Quigg (1993) tested the empirical prediction of a real option-pricing model using large samples of market prices in the real estate sector. The test was based on market data for local transactions in Seattle over 1976- 1979.

- Berger (1996) examined the empirical implication of a RO model to price an abandonment option. The test data was based on market data for companies (sales over $20million), totaling over seven thousand observations. The strong relationship, which was between market values and estimated exit prices.

- Moel and Tufano (2002) studied the decision pattern of closing and reopening gold mines in North America. The test was based on data, extracted by the authors from various database and public information that covered 285 gold mines. The study confirmed that the decisions outcome made were consistent with real option model predictions.

Philippe observes that the above-described empirical studies primarily covered the natural resources sector, noting that, "Natural resources are usually traded commodities and hence have an obvious advantage for researchers: this context is appropriate for arbitrage reasoning"[233]. He also comments on the objectives of these studies. He argues that in some cases, actual prices for the assets are not directly observable in markets (except in the Quigg study of undeveloped land, which was based on the building value). He also points out the difficulty in obtaining a tractable model. Paddock's empirical test, for example, used a rough assumption on oil price data as a proxy to estimate the standard deviation of the rate of change of the value of the underdeveloped reserves.

Philippe concludes that it is difficult for researchers empirically testing RO models to find samples of data large enough to draw valid conclusions. And since the data is limited, the empirical studies "show empirical evidence of their existence and of the relations presented in the theory, but not of their value"; moreover, he thinks the "real options are useful for many reasons and not just for valuing." The focus of empirical tests should not necessarily be on testing value but more on understanding investors' behavior.

He further classifies the options in the literature:

- Investment options (Wait and See, decrease / increase the scope of the investment);
- Operating options (abandon options as such);
- Strategic option (growth options)

He regards the Investment and Operating options as the easiest to assess and to test empirically as they are exposed to a simple asset only. Because the growth options consist of more complex options, they are more difficult to design and to value. He finally concludes that real options are more than just a valuation tool. RO also serves as a tool that can build bridges for management and cross-functional

---

[233] Real Options: Still Looking for Evidence? Henri Philippe, PhD research paper, Real Options Conference, 2005.

teams.[234] His conclusion in regard to RO empirical testing is that these studies help to confirm the existence of real options. However due to the lack of large databases and due to the subjectivity of the data validation, real options should be treated more as a strategic tool or a way of thinking, rather than as a valuation tool. He concludes that case studies are more feasible than empirical studies in the application of RO[235].

9.5 The Role of Real Options in Capital Budgeting: Theory and Practice

McDonald, Robert L. Journal of Applied Corporate Finance, 2006

In this influential 2006 article,[236] McDonald argues that some recent discussions of capital budgeting are misleading. He states that they tend to focus on large differences between discounted cash flow (DCF) and Real Options (RO), concluding that: 1) the two different methodologies should be applied in different circumstances; 2) DCF is easy and ROV is hard or unfamiliar; and 3) most corporate finance managers use DCF and rarely use ROV. These conclusions are not entirely without merit. They are supported by a widely known industry survey conducted by Graham and Harvey (2001) showing that DCF is used very widely in corporate capital budgeting in conjunction with other valuation models, such as Internal Rate of Return, payback, and P/E ratio (detailed survey result is in the later section 2.14[237]). Similar results are also demonstrated in the 2002 survey by Patricia Ryan and Glenn Ryan[238]. Although these survey results indicate that most managers do not use RO valuation when making capital

---

[234] Applications of real options in strategic planning, management are discussed in the literature review section, 2.13, *infra*.

[235] See Section 4 for a more thorough discussion of this literature's influence on this proposal.

[236] McDonald, Robert L., "The Role of Real Options in Capital Budgeting: Theory and Practice. Journal of Applied Corporate Finance, Vol. 18, No. 2, pp. 28-39, Spring 2006.

[237] De Jong, Abe, Brounen, Dirk and Koedijk, Kees C.G.,Corporate Finance in Europe Confronting Theory with Practice.

[238] Ryan, P.A., and G.P. Ryan, 2002, "Capital Budgeting practices of the Fortune 1000: How have things changed?" Journal of Business and Management, 8(4), 355-364.

budgeting decisions, McDonald argues that DCF and RO valuation are both essential in budgeting planning, and more particularly, in corporate finance managerial thinking. A key contribution of this study is the differentiation which McDonald makes within DCF methodology. He uses the term "static DCF" to describe the traditional DCF approach, and "dynamic DCF" to describe an adjustable approach that takes into account the possibility that risk changes over time. According to McDonald, when using the static DCF technique, "a constant discount rate is a correct discounting method only under the special assumption that risk resolves at a constant rate over time." In today's business world, risk develops and evolves dynamically across many dimensions at the same time, with only mature and stable industries growing at a constant rate. RO valuation addresses and enables the capture of the dynamic risks faced by most modern companies. In McDonald' words: "RO valuation addresses the problem of discounting cash flows even when risk premiums change dynamically[239]."

In his article, he uses a Project-valuation as an example. In this example, a *forward price*—the expected cash flow computed using the "risk–neutral probability[240]" is calculated. The forward price is the future value of the present price. When compared to the present value of expected future value, the difference is the risk premium. This implies that the DCF valuation is a necessary input into the risk-neutral calculation that is required to conduct the RO valuation. As a result, McDonald notes, "Even if we perform real options valuation, a DCF valuation is necessary unless there is forward price or present value that we can observe in the market.[241]"

McDonald also argues that the "difference between the DCF and real options valuation approaches are not as great as practitioners seem to believe[242]". He compares RO and DCF valuations and shows that, when used correctly, both methods provide the same answers, because both calculate the same thing: the present values of risky

---

[239] McDonald, Robert L., "The Role of Real Options in Capital Budgeting: Theory and Practice. Journal of Applied Corporate Finance, Vol. 18, No. 2, pp. 28-39, Spring 2006.

[240] Different from True Probability, McDonald, Robert L., "The Role of Real Options in Capital Budgeting: Theory and Practice. Journal of Applied Corporate Finance, Vol. 18, No. 2, pp. 28-39, Spring 2006, Pg 31.

[241] McDonald, Robert L., "The Role of Real Options in Capital Budgeting: Theory and Practice. Journal of Applied Corporate Finance, Vol. 18, No. 2, pp. 28-39, Spring 2006.

[242] Ibid

future cash flows. Nevertheless, the difference between the two methodologies is in the discount rates used. DCF uses a discount rate that reflects expected future cash flows at the expected rate of return on an asset[243], while RO uses risk-neutral valuation (based on risk neutral probabilities). RO's strength becomes more apparent when the discount rates are expected to change over time, due to changes in the project, industry, or macro-economy environments.

McDonald's closing comment is that using RO to support NPV may "encourage managers to think more broadly about the flexibility that is (or can be) built into future business decisions, and thus to choose from a different set of possible investments."[244] His point of view is also shared by some strategists[245] who think that the implementation of real options methodology can broaden the strategic direction of the company.

9.6 How Kimberly-Clark Uses Real Options

Amram, Li, and Perkins, Journal of Applied Corporate Finance, 2006

Kimberly-Clark (K-C), a leading consumer products manufacturer, has enjoyed accelerated organic growth over the past eight years, thanks to its stringent allocation of additional capital to key strategic innovations. In 2004, K-C introduced its Enterprise Growth Incubator (EGI), which is comprised of projects, corporate venture capital, and technology licensing deals characterized by great uncertainty. In their 2006 article, Amram *et al.* described K-C's evolution toward RO methodology as follows: "Careful attention to implementation of this strategic imperative led to concern about how to value risky projects, which led in turn to real options."[246] Therefore, "As a new way of

---

[243] See detailed discussion on NPV discount rates in the NPV Background section.

[244] Amram, Martha , Li, Fanfu and Perkins, Cheryl A., How Kimberly-Clark Uses Real Options. Journal of Applied Corporate Finance, Vol. 18, No. 2, pp. 40-47, Spring 2006.

[245] Tong, Reuer, 2007, "Real Options in Strategic Management—Advances in Strategic Management", vol, 24, Real Options in Strategic Management.

[246] Amram , Martha , Li, Fanfu and Perkins, Cheryl A., How Kimberly-Clark Uses Real Options. Journal of Applied Corporate Finance, Vol. 18, No. 2, pp. 40-47, Spring

thinking, as a change in both how project analyses are framed and the order in which risks are investigated and resolved"[247], RO valuation methodology was implemented by K-C. This article discusses how K-C adopted and uses the real options approach to project valuation.

In this article, Amram, Li, and Perkins use the example of RO valuation in one of K-C's potential Joint Development Agreements, pursuant to which K-C agreed to develop new products with a start-up company (ABC) by combining ABC's unique technology with K-C's manufacturing and distribution. It would be very difficult to project the future cash flows to be generated from this arrangement due to the uncertainty inherent in both ABC (due to its startup status) in particular and the marketplace in general. K-C decided to use RO analysis.

Based on RO analysis, the deal was structured as follows: the first payment of $1million would be paid only if and when a 50% technology success rate were attained (otherwise the project would be abandoned); the second payment would be paid only if and when a 75% rate were attained (otherwise the project would be abandoned); and the product launch would commence only when an 80% success rate were achieved and delivered. This structure led to a "secured" benefit of minimized downside risk while simultaneously preserving the opportunity to reap the upside by "waiting for the future." Although the project's upside potential was highly uncertain, by using RO valuation K-C was able to structure the deal in a way that enabled it to retain flexibility by delaying spending until sufficient information became available.

Amram, Li, and Perkins conclude that "K-C is uniquely positioned to support and benefit from innovations with large upside potential[248]." K-C's successful RO analysis relied on a number of factors that have more to do with corporate process than with quantitative models. In spite of this, the authors argue that this case study on real options

---

2006.

[247] Ibid.

[248] Ibid.

implementation should lead to a greater acceptance of RO as an important valuation method.

9.7 Sub-Finance: New Sources of Data for Real Options Analysis[249]

Nelson, Housel, and Mun, 2005

In this article, Nelson, Housel, and Mun address the "interlocking" issue by presenting an analytic theory and related methodology, Knowledge Valuation Analysis (KVA). This "interlocking" was raised by Dr. Steward Myers in his keynote speech at the 8th Annual Real Options Conference held in Montreal, Canada, in June 2004. Dr Myers described four interlocking issues to be addressed in RO practice: 1) problems related to developing fundamental inputs for the models; 2) a low level of computational transparency; 3) no standardized method; and 4) the need to more effectively "commercialize" the practice of RO analysis.

They propose that the KVA will provide a new source of raw data for use in real options analysis. Their analysis began by identifying a number of problems related to developing RO model input, including the following:

a) inconsistent financial languages, thought processes, and evaluation output in corporate finance;

b) accurate financial valuation constrained by "quality of data";

c) difficulty in valuation of the underlying asset due to:

   i) lack of ability to replicate the underlying asset for real options by using a market portfolio;

   ii) difficulty in estimating the net present value of cash flows of the underlying assets (this could be due to the uncertainty around the underlying assets / projects);

---

[249] Nelson, Housel, and Mun, "Sub-Finance: New Sources of Data for Real Options Analysis", Real Options Conference working paper 2005.

iii) difficulty in isolating the interdependencies and synergies; and/or

iv) difficulty in developing a sensible discount rate which can capture/reflect all risks the underlying real asset / project is exposed to;

d) the extreme difficulty in capturing the volatility of projects; and

e) difficulty in modifying traditional theoretical assumptions to fit RO settings.

The study cites an example utilized by Booz Allen Hamilton on the Mission Support Center (MSC) used by the U.S. Special Operation Forces (SOF) to demonstrate how KVA and RO can be used effectively together. The purpose of KVA analysis is "to assist strategic planners in understanding the levels of value contributed to the MSC by people, processes, and information technology." The analysis first uses the KVA approach to model the results from three possible scenarios:

1) build IT in-house; 2) buy IT from external sources; or 3) outsource software development and staff. These scenarios are then developed into a set of discounted cash flows, resulting in expected net present values. Thereafter, decision support software is used to generate probabilities for use in the RO analysis. Based on this example, the authors conclude that "KVA can be used to identify and measure the outputs of people, IT, and a core process."

In their study, the authors also address some limitations of the KVA + RO method, including the "need to capture non-directly-observable meta processes and the contribution of management" and "the need to fully standardize the data-gathering methods." As the article indicates, these needs are required to properly conduct the KVA + RO approach; in reality, however, both are difficult to meet. Another limitation might be that, due to the particular dynamics and features of the organization described, the study's results might not be readily generalizable.

9.8 Real Options in Strategic Management Advances in Strategic Management

Tong and Reuer, 2007

In their paper[250], Tong and Reuer emphasize the key role of uncertainty, particularly in financial and strategic planning. They review the strategy literature focusing on RO, with the objective of providing a forum for researchers to tackle key questions. They also map out the future research agenda for RO in strategic management.

Tong and Reuer regard RO is a unique theory that can fit in strategic management, at least in regard to three of its properties: its uncertainty; 2) its unique structure for protecting the downside risk via payment of the premium as "insurance"; and 3) its ability to provide follow-on opportunities to firms, such as stage investment and expansion investment.

The authors contend that the financial field is known for its discipline while strategic planning is known for its qualitative attributes. They contend that by "bringing the discipline of financial markets into qualitative strategic planning,"[251] RO has a great prospect of "integrating strategic and financial analyses for corporate strategy."[252]

All of these analyses build a framework that overlays three critical topics of research in international strategy (multinational, market entry mode, and market entry timing) with three major approaches used in existing RO research in the field (RO modeling/reasoning, and empirical testing). The study also discusses the potential contributions that RO theory can make that may enhance managerial and organizational capabilities to implement companies' strategic decisions. In the area of empirical studies, they conceptualize patents as technology options and examine the option value of a firm's patent

---

[250] Tong, Reuer, "Real Options in Strategic Management," Advances in Strategic Management, Vol 24 (2007), University of Toronto.

[251] Ibid

[252] Ibid

portfolios. They conclude that RO theory parameterizes sources of uncertainty; adding value to the investment choices and hence improving and directing the firm's strategic decisions. Therefore, RO can significantly contribute to strategic management research.

9.9 Management Corporate Finance Decision Making— Corporate Finance in Europe: Confronting Theory with Practice

Brounen, de Jong, & Koedijk, 2001

In 2001, Brounen, de Jong, and Koedijk cite Graham and Harvey in a widely covered survey on the corporate application of a variety of capital budgeting techniques, the discounted cash flow techniques included the following:

1) the IRR, 2) the NPV, 3) the adjusted present value, 4) the discounted payback period, 5) the profitability index, 6) hurdle rates, 7) book rates of return, 8) more advanced methods like sensitivity analysis, 9) Real Options, and 10) value at risk.

The authors of this study described the purpose of said study as follows: "To investigate the effect of the corporate governance system on individual firms and include this important issue in our overall analysis of corporate finance practices. The analysis covers a wide range of corporate finance issues, ranging from capital budgeting techniques to capital structure, and corporate governance." From the responses, the authors conclude there are differences between management corporate finance decision making in the US and in Europe (primarily in UK, Netherlands, Germany, and France).

The survey sample consists of a cross-section of 6,500 companies from the U.K., the Netherlands, France, and Germany, from which De Jong & Koedjik collected 313 responses. In this case, the sample is large and offers cross-sectional variations and the statistical power to analyze these variations. The main purpose is to provide a general guidance for the main methodology currently being used by corporate management in the financial decision making process. Selected survey questions and their answers included the following:

Survey question: "How frequently does your firm use the following techniques when deciding which projects or acquisitions to pursue?"

Results: European respondents selected <u>payback period</u> as their most frequently used capital budgeting technique. The percentage of finance executives selecting this measure was: In the U.K. 69.2%, the Netherlands 64.7%, Germany 50.0%, and France 50.9%. In Europe, the preference for payback period is followed immediately by net present value and internal rate of return methods. In the U.K., the Netherlands, Germany and France 53.1%, 56.0 %, 42.2% and 44.1% of all CFOs use the internal rate of return method respectively, while using the NPV method is comparably 47.0%, 70.0% 47.6% and 35.1%. Of U.S. firms, 56.7% declared themselves as utilizing the payback tool, but in the U.S. it was only the third most popular tool after internal rate of return and net present value.

The relative popularity of the payback period in Europe is surprising, because financial textbooks have discussed the shortcomings of the payback criterion for many decades. As is well known, the payback method ignores the time value of money and cash flows beyond the cut-off date. It is sometimes argued that the payback approach is rational for severely capital constrained firms: if an investment project does not yield positive cash flows early on, the firms will cease operation and therefore can not receive positive cash flows that occur in the distant future.

When taking firm characteristics into account, one of the interesting pieces of feedback, according to the survey, was that the use of the payback criterion is more popular among smaller firms (except for the U.K.) and among firms with management belonging to the highest age cluster. NPV is used significantly more often by large firms (except in the U.K.). Real options however, is still new to most of the CFOs, but has emerged as a widely accepted and valuable supplemental valuation methodology to NPV.

9.10 Option Valuation of Architectural Flexibility: A Case Study of the Option to Convert to Office Space

Lara Greden, PhD Candidate, Leon Glicksman, 2004

In their 2004 Real Option conference paper, Greden and Glicksman address the "potential value in flexible spaces," proposing that, "In moving towards a strategic view of space as a flexible asset, real options methodologies are promising candidates for informing decisions in the design process." They identified the goal of their paper to be helping corporate facility managers and real estate developers to recognize architectural flexibility. The research addresses the assumptions needed to apply financial-type real options models to physical design questions. "The model provides results that help decision-makers justify increased investment in designs that will cost less to renovate (i.e., are more flexible) in the future." In an example, "a case study for a corporate campus, a model is developed to determine the option value to convert a space to office space, concluding that "the governing uncertainty must be a market-based factor such as the price of rent."[253]

9.11 Mixed Uses and the Redevelopment Option

Paul D. Childs, Timothy Riddiough, and Alexander Triantis

In this research, Childs, Riddiough, and Triantis explore the potential impact of mixed uses and redevelopment on property value. They suggest that, "operating flexibility of this type is found to significantly increase property value when the correlation between payouts from different property types is low or when redevelopment costs are low."[254] The authors suggest that the "choice between mixed- use versus single-use real estate development is neglected"[255]

---

[253] Ibid.

[254] Childs, Riddiough, and Triantis , "Mixed Uses and the Redevelopment Option", Real Estate Economics, V24, 1996, pp 317-339.

[255] This statement is from the cited article written in 1996 by Childs, Riddiough, and Triantis , "Mixed Uses and the Redevelopment Option", Real Estate Economics, v24,

and that, "Given flexible zoning controls, a strong case can be made for mixed- use development as a hedging strategy—it allows for diversification between different uses that can decrease risk to the investor."[256] Not just the mixed uses of land, Childs *et al.* further point out that, "the flexibility to redevelop a property into different combinations of uses may yield additional economic value."[257]

This study investigates whether it is feasible to derive optimal proportions of alternative uses and, if so, it attempts to derive those proportions. They find that, "in the presence of relatively low costs to conversion, flexibility with respect to mixing uses and redevelopment will contribute significantly to the overall value of the built property or undeveloped land." The article develops a theory for valuing both developed and undeveloped land given the option for mixed uses (and possible redevelopment if conditions dictate). It then presents solutions that demonstrate correlations in operating cash flows, costs, and rental revenues that scale in direct proportion to the property value.

They find that, "when revenue and cost functions are linear in quantity...[and when the objective of value maximization is present] mixed-use projects will not exist." They argue that this result is consistent with the intuition of real estate development in that, "since marginal revenues are constant in scale, diversification within use is sub-optimal since doing so will never increase (and typically decreases) combined current revenues."[258] They also find that mixing uses may be optimal even in the linear revenue case. Therefore, they conclude, "The mixed-use outcomes are characterized as happening in real estate markets that are 'supply sensitive.'"[259]

The authors propose that future research can be extended in several dimensions, including the determination of optimal density

---

1996.

[256] Childs,, Riddiough, and Triantis , "Mixed Uses and the Redevelopment Option", Real Estate Economics, v24, 1996.

[257] Ibid.

[258] Ibid.

[259] Ibid.

and RO application. At least one researcher has followed this direction.[260]

9.12 Valuing Retail Shopping Center Lease Contracts Incorporating Inter-Store Externality Effects: A Real Option Approach

Cho, Hoon, 2007

In this dissertation, Cho provides a general formulation for valuing a retail-shopping center under conditions of uncertainty. The study integrates two lines of research: one line consists of the valuation of options embedded in a retail lease contract, while the other addresses the valuation of retail leases in consideration of inter-store externalities.[261] Cho regards his dissertation as the "first step in the quantification of 1) sales-demand shock parameters and all shopping-center tenants' space-demand functions." Cho's study was motivated primarily by the decrease in the number of viable department stores due to industry re-organization and/or consolidation, as well as by the flattening of department store returns on investments due to the growth and expansion of discount stores and the resulting intensified competition. These developments highlight the need for developers to "maximize returns while controlling for the risk of the variability of receiving the rents."[262]

The principal goal of Cho's dissertation is to explain how to theoretically value a sales-percentage lease, using the RO approach, by establishing a simple RO model of retail shopping-center leases—"a model whose features are necessary to efforts to value a standard percentage retail-lease contract under uncertainty."[263]

---

[260] Åke Gunnelin, "The option to change the use of a property when future property values and construction costs are uncertain", Section of Building and Real Estate Economics, Vol 22, Issue 7, pp 345-354, Royal Institute of Technology, Stockholm, Sweden.

[261] Cho, Hoon. (2007) Valuing retail shopping center lease contracts incorporating inter-store externality effects: A real option approach. Ph.D. dissertation, The University of Wisconsin, Madison, Wisconsin.

[262] Ibid.

[263] Ibid.

Cho argues that neither deterministic frameworks nor stochastic process models were able to estimate the risk / value: "these models systemically underestimate risk and overestimate value when default is an important element in the analysis."[264]

Cho asserts that "the present study integrates these two lines of research by the proposed model that "developed here treats (1) the stochastic component of stores sales in a manner similar to that of Hendershott and Ward (2000, 2002) and (2) shared and generative business within the shopping center in a manner similar to that of Brueckner (1993)."[265]

The source that Cho uses to parameterize his model is Simon Property Group Inc., which he describes as the largest publicly traded real estate investment trust (REIT) in North America and the country's largest owner, developer, and manager of high quality retail real estate. Although Cho described his model as "relatively simple", it nonetheless "helps to explain a variety of phenomena: why an increase in sales volatility may reduce shopping-center value, rather than increase it as others have suggested, etc."[266]

Businesses today are challenged by a marketplace that is changing at a rapid and unprecedented rate. Corporations compete to win both consumers and investors. Investors demand better returns on their real and financial asset investments. As one of the financial derivatives, financial options can be used normally as leverage. This allows the holder to participate in equity investments without actually buying the underlying asset outright. Financial options can also be used as a protection. This allows the option holders to guard against price fluctuations in the short term because the holders can acquire the underlying stock at a fixed price for a limited time. Real asset investment valuations have recently begun to investigate the possible benefits of utilizing BSOPM in real asset valuation, to complement the traditional valuation tools, such as NPV.

---

[264] Ibid.

[265] Ibid.

[266] Ibid.

9.13 Making Real Options Real[267]

Copeland, T. and P. Keenan, 1998, The McKinsey Quarterly

Copeland and Keenan continued to expand upon their initial research. In 1998, they pointed out that Real Options are especially valuable for projects that involve both a high level of uncertainty and opportunities to dispel that uncertainty as new information becomes available. To bring practicality and detail to thinking about real options, Copeland and Keenan worked through a series of cases that capture the business problems and realities they involve. In their 1998 article, Copeland and Keenan focus on three different types of real options: compound options, learning options, and staged investments.

1) Compound options can help management understand whether and when to proceed with the later phases of projects that have already been initiated. This application is particularly useful when the NPV is close to breakeven because breakeven results tend to result in overly subjective decision-making. In general, compound options involve sequenced or staged investments. Making the first investment gives a company the right but not the obligation to make a second investment, which in turn confers the right to make a third, and so on. This differs from simple options, which gives their holders the right to buy or sell an item at a particular price on only one occasion, at or before a particular expiration date.

2) Learning options are those where the holder pays to learn about an uncertain quantity or technology. An oil company may own the rights to a plot of land without knowing exactly how much oil it contains. Rather than trying to predetermine a particular level of production capacity, the company might find it worthwhile to spend money discovering the actual extent of the reserves. This might involve drilling to

---

[267] Copeland, Thomas E. and Philip T. Keenan (1998) "Making Real Options Real", McKinsey Quarterly, no. 3, 128-141.

learn more about the quantity of natural resources located under the surface. This would allow development of the field without wasting resources building facilities designed to process more oil than is actually there. Conversely, it would avoid delayed profits from constraining production rates for fear of depleting wells that in reality contain more oil than was believed to be there. Similarly, companies with R&D programs invest to reduce technological or knowledge-based uncertainty.

3) Staged investments give managers the option to abandon or scale up projects well into their lifetimes. These compound options can be highly valuable. Similar factors apply in any manufacturing industry when a new factory or a large capital investment is under consideration. Decisions about expanding into new geographic areas and investing in research and development also involve staged investments of this kind. A sequence of acquisitions constitutes a staged series of investments. At each stage, it is not clear that an acquisition will provide the anticipated growth platform. If it does, the company that makes the acquisition can proceed with the next one. If it does not, the acquirer has the option of selling the latest acquisition, though not necessarily recouping its full cost. Real Option valuation can be used to value all possible contingencies.

9.14 Using Real Options In Strategic Decision Making

Chris Walters and Tim Giles, 2000,
Amos Tuck School of Business at Dartmouth

The tools most commonly used to value investments are: payback rules, rates of return, net present values (NPV) and Real Options. In this study, Walters and Giles suggest that the application of Real Option methodology contributes not only to financial valuation, but also to strategic vision by providing a useful planning framework to address growth and timing of, and exit from, investment opportunities.

- Growth: Real Options place a value on the ability to invest now and make follow-up investments later if the original project is successful. Examples are: high investment experimental R&D, such as new product development in pharmaceutical or high technology industries.

- Exit: Real Options can also enable valuation of the ability to abandon a project if it is unsuccessful. Examples include mining or oil exploration investment.

- Timing: Real Options can value the ability to wait and learn, resolving uncertainty, before investing.

Walters and Giles also compare Real Options with Decision Tree analytical methodology. They state, "Decision-tree analysis tends to consider great detail in the cash flow models and many uncertainties, but relatively little in the way of dynamic decision making" and that "this dynamic complexity is generally more important than detail complexity".[268] Real Options analysis, on the other hand, can help the business focus on a few key dynamic processes while decision-tree analysis would overflow the largest boardroom whiteboard. They suggest/conclude that using NPV does not take account of managerial options and the Real Options approach can help by valuing these managerial intangibles and preventing mistakes.

9.15 Managerial Implications of Implementing Real Options Thinking In Resource Allocation

Jacquet, 2000

In his paper, Jacquet raises the following two points:

1) Why organizations have restrained themselves in the introduction of Real Option thinking in capital budgeting and

---

[268] Using Real Options in Strategic Decision Making, Chris Walters and Tim Giles, London Economics, Tuck Paradigm, Amos Tuck School of Business at Dartmouth, Spring 2000.

2) How companies fully integrate Real Options into their business models.

He regards the traditional approach—utilization of the cost of capital and its application in the valuation of assets (Discounted Cash Flows, Net Present Value)—as less than optimal in the long run, and he argues that Real Option thinking should be embedded in the resource allocation processes for the short- and medium-run.

In this respect, the RO approach would be a way to understand:

- The manner in which management reacts, to future evolutionary changes, and how management can be assisted to understand which actions to take to react to such changes, adds value.

- How alternative options should be taken into account when the initial investment is made.

Jacquet argues there is an important organizational consequence of that behavioral issue. Introducing an "option-mentality" in a company will probably increase the percentage of risky projects accepted. If the company wants to encourage its employees to take "good" risks, it has to protect them against an adverse evolution.

9.16 Decision Making for Technology Executives, Artech House

Linstone, 1999

In his book, "Decision Making for Technology Executives, "Linstone proposes that three distinct perspectives are inherent in any system and that all three must be understood to fully understand the system. These three views are identified as the Technical (T), Organizational (O), and Personal (P) perspectives. Each perspective yields insights about the system not obtainable via the others, and for a full comprehension of the system all three perspectives must be integrated; the implication is that the integrated view enables the whole system to be greater than the sum of its parts. The author emphasizes that it is necessary to balance attention across all three perspectives. Balancing the perspectives help to avoid problems such as technologists attempting to perceive all problems through the technological lens that comes naturally to them, with the result those technological solutions are applied to problems that may not be technological in nature. It is often said that to a worker with only a hammer, every problem looks like a nail. Workers with an understanding of the organizational and personal perspectives may seek other tools to solve problems.

Linstone describes the three perspectives thusly:

- The Technical perspective refers to the world as seen in quantitative ways, such as curves or computer models. Problems and proposed solutions are described in terms of alternatives, trade-offs, optimization, data and models.

- The Organizational perspective perceives the world through the viewpoint of affected and affecting organizations. Organizations, from this perspective, may be formal or informal, hierarchical or egalitarian, or permanent or ad hoc. Linstone asserts that the O perspective also reflects the culture and myths that have helped to mold and bind the organization, group, or society as a distinct entity in the eyes of its members. He notes that, normally, outstanding companies have strong cultures that reflect their values.

- The Personal perspective is the most subtle and elusive, and the most difficult to define, because it is stems from the individual personality. According to Linstone, self- interest motivates most individuals, although that motive may often be hidden or disguised. Disguised self-interest may manifest itself in the pursuit of prestige, profit, power, or pleasure.

The purpose of understanding the three perspectives is to help a person with one of those perspectives to recognize that his or her point of view is not the only significant way of looking at the situation. An understanding of the three perspectives should also reveal to the person why he or she holds his or her own position.

Linstone points out, for example, that people associated with the Technical perspective tend to want to reduce issues to questions of fact, to undertake some kind of research, or gather data, or do tests, all to clarify situations from a scientific or technical point of view so they can move on to a solution. The reality is that in complex situations there are relatively few situations that lend themselves to purely technical solutions. Rather, in most complex situations there are some technical problems, but the most important concerns usually involve assumptions and goals that may not be technical in nature. In these issues, technical solutions are rarely to be found. More likely to be found is a point of resolution, a point which satisfies everyone to some extent, but no one completely.

From the Organizational perspective, the primary priority is the well-being of the organization. When organizations are faced with crises, their priority is not to seek technical solutions or solutions that satisfy every individual. Rather, they seek to minimize damage to organizational well-being, even at the cost of personal hardships to organizational members and even if technical solutions may be available to help ameliorate the crisis. If the solution does not help the organization as a whole, it does not satisfy those who embody the Organizational perspective.

The Personal perspective is the most broad and diversified, since it has to do with how any person who has a connection with the socio-technical system at issue thinks, feels, believes, or may act. Those personal factors are often the most difficult to comprehend fully because they are often extremely divergent. They come from people with varying levels of concern, interest and commitment to the system. Ultimately, it is essential to understand those personal perspectives to achieve a workable resolution to a problem.

Based on the foregoing, it can be seen that T perspective looks to the logic of problem solving and optimizing involving trade-offs; the O perspective is action-focused on the group and oriented towards incremental organizational change; and the P perspective relates to the individual, accepting his/her power and influence and limited cognitive ability to handle more than a few alternatives. Thus T relies on logic, observation and analysis, O emphasizes justice and bargaining, while P has morality as a core value leading to intuition and learning. A key attribute of TOP theory is that because it emphasizes that all three perspectives must be integrated, none of the individual perspectives can be allowed to dominate the rest, so that all three contribute to pursuit of a more nuanced and balanced solution than would be obtainable without applying all three perspectives.

In this study, the investment decisions involved clearly benefit from incorporation and integration of all three perspectives. When the NPV is negative (T perspective), management may nonetheless decide to invest (P perspective) based on their business instinct that the investment aligns with the company's long term strategic goal (O perspective).

Because management's instinctive "P" view is subjective, it is not easy to determine whether it is correct or not, unlike the "T" analysis that is provided by NPV. Hence a supplementary T perspective tool, RO analysis, is very helpful and useful in testing the alignment between the P and O perspectives.

10. References

Abel, A. B., A. Dixit, et al. (1995). "Options, the Value of Capital, and Investment." NBER Working Paper.

Alimov, A. (2007). Innovations, Real Options, Risk and Return: Evidence from the Pharmaceutical and Biotechnology Industries, University of Oregon.

Amram, M. and N. Kulatilaka (1999). Real options, Harvard Business School Press. Amram, M. and N. Kulatilaka (1999). "Disciplined Decisions: Aligning Strategy with the Financial Markets." Harvard Business Review 77: 95-104.

Amram, M. and N. Kulatilaka (1999). Real Options: Managing Strategic Investment in an Uncertain World, Harvard Business School Press.

Amram, M. and N. Kulatilaka (1999). "Uncertainty: The New Rules for Strategy." Journal of Business Strategy 20(3): 25–32.

Amram, M. and N. Kulatilaka (2001). "Real Options: Managing Strategic Investment in an Uncertain World", Harvard Business School Press. Also published by Oxford University Press.

Amram, M., F. Li, et al. (2006). "How Kimberly-Clark Uses Real Options." Journal of Applied Corporate Finance 18(2): 40-47.

Angelis, D. (2000). "Capturing the Option Value of RD." Research-Technology Management 43(4): 31-34.

Armstrong, M., A. Galli, et al. (2004). "Incorporating technical uncertainty in real option valuation of oil projects." Journal of Petroleum Science and Engineering 44(1-2): 67-82. Baeyens, K. (2006). "Essays on the Determinants and Long-term Effects of Entrepreneurial Financing Choices." Ghent Unversity, Belgium.

Baghai, M., S. Coley, et al. (1996). "Staircases to growth." The McKinsey Quarterly 4: 54-61.

Balasubramanian, P., N. Kulatilaka, et al. (2000). "Managing information technology investments using a real-options approach." Journal of Strategic Information Systems 9(1): 39-62.

Basu, S. (2007). Corporate Venture Capital: Towards Understanding Who Does It, Why and How, University of Washington.

Benaroch, M. and R. J. Kauffman (1999). "A Case for Using Real Options Pricing Analysis to Evaluate Information Technology Project Investments." Information Systems Research 10: 70-86.

Benninga, S. and E. Tolkowsky (2002). "Real Options—An Introduction and an Application to R&D Valuation." The Engineering Economist 47(2): 151-168.

Black, F. and M. Scholes (1973). "The Pricing of Options and Corporate Liabilities." Journal of Political Economy 81(3): 637.

Blake, G. (1999). "Ten 'biggest' Problems Technology Leaders Face." Research Technology Management 42(6): 13–14.

Boer, F. (2000). "Valuation of Technology Using" Real Options."" Research-Technology Management 43(4): 26-30.

Boer, F. (2002). The Real Options Solution: Finding Total Value in a High-Risk World, Wiley.

Boer, F. (2002). "Real Options: The IT Investment Risk-Buster." Optimize Magazine, July 1.

Boquist, J., T. Milbourn, et al. (1998). "How do you win the capital allocation game." Sloan Management Review 39(2): 59-71.

Bouteiller, C. (2000). The evaluation of intangibles: advocating for an option based approach.

Boyle, P. (1977). "Options: A Monte Carlo Approach." Journal of Financial Economics 4(3): 323-338.

Brabazon, T. (1999). "Real Options-Valuing flexibility in capital investment decisions:

Do you feel uncomfortable when you are asked to appraise an investment in IT, in research and development, or in brand development?" Accountancy Ireland 31: 16-18. Brennan, M. and E. Schwartz (1985). "Evaluating Natural Resource Investments." Journal of Business 58(2): 135.

Brennan, M. and L. Trigeorgis (2000). Project Flexibility, Agency, and Competition: New Developments in the Theory and Application of Real Options, Oxford University Press. Brennan, M. J. and E. S. Schwartz (1976). "The pricing of equity-linked life insurance policies with an asset value guarantee." Journal of Financial Economics 3(3): 195–214. Brennan, M. J. and E. S. Schwartz (1977). "The valuation of American put options." Journal of Finance 32(2): 449-462.

Brennan, M. J. and E. S. Schwartz (1978). "Finite Difference Methods and Jump Processes Arising in the Pricing of Contingent Claims: A Synthesis." Journal of Financial and Quantitative Analysis 13(3): 461-474.

Brennan, M. J. and E. S. Schwartz (1979). "A Continuous Time Approach to the Pricing of Bonds." Journal of Banking and Finance 3(2): 133-155.

Brennan, M. J. and E. S. Schwartz (1982). "An equilibrium model of bond pricing and a test of market efficiency." Journal of Financial and Quantitative Analysis 17(3): 301-329. Brennan, M. J. and E. S. Schwartz (1985). "Evaluating Natural Resource Investments." Journal of Business 58(2): 135.

Brennan, M. J. and E. S. Schwartz, et al. (1991). "Analyzing Convertible Bonds." Proceedings Issue 15(4).

Brennan, M. J., E. S. Schwartz, et al. (1997). "Strategic asset allocation." Journal of Economic Dynamics and Control 21(8-9): 1377-1403.

Brennan, M. J. and L. Trigeorgis (2000). "Real Options: Development and New Contributions." Project Flexibility, Agency, and Competition 11.

Brennan M, and Trigeorgis (1998), Infrastructure and Strategic Options, Oxford University Press, New York.

Brennan M, and Trigeorgis L (1999), Project Flexibility, Agency, and Competition: New Developments in the Theory and Applications of Real Options. Oxford University Press, New York.

Brounen, de Jong & Koedjik (2001), "Management Corporate Finance Decision Making—Corporate Finance in Europe: Confronting Theory with Practice", Financial Management Winter 2001.

Bulan, L. T., C. J. Mayer, et al. (2008). "Irreversible Investment, Real Options, and Competition: Evidence from Real Estate Development." Journal of Urban Economics. Campbell, J. A. (2001). "Identifying an optimal start-up date for information technology projects: a real options approach." Management of Engineering and Technology, 2001. PICMET '01, Vol. 1: 37.

Carr, P., R. Jarrow, et al. (1992). "Alternative Characterizations of American Put Options" Mathematical Finance 2(2): 87-106.

Carter, J., M. Dijk, et al. (1996). "Capital Investment: How Not to Build the Titanic." The McKinsey Quarterly(4): 147-148.

Casassus, J. and P. Collin-Dufresne (2003), Maximal affine model of convenience yields implied from interest rates and commodity futures, Tech. report, Carnegie Mellon University, Preprint.

Casassus, J. and P. Collin-Dufresne (2005). "Stochastic Convenience Yield Implied from Commodity Futures and Interest Rates." The Journal of Finance 60(5): 2283-2331.

Cassimon, D. and P. J. Engelen (2001). "A Real Option Approach to Valuing Pharmaceutical Investment and Firms." Value in Health 4(6): 428.

Cassimon, D., P. J. Engelen, et al. (2004). "The valuation of a NDA using a 6-fold compound option." Research Policy 33(1): 41-51.

Chan, S., J. Martin, et al. (1990). "Corporate Research and Development Expenditures and Share Value." Journal of Financial Economics 26(2): 255-276.

Childs, P. D., T. J. Riddiough, et al. (1996). "Mixed Uses and the Redevelopment Option." Real Estate Economics 24(3): 317-339.

Childs, P. D. and A. J. Triantis (1999). "Dynamic R&D Investment Policies." Management Science 45(10): 1359-1377.

Cho, H. (2007). Valuing Retail Shopping Center Lease Contracts Incorporating Inter- store Externality Effects: A Real Option Approach, University of Wisconsin—Madison. Cobb, B. and J. Charnes (2004). "Real

Options Volatility Estimation with Correlated Inputs." The Engineering Economist 49(2): 119-137.

Copeland, T. and V. Antikarov (2001). "Real Options-A Practitioner's Guide", Texere LLC, New York.

Copeland, T. and P. Keenan (1998). "How Much is Flexibility Worth?" The McKinsey Quarterly 2(1998): 38-49.

Copeland, T. and P. Keenan (1998). "Making Real Options Real." The McKinsey Quarterly no. 3: 128–41.

Copeland, T. and P. Tufano (2004). "A Real-World Way to Manage Real Options." Harvard Business Review 82(3).

Copeland, T. E. (2002). "What Do Practitioners Want?" Journal of Applied Finance 12(1): 5-12.

Cortazar, G. and J. Casassus (1998). "Optimal Timing of a Mine Expansion: Implementing a Real Options Model." Quarterly Review of Economics and Finance 38: 755-769.

Cortazar, G. and E. Schwartz (1993). "A Compound Option Model of Production and Intermediate Inventories." Journal of Business 66(4): 517.

Cortazar, G., E. S. Schwartz, et al. (2001). "Optimal exploration investments under price and geological-technical uncertainty: a real options model." R&D Management 31(2): 181-189.

Cortazar, G., E. S. Schwartz, et al. (1998). "Evaluating environmental investments: A real options approach." Management science 44(8): 1059-1070.

Damodaran, Aswath (2000). "The Promise of Real Options" Journal of Applied Corporate Finance 13(2): 29-44.

Damodaran, Aswath (2005), "The Promise and Peril of Real Options." NYU Working Paper No. S-DRP-05-02.

Davis, G. (1998). "Estimating Volatility and Dividend Yield When Valuing Real Options to Invest or Abandon." Quarterly Review of Economics and Finance 38: 725-754.

Davis, G. (2002). "The Impact of Volatility on Firms Holding Growth Options." The Engineering Economist 47(2): 213-231.

Davis, G. A. (1998). "Estimating Volatility and Dividend Yield When Valuing Real Options to Invest or Abandon." Quarterly Review of Economics and Finance38: 725-754. Dubofsky, David A., and Thomas W. Miller, Jr. (2002). Derivatives: Valuation and Risk Management, Oxford University Press, New York, NY.

Dillon, R. and J. Owers (1997). "EVA as a Financial Metric: Attributes, Utilization, and Relationship to NPV." Financial Practice and Education 7(1): 32–40.

Dixit, A. and R. Pindyck (1995). "The Options Approach to Capital Investment,." Harvard Business Review 73(3): 105-116.

Dixit, A. K. and R. S. Pindyck (1994). Investment under uncertainty, Princeton University Press Princeton, NJ.

Dixit, A. K. and R. S. Pindyck (1997). Expandability, Reversibility, and Optimal capacity choice. Academic paper.

Doukas, J. and L. Switzer (1992). "The stock market's valuation of R&D spending and market concentration." Journal of Economics and Business 44(2): 95-114.

Eisenhardt, K. M., A. Etzioni, et al. (1985). "Strategy as Strategic Decision Making." Theory and Decision 18(2).

Engelen, P. J. and D. Cassimon (1999). "The valuation and financing of high-risk startup ventures: an option perspective matching real and financial options." Business & economics for the 21st century", Business & Economics Society International, Worcester: 345-355.

Fama, E. F. (1996). "Discounting Under Uncertainty." Journal of Business 69(4): 415. Faulkner, T. W. and R. (1996). "Applying 'Options Thinking' To R&D Valuation: Used properly, options pricing can identify important sources of value that are missed by the traditional DCF approach." Research Technology Management 39: 50-56.

Faulkner, T. W. (1996). "Options pricing theory and strategic thinking: Literature review and discussion." report (version 3.3), Eastman Kodak Company.

Figlewski, S. (1989). "Options Arbitrage in Imperfect Markets." Journal of Finance 44(5): 1289–1311.

Foster, R., L. Linden, et al. (1985). "Improving the return on R&D." Research Management 28(1): 12-17.

Glasserman, P. and J. Staum (2001). "Conditioning on One-Step Survival for Barrier Option Simulations." Operations Research 49(6). 923-937.

Godinho, P. (2006). "Monte Carlo Estimation of Project Volatility for Real Options Analysis." Journal of Applied Finance 16(1): 15-30.

Greden and Glicksman (2004), Options Valuation of Architectural Flexibility: A Case Study of the Option to Convert to Office Space, conference paper.

Grinyer, J. and M. Walker (1990). "Deprival Value Accounting Rates of Return." Economic Journal 100(3): 918–22.

Harmantzis, F. and T. V. Praveen (2004). Real Options Analysis for GPRS Network with Wi-Fi Integration, 31 st Annual Conference of the Northeast Business & Economics Association, New York, NY.

Harmantzis, F. and V. P. Tanguturi (2004). Delay in the Expansion from 2.5 G to 3G Wireless Networks: A Real Options Approach, International Telecommunications Society 15th Biennial Conference, Berlin, Germany.

Harmantzis, F. C. and V. P. Tanguturi (2007). "Investment decisions in the wireless industry applying real options." Telecommunications Policy 31(2): 107-123.

Hartmann, M. and A. Hassan (2006). "Application of real options analysis for pharmaceutical R&D project valuation—Empirical results from a survey." Research Policy 35(3): 343-354.

Hayes, R. and W. Abernathy (2007). "Managing Our Way to Economic Decline." Harvard Business Review 85(7/8): 138.

Hayes, R. and D. Garvin (1982). "Managing as if tomorrow mattered." Harvard Business Review 60(3): 71-79.

Haylett, J. (2001). Calculating the Real Option Value of an Exploration Mineral Rights Lease Using Monte Carlo Simulation, Texas A & M University.

Herath, H. and C. Park (1999). "Economic Analysis of R&D Projects: An Options Approach." The Engineering Economist 44(1): 1-35.

Herath, H. and C. Park (2002). "Multi-State Capital Investment Opportunities as Compound Real Options." The Engineering Economist 47(1): 1-27.

Herath, H. S. B. and C. S. Park (2001). "Real Options Valuation and its Relationship to Bayesian Decision-Making Methods." The Engineering Economist 46(1): 1-32.

Hoe, S. (2006). Strategic Exercise of Options on Non-traded Assets and Stochastic Volatility in an Incomplete Market: Indifference Pricing and Entropy Methods, University of Texas, Arlington, Texas

Hull, J. (2005). Fundamentals of Futures and Options Markets. Upper Saddle River, NJ, Pearson Prentice Hall.

Iversen, E. and A. Kaloudis (2006). "IP Valuation as a Tool to Sustain Innovation." The Management of Intellectual Property. Edward Elgar: Aldershot.(forthcoming).

Jagannathan, R. (1984). "Call Options and the Risk of Underlying Securities." Journal of Financial Economics 13(3): 425-434.

Jacquet, D. (2000). Managerial Implications of Implementing Real Options Thinking in Resource Allocation. Working Paper 00 25, University of Ottawa.

Linstone, H.A., (1999). Decision Making for Technology Executives. Artech House, Boston.

Kaplan, R. and D. Norton (1996). "Using the Balanced Scorecard as a Strategic Management System." Harvard Business Review 74: 75-87.

Kaplan, R. and D. Norton (2001). The Strategy-Focused Organization: How Balanced Scorecard Companies Thrive in the New Business Environment, Harvard Business School Press.

Kaplan, R. and D. Norton (2001). "Transforming the Balanced Scorecard from Performance Measurement to Strategic Management: Part I." Accounting Horizons 15(1): 87-104.

Kaplan, R. and D. Norton (2001). "Transforming the Balanced Scorecard from Performance Measurement to Strategic Management: Part II." Accounting Horizons 15(2): 147-160.

Kaplan, R. and D. Norton (2005). "The Balanced Scorecard: Measures that Drive Performance." Harvard Business Review 83(7): 172.

Kellogg, D. and J. Charnes (2000). "Real-Options Valuation for a Biotechnology Company." Financial Analysts Journal 56(3): 76-84.

Kemna, A. G. Z. (1993). "Case Studies on Real Options." Financiall Management 22: 259-259.

Kerssens-van Drongelen, I. and J. Bilderbeek (1999). "R&D performance measurement: more than choosing a set of metrics." R&D Management 29(1): 35-46.

Kerssens-van Drongelen, I., B. Nixon, et al. (2000). "Performance measurement in industrial R&D." International Journal of Management Reviews 2(2): 111-143.

Kogut, B. and N. Kulatilaka (2001). "Capabilities as Real Options." Organization Science 12(6): 744-758.

Kogut, B. and N. Kulatilaka (2004). "Real Options Pricing and Organizations: The Contingent Risks of Extended Theoretical Domains." Academy of Management Review 29(1): 102-110.

Kulatilaka, N. (1993). "The Value of Flexibility: The Case of a Dual-Fuel Industrial Steam Boiler." Financial Management 22(3): 271-280.

Kulatilaka, N. (1995). "The Value of Flexibility: A General Model of Real Options." Real Options in Capital Investment: Models, Strategies, and Applications: 89–107, Westport, CT, US.

Kulatilaka, N., P. Balasubramanian, et al. (1996). Managing Information Technology Investments: A Capability-based Real Options Approach, Boston University, School of Management, Boston, MA, US.

Kulatilaka, N. and E. Perotti (1998). "Strategic Growth Options." Management Science 44: 1021-1031.

Kuske, R. and J. Keller (1998). "Optimal exercise boundary for an American put option." Applied Mathematical Finance 5(2): 107-116.

Laate, E. A., E. Dept. of Rural, et al. (2006). Valuing Agricultural Biotechnology Investments a Real Options Approach, Library and Archives Canada= Bibliothèque et Archives Canada.

Lander, D. and G. Pinches (1998). "Challenges to the Practical Implementation of Modeling and Valuing Real Options." Quarterly Review of Economics and Finance 38: 537-568.

Lander, D., P. Shenoy, et al. (1999). "Modeling and Valuing Real Options Using Influence Diagrams." University of Kansas, Kansas.

Lee, S.-H. (2002). Real Options Theory: Implications on Entrepreneurship Development and Options Value Under Uncertainty. Ohio State University, Ohio

Leslie Keith, J. and P. Michaels Max (1997). "The Real Power of Real Options." The McKinsey Quarterly, New York 3: 97-108.

Leung, Nga-Na (2007) Real Options Framework for Acquisition of Real Estate Properties with Excessive Land. University of Florida, Florida.

Li, Y. and G. Sick "Equilibrium Investment Decisions in A Real-Options Sequential Bargaining Game with Network Effects.", 2006 FMA Annual Meeting Preliminary Academic Program, Conference working paper.

Luehrman, T., E. Schwartz, et al. (2004). "Strategy as a Portfolio of Real Options." Real Options And Investment Under Uncertainty: Classical Readings and Recent Contributions.

Luehrman, T. A. (1998). "Strategy Portfolio of Real Options." Harvard Business Review: 89-99.

Luehrman, T. A., A. K. Dixit, et al. (1997). "A General Manager's Guide to Valuation." Harvard Business Review 75(3): 133-154.

Luehrman, T. A., E. S. Schwartz, et al. (2004). "Strategy as a Portfolio of Real Options." Real Options And Investment Under Uncertainty: Classical Readings and Recent Contributions.

Martín, G. R. and P. L. Fernández (2006). "Real Option in Biotechnological Firms Valuation. An Empirical Analysis of European Firms." Journal of Technology Management & Innovation 1(2): 27.

Martzoukos, S. and L. Trigeorgis (2002). "Real (investment) options with multiple sources of rare events." European Journal of Operational Research 136(3): 696-706. Maya, C. (2004). In Search of the True Value of Start-up Firms: Creative Destruction and Real Options Approach, Brandeis University, Waltham, MA.

McAllister, P., B. O'Roarty, et al. (1999). Pricing break clauses: a fundamental approach, RICS Cutting Edge Conference, Cambridge.

McCahery, J. and L. Renneboog (2003). Venture Capital Contracting and the Valuation of High-technology Firms, Oxford University Press, USA.

McConnell, J. (2007). A Life-Cycle Flexibility Framework For Designing, Evaluating and Managing Complex Real Options: Case Studies In Urban Transportation and Aircraft Systems. MIT Engineering Systems Division, Cambridg, MA

McDonald, R. (2006). "The Role of Real Options in Capital Budgeting: Theory and Practice 1." Journal of Applied Corporate Finance 18(2): 28-39.

McDonald, R. and D. Siegel (1984). "Option Pricing When the Underlying Asset Earns a Below-Equilibrium Rate of Return: A Note." Journal of Finance 39(1): 261-265.

McDonald, R. and D. Siegel (1985). "Investment and the valuation of firms when there is an option to shut down." International Economic Review 26(2): 331-349.

McGrath, R. G. (1997). "A Real Options Logic for Initiating Technology Positioning Investments." Academy of Management Review 22: 974-996.

Merchant, K. (1998). Modern Management Control Systems: Text and Cases, Prentice Hall.

Merton, R. (1973). "Theory of Rational Option Pricing" Bell Journal of Economics and Management Science 4(1): 141-183.

Merton, R. (1974). "On the Pricing of Corporate Debt: The Risk Structure of Interest Rates." Journal of Finance 29(2): 449-70.

Merton, R. (1998). "Applications of Option-Pricing Theory: Twenty-Five Years Later (Digest Summary)." American Economic Review 88(3): 323-349.

Miltersen, K. (2000). "Valuation of Natural Resource Investments with Stochastic Convenience Yields and Interest Rates. Project Flexibility, Agency, and Competition." New York. Oxford University Press 183: 205.

Miltersen, K. and E. Schwartz (1998). "Pricing of Options on Commodity Futures with Stochastic Term Structures of Convenience Yields and Interest Rates." Journal of Financial and Quantitative Analysis 33: 33-60.

Moser, M. (1985). "Measuring performance in R&D settings." Research Management 28(5): 31-33.

Myers, S. (1977). "Determinants of Corporate Borrowing" Journal of Financial Economics 5(2): 147-175.

Myers, S. (1984). "Finance Theory and Financial Strategy." Interfaces 14(1): 126. Nelson, Housel, and Mun (2005), "Sub-Finance: New Sources of Data for Real Options Analysis", Real Options 2005Conference working paper.

Olmsted Teisberg, E. (1994). "An option valuation analysis of investment choices by a regulated firm." Management Science 40(4): 535-548.

Paddock, J. L., D. R. Siegel, et al. (1988). "Option Valuation of Claims on Real Assets: The Case of Offshore Petroleum Leases." Quarterly Journal of Economics 103(3): 479- 508.

Paris Champs-Élysées Street, by the author
https://commons.wikimedia.org/wiki/File:Nike_Store,_67_Avenue_des_Champs-%C3%89lys%C3% A9es,_75008_Paris,_October_2014.jpg

Pengfei, H. and H. Yimin (2000). Real Option Valuation in High-Tech Firm. Göteborg University. School of Business, Economics and Law, Sweden.

Philippe, Henri (2005), "Real Options: Still Looking for Evidence?" Real Options Conference, 2005.

Pindyck, R. "Irreversibility, uncertainty, and investment, 1991." Journal of Economic Literature 29: 1110–1152.

Pindyck, R. S. (1986). "Irreversible Investment, Capacity Choice, and the Value of the Firm." NBER Working Paper.

Pindyck, R. S. (1998). "The long-run evolution of energy prices." Sloan School of Management, Massachusetts Institute of Technology, Issue December.

Pindyck, R. S. and A. K. Dixit (1994). Investment under uncertainty, Princeton University Press.

Pindyck, R. S. and B. World (1990). Irreversibility, uncertainty, and investment, World Bank.

Pitts, C. and J. Busby (1997). "Real options in practice: an exploratory survey of how decision makers in industry think about flexibility." Management Accounting Research 8: 169-186.

Porter M. (1980), Competitive Strategy, New York: Free Press. Porter M. (1986), Competitive Advantage, New York: Free Press.

Power, B., G. C. Reid, et al. (2005). "A Test of Real Options Logic." Discussion Paper Series 9, University of Standrews Center for Research into Industry Enterprise Finance, University College Cork, Cork, Ireland.

Prokesch, S. (1997). "Unleashing the Power of Learning. An Interview with British Petroleum." Harvard Business Review 75(5): 146-68.

Qin, R. (2007). Attaining Knowledge Workforce Agility in a Product Life Cycle Environment Using Real Options, Pennsylvania State University.

Quigg, L. (1995). "Optimal Land Development." Real Options in Capital Investment: Models, Strategies, and Applications: 265–280.

Quigg, L. and U.-C. University of Illinois at (1993). "Empirical Testing of Real Option- Pricing Models." Journal of Finance-New York 48: 621-621.

Reifer, D. (2004). Use of Real Options Theory to Value Software Trade Secrets, University of Southern California, California.

Ross, M. and M. Rubinstein (1979). "Option pricing: A simplified approach." Journal of Financial Economics 7: 229-263.

Ryan, P. and G. Ryan (2002). "Capital budgeting practices of the Fortune 1000: How have things changed." Journal of Business and Management 8(4): 355-364.

Samis, M., G. A. Davis, et al. (2005). "Valuing uncertain asset cash flows when there are no options: A real options approach." Resources Policy 30(4): 285-298.

Sarkar, S. (2000). "On the investment–uncertainty relationship in a real options model." Journal of Economic Dynamics and Control 24(2): 219-225.

Schwartz, E. and J. E. Smith (2000). "Short-Term Variations and Long-Term Dynamics in Commodity Prices." Management Science 46(7): 893-911.

Schwartz, E. S. (1997). "The Stochastic Behavior of Commodity Prices: Implications for Valuation and Hedging." Journal of Finance—New York 52: 923-974.

Schwartz, E. S. (2004). "Patents and R&D as Real Options." Economic Notes 33(1): 23-54.

Schwartz, E. S. and M. Moon (2000). "Evaluating Research and Development Investments." Project Flexibility, Agency, and Competition–New Developments in the Theory and Application of Real Options, New York and Oxford.

Schwartz, E. S. and M. Moon (2000). "Evaluating Research and Development Investments—Project Flexibility, Agency, and Competition—New Developments in the Theory and Application of Real Options", New York und Oxford Press.

Schwartz, E. S. and M. Moon (2000). "Rational Pricing of Internet Companies." Financial Analysts Journal 56(3): 62-75.

Schwartz, E. S. and M. Moon (2001). "Rational Pricing of Internet Companies Revisited." Financial Review 36(4): 7-26.

Schwartz, E. S. and L. Trigeorgis (2004). Real Options And Investment Under Uncertainty: Classical Readings and Recent Contributions, MIT Press.

Schwartz, E. S. and C. Zozaya-Gorostiza (2003). "Investment Under Uncertainty in Information Technology: Acquisition and Development Projects." Management Science 49(1): 57.

Senge, P. and B. Audio (1990). The fifth discipline, Doubleday New York, NY.

Sharp, D. (1991). "Uncovering the hidden value in high-risk investments." Sloan Management Review 32(2): 69-74.

Sick, Gordon (1994). Real Options. Working paper series F, working paper # 45, Yale School of Management, New Haven, Conn.

Smit, H. and L. Ankum (1993). "A Real Options and Game-Theoretic Approach to Corporate Investment Strategy Under Competition." Financial Management 22: 241-241. Smit, H. and L. Trigeorgis (1999). "Flexibility, Strategic Options and Dynamic Competition in Technology Investments." Strategic Management Journal (under revision).

Smit, H. A. N. (2003). "Infrastructure Investment as a Real Options Game: The Case of European Airport Expansion." Financial Management 32(4).

Smit, H. T. J. (2003). "Airport Expansion." Financial Management: 27-57.

Smit, H. T. J. and L. A. Ankum (1993). "A Real Options and Game-Theoretic Approach to Corporate Investment Strategy Under Competition." Financial Management 22: 241- 241.

Smit, H. T. J. and L. Trigeorgis (2001). R&D Option Strategies.

Smit, H. T. J. and L. Trigeorgis (2004). "Real Options: Examples and Principles of Valuation and Strategy", Erasmus University Rotterdam and NIAS, The Netherlands Smit, H. T. J. and L. Trigeorgis (2004). Strategic Investment: Real Options and Games, Princeton University Press.

Smit, H. T. J. and L. Trigeorgis (2006). "Real options and games: Competition, alliances and other applications of valuation and strategy." Review of Financial Economics 15(2): 95-112.

Smit, H. T. J., L. Trigeorgis, et al. (1995). Flexibility and Commitment in Strategic Investment, Tinbergen Institute.

Stark, A. (2000). "Real Options,(Dis) Investment Decision-Making and Accounting Measures of Performance." Journal of Business Finance & Accounting 27(3-4): 313-331. Starkov, V. (2001). Essays on the Restructuring of the Electricity Industry in the United States, West Virginia University.

Sterman, J. (2000). Business Dynamics: Systems Thinking and Modeling for a Complex World, Irwin McGraw-Hill.

Tanguturi, V. P. (2005). Real Options for Migration to 3G Wireless Broadband Internet: The Case of an Operator in India, Stevens Institute of Technology.

Titman, S. (1985). "Urban Land Prices." American Economic Review 75: 505-514. Titman, S., C. Los Angeles University of, et al. (1984). Urban Land Prices Under Uncertainty, University of California, Los Angeles, Graduate School of Management. Tourinho, O. (1979). The valuation of reserves of natural resources: an option pricing approach, University of California, Berkeley.

Tong, Reuer (2007), "Real Options in Strategic Management—Advances in strategic Management", 24, Real Options in Strategic Management.

Trigeorgis, L. (1993). "Real Options and Interactions with Financial Flexibility." Financial Management 22: 202-202.

Trigeorgis, L. (1995). Real Options in Capital Investment: Models, Strategies, and Applications, Praeger/Greenwood Press.

Trigeorgis, L. (1996). Real options, MIT Press Cambridge, Mass.

Trigeorgis, L. (1996). Real Options: Managerial Flexibility and Strategy in Resource Allocation, MIT Press.

Trigeorgis, L. (2001). "A Log-Transformed Binomial Numerical Analysis Method for Valuing Complex Multi-Option Investments." Real Options and Investment under Uncertainty: Classical Readings and Recent Contributions. Cambridge: 539-558.

Trigeorgis, L. (2004). "A Conceptual Options Framework for Capital Budgeting." Real Options And Investment Under Uncertainty: Classical Readings and Recent Contributions.

Trigeorgis, L. (2004). "The Nature of Option Interactions and the Valuation of Investments with Mutiple Real Options." Real Options And Investment Under Uncertainty: Classical Readings and Recent Contributions.

Van Putten, B. Alexander and C. MacMillan (2004), "Making Real Options Really Work," Harvard Business Review, 82, (12), pp. 134-141.

Wang, T., G. W. University, et al. (2007). Comparison of Methods for Valuating Technology Innovation and Adoption Projects, George Washington University.

Walters, Chris and Giles, Tim, (2000). Using Real Options In Strategic Decision Making. Tuck Paradigm, Spring 2000. Retrieved from http://mba.tuck.dartmouth.edu/paradigm/ spring2000/articles/walters-decision_making.html

Wilkinson, Christine Alicia (2006). Capital Budgeting, Real Options and Escalation of Commitment: A Behavioral Analysis of Capital Investment Decisions, Iowa State University, Iowa.

Wu, M. C. and C. Y. Tseng (2006). "Valuation of patent–a real options perspective." Applied Economics Letters 13(5): 313-318.

Wang, Tiehong (Ann) (2007) Comparison of methods for valuating technology innovation and adoption projects. (Ph.D. dissertation, The George Washington University, United States).

Y. AmKt-Sahalia, Y., Y. Wang, et al. (2001). "Do Option Markets Correctly Price the Probabilities of Movement of the Underlying Asset?" Journal of Econometrics 102(67): 110.

Zhang, Duoxing (2008) Real options evaluation of financial investment in flexible manufacturing systems in the automotive industry, Auburn University, Alabama.

Appendix A: Sportswear Industry

A-1   Industry Analysis

A-1.1   Retail industry overview—Porter's five forces analysis.

1) **Threat of New Entrants**—One trend that started over a decade ago has been a decrease in the number of independent retailers. While the barriers to starting up a store are not impossible to overcome, the ability to establish favorable supply contracts, leases, and compete is becoming virtually impossible. Their vertical structure and centralized buying gives chain stores a competitive advantage over independent retailers.

2) **Power of Suppliers**—Historically, retailers have tried to exploit relationships with suppliers. A great example was in the 1970's when Sears sought to dominate the household appliance market. Sears set very high standards for quality, and the suppliers who did not meet their standards were dropped from the Sears line. A contract with a large retailer such as Sears can make or break a small supplier. Generally speaking, suppliers in the retail industry have very little power, although this is changing. However, this is a little different in the sportswear retail industry. The dominant suppliers, such as Nike and Adidas, do command great power. As the suppliers continue to integrate forward by opening their own retail stores, their power (in relation to that of their retail customers) increases as their dependency on the independent retailers decreases.

3) **Power of Buyers**—Individually, customers have very little bargaining power with retail stores. However, as a whole, the consumer groups have been empowered with a much stronger bargaining power. As consumers become more educated, they demand more: quality products, better services, and better values; in addition, as the competition intensifies

amongst retailers, the power of buyers has been increasing significantly over the past decade.

4) **Availability of Substitutes** -The tendency in retail is not to specialize in one good or service, but to deal in a wide range of products and services. This means that what is on offer in one store can more than likely be found at another store. Retailers offering products that are unique and cannot be found elsewhere have a distinct or absolute advantage over their competitors. In sportswear retailers, this trend has been influencing and shaping the main retailers, particularly in supplier-owned retail stores.

For instance, in Adidas's Shanghai glamour Brand-Flagship *(mega-store)* stores, consumers are welcomed with celebrities' endorsement advertisements; in Niketown London, consumers can use the NikeID studio to design their own personalized shoes. These "Premium consumer experiences" cannot be replicated elsewhere, such as in the shoe sections of department stores.

5) **Competitive Rivalry**—Retailers always face stiff competition. The slow market growth for the retail market means that firms must fight each other for market share. More recently, they have tried to reduce the cut-throat pricing competition by offering Frequent Flyer points, memberships, and other special services to try to gain the customers' loyalty. Rivalry is fierce, and there are a number of standard reasons why it is—relatively small number of competitors and so on.

A-2   Retail Industry Growth—Global Retail Outlook

A-2.1   Regional growth.

Asia: The Asian market is prevalent in the rankings partly due to demographics, because Asian countries tend to have a higher number of younger people than developed markets.

Europe: Europe has slipped down the rankings generally with established markets such as France, the Netherlands and Sweden showing restrained growth. Russia and the UK are the leaders and Turkey is climbing (up from 16th to 12th).

North America: The North American market is characterized by saturation and intense competition, but it still remains a very attractive market for international retailers.

Latin America: The Latin American market is developing slowly; while Argentina and Brazil are improving their rankings slightly, they are very much at the bottom end of the table.

A-2.2   U.S. retail industry overview.

The U.S. shows the biggest forecast volume growth for clothing and footwear from 2006 to 2011: clothing and footwear sales are projected to increase by $74bn from $345bn in 2006 to $419bn in 2011, up 3.9%. The US has slipped down to second due to saturation and intense competition, but still remains a very attractive market for international retailers.

The U.S. retail industry generates $3.9 trillion in retail sales annually ($4.2 trillion if food service sales are included). One of the biggest contributions that retail industry brings to a country is employment. In the US, the retail industry accounts for about 11.6 percent of U.S. employment. Annual retail employment averaged 15.3 million people in 2005. Ten year employment projections expect retail sales to increase 11.0 percent, versus 14.8 percent overall.

Table A-1: Total Retail Sales (excluding Gasoline Stations, US Census) 2000-2022

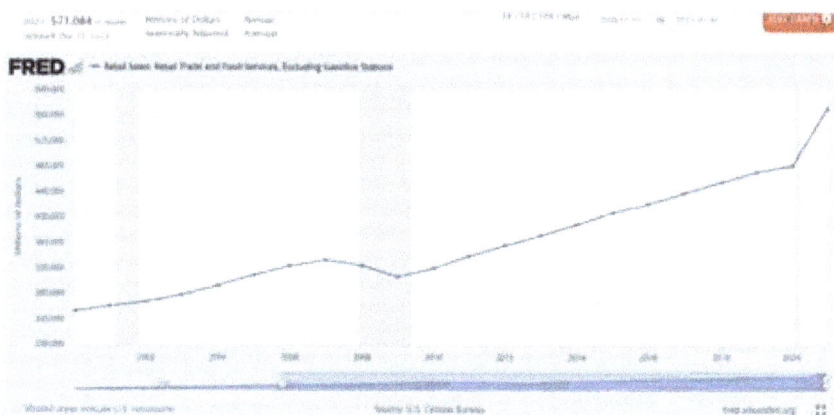

Source: US Census.

A-2.3 Global market overview on sportswear industry

A-2.3.1 History & trending.

The first complete survey conducted by WSGI (World Sporting Goods Industry Association, 2002 survey) estimated that consumer spending on sportswear will grow by a modest 18% to reach US$105bn in 2003. This estimate is proved to be conservative in the very next year: the world market for total active sportswear and athletic footwear in 2003 amounted to US$145bn, and grew to US$235bn in 2005.

A-2.4   Global market: sportswear retail industry.

Sportswear benefits from the substantial retailing sector that developed in the 1990s, now consolidated into several major multiple operators: JJB Sports, Blacks Leisure and JD Sports are the largest. The early 2000s have generally been a period of consolidation for the sportswear industry. Into the 21st century, the Retailing of sportswear is more fragmented than ever, through sports shops, general stores and e-commerce, with multiple grocers making inroads.

A-2.4.1 Product demand.

Demand is cyclical for various sports products and ˋlooks', such as the classic white trainer or running shoe, or hooded top originally used for warming up. Such products will come and go in a mature market emphasized by the popular "retro" styles but the recent publicity surrounding the need for physical activity to tackle obesity and poor health should stimulate demand for "performance sportswear."

The active sportswear and athletic footwear product group is one of the most heavily branded areas of apparel, consisting of the international brands, competing with a multitude of second division players. This is an area of clothing where the purchasing choice is frequently determined by the sports figure person admired, and the brand that person chooses to wear.

The active sportswear and athletic footwear product group is one of the most heavily-branded areas of apparel. There are only two truly global players: Nike and Adidas-Reebok. They compete with each other not only just product innovation, but also retailing their own products. They also compete with a multitude of smaller and regional sports brands, and also with the sports ranges of casual wear brands.

With growth in these apparel sectors being very much marketing-driven, major sporting events and/or world champion events for the active sportswear and athletic footwear industry. From the European Football Championship to Olympic, and other world's major sporting events, all create unique selling-opportunities for this industry. Beijing Olympic 2008 is one of the examples that the sportswear industry is expanding its influence to the young consumers in the new markets, from developed market moving into emerging developing countries.

A-2.4.2 Key global players

Sportswear is a global industry, largely revolving around three dominant brands: Nike, Adidas & Reebok, and Puma. These brands are leaders in both active sportswear and fashionable leisurewear. There are many other, more specialized brands as well, usually oriented toward a particular sport. The UK's leading companies include Umbro (football kit based in UK, acquired by Nike in 2007), Hi-Tec (trainers and outdoor footwear) and Pentland Group (through subsidiaries such as Speedo, Berghaus and Ellesse). Generally, the sportswear industry concentrates its production centers in the Far East, particularly in China.

A-2.5   US sportswear retail market analysis[269]

The retail sporting goods industry in the US includes about 20,000 companies with combined annual revenue of $25 billion (all sports related, including bicycles related, fitness equipments, etc). Large chain operators include Sports Authority, REI, and Hibbett Sporting Goods. The industry is highly fragmented: the 50 largest companies hold less than 50 percent of the market. Only about 150 companies have more than five stores. A typical store has $5 million of annual sales.

A-2.5.1 Competitive landscape.

Dick's is one of the largest specialty retailers in the U.S. Dick's competes in fragmented industry, with the top six sporting goods retailers holding only 19% of the estimated $52 billion market. Other

---

[269] Sources: D&B Research Group; First Research Inc.; Hoover's Inc, other strategic planning sources.

companies that Dick's compete with in the sporting goods retail market include the following firms:

- Academy Sports & Outdoors: Academy is a private company operating throughout the South and Southwest regions of the U.S. Academy's product offerings focus on apparel and equipment for outdoor activities such as camping, hunting, fishing and boating.

- Recreational Equipment, Inc.: REI operates about 90 stores heavily concentrated in the Western half of the US. REI sells mostly apparel and equipment used for hiking, climbing, kayaking and other similar outdoor activities.

- Big 5 Sporting Goods: This small-store neighborhood style retailer leads the sporting goods market in Western states such as Washington, California and Arizona. It operates over 300 stores throughout the Western region.

- Hibbett Sports: Hibbett boasts over 600 small-format stores based primarily in the Southeast region of the US. These stores are traditionally located in indoor and strip malls and sell a variety of sporting equipment and apparel.

In addition, there are footwear retailers: Foot Locker and Finish Line. Department store chains: Wal-Mart, Target, and Amazon who sell a selection of sporting equipment and apparel in their stores as well.

Demand is driven by population demographics and consumer income. The profitability of individual companies depends on me

Merchandising and marketing skills. Large chains have an advantage in stocking a wide variety of goods. Small companies can compete successfully by carrying a deeper product line in specialized sports, or by serving a local market.

A-2.6 Time series of the yearly change rate of total annual sales

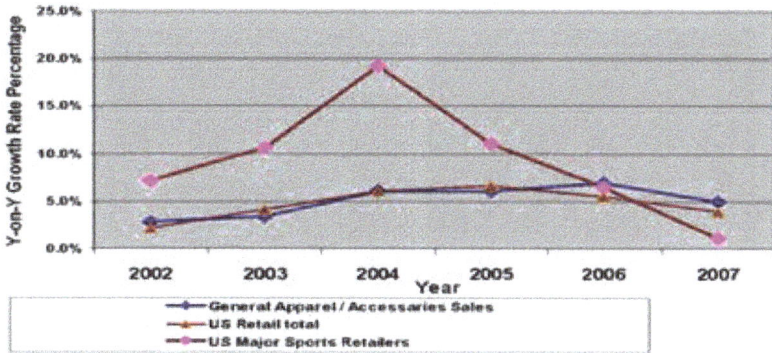

US Retail Total Annual Sales vs. General Apparel vs. US Major Sporting Goods Retailers Y-on-Y Growth Rate
Souce: US Census & Internal Retailers financial Statements

Figure A-1: US Retail Total Annual Sales vs. General Apparel vs. US Major Sporting Goods

Retailers Y-on-Y Sales Changes Rate 2002-2007

Figure A-1-1: 2020 EBIT Margin global major players—McKinsey

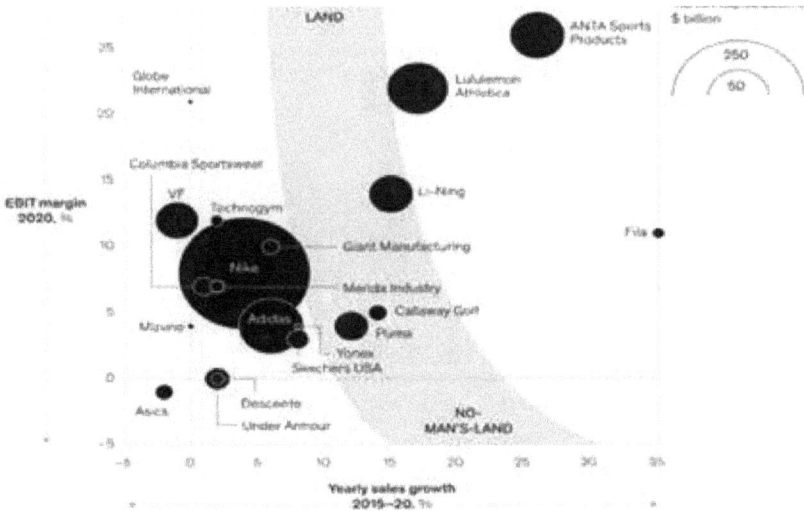

A-2.6.1 Products, operations & technology.

Major products are outdoor clothing and shoes, firearms, golf equipment, and bicycles. Clothing and shoes together account for about 25 percent of industry revenue, firearms 10 percent, bicycles and golf equipment 8 percent each. Other products include exercise, camping, and ski equipment; fishing tackle; and team sports equipment. In this study, main focus is on the footwear, apparel, and fitness accessories.

Format and merchandise vary. Most chains operate stores of a single type. Large- format stores are from 20,000 to 100,000 square feet, stock a large number of items, and are typically found as anchor stores in strip malls or in stand-alone locations.

Traditional sporting goods retail stores vary in size from 5,000 to 20,000 square feet, carry a more limited number of items, and are normally found in strip or enclosed malls. Specialty stores have a wide selection of items for just one or two sports, such as golf, tennis, skiing, camping, etc.; are typically 1,000 to 10,000 square feet; and located in enclosed and strip malls. Large-format stores typically have more than $5 million in annual revenue and more than 50 employees.

Specialty stores have less than $1 million in annual revenue and fewer than ten employees.

Although large chains can sell a broad range of merchandise at lower prices, small local stores can successfully compete by offering better service or specializing in a particular sport. Because the equipment for many sports is very technical, knowledgeable salespeople are a strong competitive factor. The operations of sporting goods stores are fairly straightforward: companies acquire merchandise, determine store layout, train employees, advertise goods, provide services, sell goods, and manage inventory.

Product is acquired from manufacturers and about 1,000 wholesale distributors. Manufacturers regularly introduce new models, which often have only minor changes from older models. Trade shows are an important way of finding out about new products. The type of merchandise purchased varies according to the season and regional and local preferences. Large-format stores may carry up to 100,000 separate items (stock keeping units—SKUs). Sports Authority stores usually carry 40,000 SKUs, with a range of brands in about 30 different sports categories. Sports Authority buys from 750 vendors. Specialty stores carry significantly fewer items. In addition to equipment, most retailers sell sports apparel and shoes. Nike, mainly a manufacturer of shoes and sports clothing, is one of the biggest vendor to Sports Authority, accounting for more than 10 percent of its merchandise. Store layouts and merchandise presentation are often changed, especially in large-format stores that try to maintain the atmosphere of a collection of specialty departments. Layout and presentation may be designed with the help of special software from companies like Marketmax. Because much sports equipment is highly specialized, employees must be trained to understand and explain differences. Companies typically try to recruit employees who are avid sports participants. Many companies rely on part-time employees for 50 percent or more of their workforce.

Inventory management is a major concern for all sporting goods retailers because of the large numbers of items they sell and the short selling season for many sports. Chains usually supply their stores from a central distribution facility, with weekly re-supply based on sales. Hibbett Sports supplies 280 stores from a single 200,000 square foot distribution facility. Many companies use highly sophisticated computerized inventory management systems that include point-of-sale (POS) terminals, scanners, and handheld radio frequency terminals to record merchandise receipts, print pricing labels, monitor inventory levels, facilitate automatic inventory replenishment, and identify popular items.

A-4   Sportswear Retail Characteristics Overview

The overall economic environment has a great impact on the retailing industry, and an even greater impact on the sportswear retailing. Retailer profits have a close correlation with the overall performance of the economy. The trends for GDP growth, inflation, consumer confidence, personal income, and interest rates are extremely important when thinking about investing in the retail industry.

The sportswear retail industry has been changing towards high-investment and high-risk industry. The logistical advances enable the sportswear suppliers to expand towards the retail front and retailers to integrate backwards along the supply chain to produce own brands. The industry is therefore consolidating itself towards main big players. They compete to attract consumers. At the same time, the technology advances information flow (there have been technological advances made in the flow of information). As consumers are becoming much more informed than ever before, they can find information about better value bargains on a broader and larger scale and can identify the latest new inventions much more quickly. They demand quality products, premium services, and most importantly, the combination of these two along with a better value. The once "led" consumers are now "leading" the industry trend.

All these developments are starting to shorten industry cycles (overall sales values and volume). Consumers' purchasing behavior is changing more quickly than ever before. As a result, the product "shelf-life" cycles are getting much shorter. The shortness of these cycles is relatively new and the industry is in the process of adapting to this change, resulting in retailers forming different types of stores to attract consumers, to create premium consumer experiences, and to take the advantage over competitors.

Some of the main "competitive advantages" are: faster logistic management, an improvement in store presentation, and better store fixtures. Creating these advantages requires heavier investment, and more flexible investment formats appear. Some of the new investment vehicles are: expansion in stage, lease contract with breach option term, and/or with optional renovation, and/or contract with distributors.

As the competition in the business environment intensified, the investment risk also increases. Not only do investors need to have an instinctive and rational understanding of the selected store values, they also need to know the potential opportunities and risk that come along with the investment. They are willing to pay a premium to secure the opportunity to avoid the risk. They do this by buying an option, thus securing the investment opportunity while not having to commit the full investment. A simple example would be: buying an option to acquire a company in 4-months' time instead of buying right now. As it is still unknown whether the result of a major sporting event is favorable to the acquisition.

In conclusion, the evolution in the Sportswear Retail Industry (consolidating trends and rapid changes in the marketplace) has led to a more unstable investment environment. This in turn creates complexity in investment valuation.

A-5   Sportswear Retail Industry Investment Valuation

The traditional planning model, NPV or IRR captures market risk via a "discount rate," which does indeed enable the management in the decision-making process; but in an ever-changing retail business environment companies and management need to be able to respond proactively to the market changes in a more timely and accurate manner.

When the NPV is close to zero, it is difficult for the management to evaluate the financial benefit and investment trade off. And when new information related to the new store is still pending, managers need to (be able to) fully explore options that are other than just Go or No-Go. Of equal importance is the strategic long-term benefit gained from freeing up committed investment to pursue other investment opportunities in divesting in certain projects. Abandoning or deferring an investment can free up the cash that might have to be tied up and therefore strengthen the business' ability to be reactive or even to be pre-active to the changes in the marketplace.

Retail investors and management are challenged to explore all investments alternatives including option value investment. Particularly when the NPV is close to zero. However as discussed in the RO methodology section, there is a lack of attention to Real Option analysis in the sportswear retail environment due to:

- The irreversibility of the investment option premium—that is, the premium paid is non re-fundable in normal practice;

- The complexity of the new methodology and the effort needed to educate management about it:

- The data required to complete RO takes effort and more time.

Diagram: Methodology Flow & Output Comparison

Process and Steps to Prove Hypothesis: RG methodology can be used in SRI investment valuation, in comparison to the NPV methods, to improve SRI investment valuation accuracy and assist managerial decision-making, particularly a) when a new investment has a NPV that is b) compared by great uncertainty, b) when a new investment has a negative NPV that has strategic value embedded.

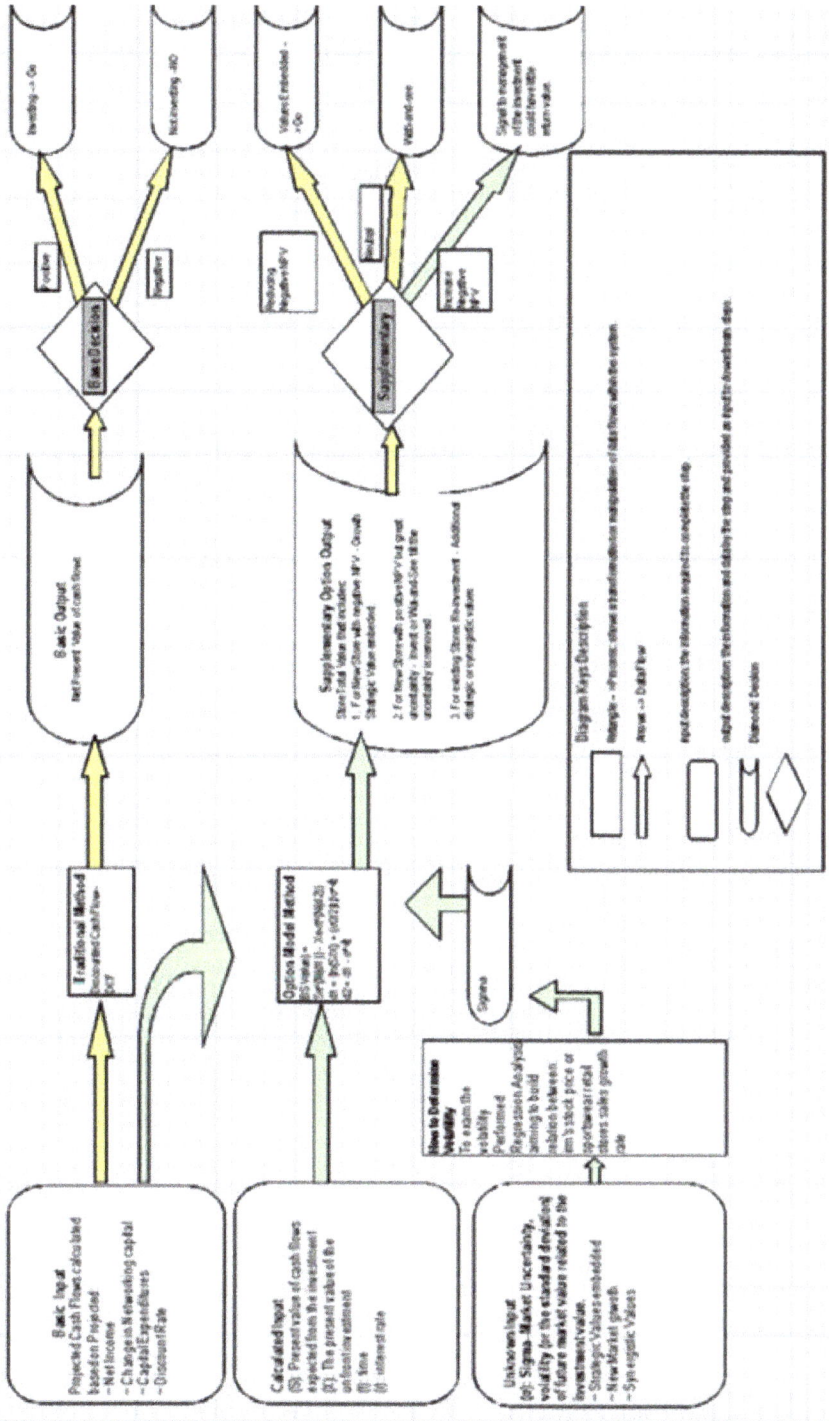

Basic Input:
Projected Cash Flows calculated based on Projected
– Net Income
– Changes in Net working capital
– Capital Expenditures
– Discount Rate

Calculated Input:
(S) Present value of cash flows expected from the investment
(X) The present value of the unfused investment
(i) time
(i) interest rate

Unknown Input:
(σ): Sigma: Market Uncertainty, volatility for the standard deviation of future market value related to the investment value.
– Strategic Values embedded
– New Market growth
– Synergistic Values

How to Determine Volatility:
To examine the volatility Performed Regression Analysis aiming to build relation between firm's stock price of top-of-award retail share sales growth rate

Traditional Method
Discounted Cash Flow – NPV

Option Model Method

Basic Output:
Net Present Value of cash flows

Supplementary Option Output:
Store Total Value that include:
1. For New Store with negative NPV – Growth Strategic Value obtained
2. For New Store with positive NPV but great uncertainty – invest or Wait-and-See till the uncertainty removed
3. For existing Store Re-Investment – Additional strategic or synergistic value

Basic Decision — Invest → Go / Not Investing – NO

Supplementary — Value if needed – Go / Wait-and-see / Signal to management of the investment could have little return value

Diagram Keys Description

Shape – «Process: shows a transformation manipulation of data flows within the system

Arrow – «Output Flow

Input description: the information required to complete the step

output description: the information and data by the step and provided as input to downstream steps

Delayed: Decision

Appendix B: Nike Sport Brand Key Athletes Endorsed[270]

Basketball: Michael Jordan, Kobe Byrant, LeBron James, Kevin Durant, Jordan Chris Paul, Carmello Anthony, Ray Allen, Dwayne Wade

Football: Tom Brady, Adrian Peterson, LaDanian Tomlinson, Jordan Terrell Owens, Jason Taylor

Baseball: Jordan Derek Jeter, Andruw Jones, CC Sabathia

Golf: Tiger Woods, Anthony Kim, Trevor Immelman, Michelle Wie

Soccer: Ronhaldhino, Cristiano Ronaldo, Wayne Rooney **Tennis**: Roger Federer, Rafael Nadal, Serena Williams **Running**: Asafa Powell, Walter Dix, Paula Radcliffe **Cycling**: Livestrong Lance Armstrong

---

[270] Source: Company data.

Appendix C: Nike Best Positioned in Footwear Product Innovation History[271]

1974   The "Waffle trainer" is introduced.

1978   The first Air-Sole units are created, resulting in Nike Air cushioning.

1979   Nike introduces the Tailwind, the first running shoe with Nike Air.

1982   Air Force 1, the first Nike basketball shoe to incorporate Nike Air cushioning, is introduced.

1986   Nike debuts two apparel collections, one featuring John McEnroe and the other Michael Jordan.

1987   The Air Trainer High Shoe and the Air Max shoe are introduced.

2000   The Nike Air Presto, and its revolutionary approach to fit, is launched.

2000   Nike unveils its Shox technology.

2000   At the Olympics in Sydney, Nike reveals the lightest track spike ever made, the aerodynamic and thermo-regulatory Swift Suit, and the recyclable Marathon Singlet.

2002   Nike introduces its first golf clubs with forged blade irons, forged wedges, and forged Titanium drivers.

2005   Nike Free, footwear that emulates the leg-strengthening benefits of barefoot running, is launched.

2006   Nike launches Air Max 360, which uses a new method of creating Air-Sole units.

2006   Nike+ is launched.

2008   Flywire technology is launched.

2009   Pro Combat performance apparel is launched.

---

[271] Source: Company data.

Appendix D: Nike Timeline

D-1 The 1960s-70s

1964   Nike's predecessor, Blue Ribbon Sports, is incorporated in Oregon.[1]

1971   The Swoosh first appears on Nike shoes

The first line of Nike footwear is introduced, including the so-called "Moon Shoe" that features a waffle sole, which is distributed to athletes competing in the US Olympic Track & Field Trials in Eugene, Oregon

Romanian tennis star Ilie Nastase becomes the first athlete to sign an endorsement contract with Blue Ribbon Sports to wear its Nike tennis shoes.

1972   American record-holder Steve Prefontaine becomes the first major track athlete to wear Nike shoes.

1975   The Waffle Trainer is introduced, quickly becoming the best-selling training shoe in the U.S.

Nike print ad with the tag "There is no finish line" is introduced.

1978   Tennis "bad boy" John McEnroe is signed by Nike to an endorsement contract.

1979   Nike's Air technology patented by inventor M. Frank Rudy is introduced in the Tailwind running shoe. Gas-filled plastic membranes are inserted into the sole of running shoes to provide cushioning.

D-2 The 1980s

1980   Nike completes an initial public offering of 2,377,000 shares of Class B common stock on December 2.

Nike hires the first industrial designers into the footwear industry to work out of their Exeter, NH R&D facility.

1981   BRS, Inc. merges into Nike, Inc. on December 31, and the company officially becomes known as Nike, Inc.

1982   Dan Wieden and Dave Kennedy start their own advertising agency, Wieden+Kennedy, taking with them the Nike account on April 1. In October, Nike airs its first national television ad during the New York Marathon.

1982   The Air Force 1 basketball shoe becomes the first Nike court shoe to make use of the Air technology.

1984   Nike signs Michael Jordan to an endorsement contract. The first model of his signature shoe, the Air Jordan, originally is banned by the NBA, drawing a tremendous amount of publicity.

1986   Corporate revenues surpass $1 billion for the first time.

1987   The Nike Air Max shoe is introduced, which for the first time makes visible the Nike air bag. A television ad featuring the Beatles' song "Revolution" is the first time that a song performed by the Beatles is used in a TV ad.

1988   The famous tagline, "Just do it", is introduced at the suggestion of 4th grader Tiffeny Speir from Urban Park Elementary School in Dallas, TX.

1989   Nike enters the European football market, signing a kit deal with Paris Saint- Germain Bo Jackson appears in Nike's Bo Knows ad campaign to support the launch of its cross-training shoe.

D3   The 1990s

1990   The first Niketown store opens in downtown Portland.

Nike opens its world headquarters in unincorporated Washington County, just west of Portland, on 74 acres (0.3 km²) of land.

1993   Nike introduces Reuse-A-Shoe, which collects athletic shoes, separates and grinds them up into Nike Grind, used in the making of athletic courts, tracks and fields.

1994   Nike wins Advertiser of the Year at the Cannes Advertising Festival.

Nike enters the ice hockey market after acquiring Canstar, the parent company of hockey equipment manufacturer Bauer Hockey. Previously, Nike had only made hockey jerseys, specifically those of the Edmonton Oilers at the height of Wayne Gretzky-mania, but now began to make all equipment.

1995   Nike signs long-term partnerships with the Brazilian and United States soccer teams, and moves into English football, signing a kit (uniform/apparel) deal with Arsenal.

1996   Nike signs Tiger Woods soon after he gives up his amateur golf status.

Nike causes controversy with its advertising campaign during the Summer Olympics in Atlanta which features the slogan, "You Don't Win Silver—You Lose Gold." Nike's use of this slogan draws harsh criticism from many sources, including—not surprisingly—several former Olympic silver and bronze medalists.

Niketown Los Angeles opens in Beverly Hills.

1997   Nike signs several hockey stars, including Sergei Fedorov and Jeremy Roenick, to endorsement deals to wear their new line of skates, which are quickly lambasted for the fact that they are mostly white, traditionally the color of women's figure skates. This sartorial quirk, coupled with problems with the soles of the skates, leads Nike to relent and allow Fedorov to wear Graf-brand skates with a Nike swoosh applied to them. In the future, Nike's hockey skates become simply restyled Bauer products until the two brands are combined in 2005.

1998   Phil Knight commits Nike to standards for its affiliated manufacturing facilities, including: minimum age; air quality; education programs; expansion of microloan program; factory monitoring; and enhanced transparency of Nike's corporate social responsibility practices.

1999   Bill Bowerman, co-founder of Nike, dies on Dec. 24 at age 88.

D4 The 2000s

2000   Nike Shox cushioning/support system is introduced, initially worn by Vince Carter and others on the US Olympic basketball team.

2002   Nike purchases Hurley International, an action sports clothing company, for an undisclosed amount.

NikeGO launches, a grassroots initiative to increase physical activity among youths aged 9-15.

Nike become the apparel sponsor of Manchester United until 2010. Nike SB, Nike's Skateboarding line, debuts.

2003   Nike acquires once-bankrupt rival Converse for $305 million on July 9.

For the first time in the company's history, international sales exceed USA sales.

Nike is again (also in 1994) named "Advertiser of the Year" by the Cannes Advertising Festival.

Nike signs NBA player LeBron James with an unprecedented $87 million endorsement contract.

2004   Phil Knight steps down as CEO and President of Nike, but continues as chairman. Knight is replaced by William D. Perez as CEO of Nike, effective Dec. 28.

Nike creates the Exeter Brands Group, a wholly owned subsidiary for athletic footwear and apparel brands for lower price points. Brands include Starter, Team Starter, Asphalt, Shaq, and Dunkman.

Annual revenues exceed $ 12.25 billion.

2005   Nike reports annual revenue for fiscal year 2005 (ending May 31) of $13.74 billion, a 12% increase over the previous fiscal year.

Nike Signs Tennis Pro Rafael Nadal.

2006   Nike enters the cricket market with a 5-year sponsorship of the Indian cricket team for US$43m.

CEO William Perez leaves Nike on January 23, 2006. Perez said in the statement that he and Knight "weren't entirely aligned on some aspects of how to best lead the company's long-term growth. It became obvious to me that the long-term interests of the company would be best served by my resignation."

Mark Parker replaces Perez as CEO. Parker previously was brand co- president of the company, and joined Nike in 1979.

Nike and Apple release the Nike+iPod sports kit, enabling runners to log and monitor their runs via iTunes and the Nike+ website.

Nike reports annual revenue for fiscal year 2006 (ending May 31) of $15 billion.

2007   Nike introduces the Second Coming, a group of NBA basketball players who best represent the Nike Basketball.

Nike introduces AF25, after 25 years of Air Force shoe line. Nike become the kit sponsor of Aston Villa.

2008   Nike sells its Nike Bauer hockey equipment division.

Nike introduces shoes featuring new Flywire and Lunarlite Foam materials. Flywire is a new technology made up of thin wires of vectran fibers, which are 5 times stronger than steel and never lose strength. Lunar Foam is a material developed by NASA that gives the shoe excellent shock absorption and a great feel with minimal weight.

Nike reports annual revenue for fiscal year 2008 (ending May 31) of $18.6 billion, a 14% increase over the previous fiscal year

2009   Nike laid off 4% of its labor worldwide; restructured its geography structure and management.

Appendix E: Correlation

The correlations of between rates of return of the "underlying asset" calculation is shown below. Correlation relationship on the year on year growth change percentage among NTL Sales, Nike Sales, Nike Stock Price, and ROIC[272].

Table E-1: Supplement Correlation—NTL & Nike Yearly Growth % & Nike Sales &. Nike Stock Price & ROIC

Data	Period—Year	NTL Growth%	Nike Stock Price Change	ROIC
	2007	8.00%	28.70%	25.80%
	2006	-8.50%	12.90%	26.70%
	2005	-4.30%	4.40%	24.10%
	2004	9.00%	25.70%	20.50%
	2003	0.00%	32.905	17.00%
	2002	-7.00%	-8.00%	15.20%
	2001	1.30%	10.80%	13.90%
	2000	3.20%	4.30%	14.30%
Correlation				
	NTL Sales	vs nike Stock		
	Nike Sales	vs. Stock		
Reference:				
		NTL Sales	vs. Nike Sales	26.5%
		NTL Sales	vs. ROIC	-6.5%
		Nike Sales	vs. ROIC	65.4%
		Nike Stock	vs. ROIC	32.1%

---

[272] ROIC: Return on Invested Capital, an accounting measurement of return on investment. to assess a company's efficiency at allocating the capital under its control to profitable investments.
ROIC = (Net Operating Profit After Taxes—NOPAT) / (Invested Capital—IC)
NOPAT = (Operating Profit) x (1—Tax Rate)
IC = (Total Assets)—(Excess Cash)—(Non-Interest-Bearing Current Liabilities)

As can be seen from the table, the correlation between Nike sales and the Nike stock price and between NTL sales to the Nike stock price demonstrate strong correlation relation.

Appendix F: Other Approach to define Sigma

F-1   UK Retail index

In this study, the United Kingdom Retail Sales Index (RSI) is the industrial group index. In past studies, an industry index has been used to estimate the volatility of a project's value. However, as we discussed in the previous section: the distinguishing characteristics of the sportswear retail industry differentiate itself from the general apparel and footwear retail industry. We will further elaborate sportswear characteristics in the following discussion, leading to the conclusion the RSI would not be an appropriate definition of sigma in this study.

The Retail Sales Index is a measure of the consumer spending and retail output in the United Kingdom. It is derived from a monthly survey, conducted by the Office for National Statistics, of 5,000 businesses in Great Britain, including all large retailers and a representative sample of smaller businesses. This is a key indicator[273] of the state and direction of the economy. It is also used to help estimate consumer spending on retail goods and the output of the retail sector, both of which feed into the compilation of the National Accounts. Accordingly, the Retail Sales Index initially appears promising as a proxy for NTL investment rate of return.

---

[273] The value of retail sales reported via the monthly survey is converted to a chained volume basis using weighted contributions of price indices for various categories of retail goods. These commodity price indices are consistent with the consumer price indices published by the ONS every month.

For each four-or-five-week period, respondents report their total value of retail sales for all their outlets and by mail order (including via the internet). The statistics include VAT. The reference year has been set at 2005=100.

Installment credit sales are valued at the credit price of the goods, that is including deposits and, where credit is provided by the shop, credit charges. Figures of credit sales relate only to the period during which the transactions took place; cash received from credit sales in previous periods is not included. Sales by chemists and opticians exclude receipts under the National Health Service. Sales of automotive fuel are also included.

However, unlike the regular large retailers and smaller retailing businesses whose retail data are encapsulated by the Retail Sales Index, the Sportswear Retail Industry (particularly flagship stores such as NTL) has its own distinguishing characteristics that render the Retail Sales Index an inappropriate proxy.

F-2   Other Sigma definition approaches

Various RO Calculation results based on different was to define sigmas. Examples are as the following. However these variables establish less significant correction / regression with the underlying assets; hence, being excluded.

Applying the BSOPM, when sigma is defined as –

1. Std_Dev of VFTSE[274]: the real investment value of the refitting investment is $** million; standard capital budgeting analysis yields a net present value of negative $4.4 million.

2. Std_Dev of 10-Year Nike Company Cash Flow rate of change: the real investment value of the refitting investment is $** million; standard capital budgeting analysis yields a net present value of negative $4.4 million.

3. Std_Dev of 1-Year Nike Net Income: the real investment value of the refitting investment is $** million; standard capital budgeting analysis yields a net present value of negative $4.4 million.

---

[274] VFTSE reflects the general beliefs and risk-preferences of investors that underlie their investment equity index returns in UK. It is a "market forecast". However it is because of its "generalization", it imposes the limitation of using this index as the proxy to represent the rate of return of the NTL. While VFTSE can be considered as one of the ways to define sigma, we realize the limitation of using this index as the proxy to represent the rate of return of the underlying asset.

Table F-1: NPV & RO NTL Calculation Result–Std Dev VFTSE

Total Investment Construction Cost (USD Thousand)	$	(17.45)
PV of Projected Cash Flows: (USD Thousand)	$	12.98
NPV (USD Thousand)	$	**(4,467)**
RO (USD Thousand)	$	**2,770**

Table F-2: NPV & RO NTL Calculation Result–Std Dev Cash Flow

Total Investment Construction Cost plus Fit-out	$	(17.48)
PV of Projected Cash Flows:	$	12.98
Lease Term: 35 year with 10 years breach option	$	
NPV	$	(4.468)
RO	$	5,587

Table F-3: NPV & RO NTL Calculation Result–Std Dev Net Income

Total Investment Construction Cost plus Fit-out	$	(17.48)
PV of Projected Cash Flows:	$	12.98
Lease Term: 35 year with 10 years breach option	$	
NPV	$	(4.468)
RO	$	6,220

Appendix G: RO testing example—"Flushed Data."

Assume that a proposal to build a stadium in one year's time is pending before the city council of a major metropolitan area, and sportswear retailer X must decide whether to construct a new store in the city. If the stadium is constructed, a store's sales are is expected to generate an NPV of $10M; if the city council decides to build the stadium a year later, then the new store is expected to have an NPV of $9M; if the City decides not to build the stadium, however, the new store is expected to have an NPV of -$14M. If the likelihood of construction approval is 50%, defer building stadium is 5%, and remaining 45% is not to build stadium. An "Expected NPV Analysis" is demonstrated in Figure[275].

If sportswear retailer Y has a greater appetite for risk and decides to build a store, though, and the city council does approve the stadium, the competitor may be able to exploit its first mover advantage to gain market share that may be hard to retake. Nonetheless, sportswear retailer A's decision not to build was the "right" one given the information available at the time it was made.

On the other hand, if competitor X had an option to delay its ultimate decision whether to build or not until after the city council made its decision, it could substantially eliminate its uncertainty. It might be able to do this, for example, by spending a nonrefundable $1.5M to purchase an option to lease the most desirable retail premises and to obtain commitments by architects and construction firms to build the store if approval is granted by the city council. This "wait-and-see" approach determines the NPV of the store if the stadium is approved and subtracts the nonrefundable up-front costs, and then repeats the process under the condition that the city council decides not to build the stadium, as follows: in essence, this is a Real Option concept: it incorporates data regarding expected cash flows and variation or volatility in those cash flows to produce a reliable estimate of fair value. Real Options analysis addresses the uncertainty of projects through payment of a premium to secure the right to invest until the uncertainty is removed or solved.

---

[275] This format is originated from Strategic Flexibility in Financial Industry, Deloitte.

Figure G-1: Example of a Sportswear Retail Industry Investment Valuation Using RO

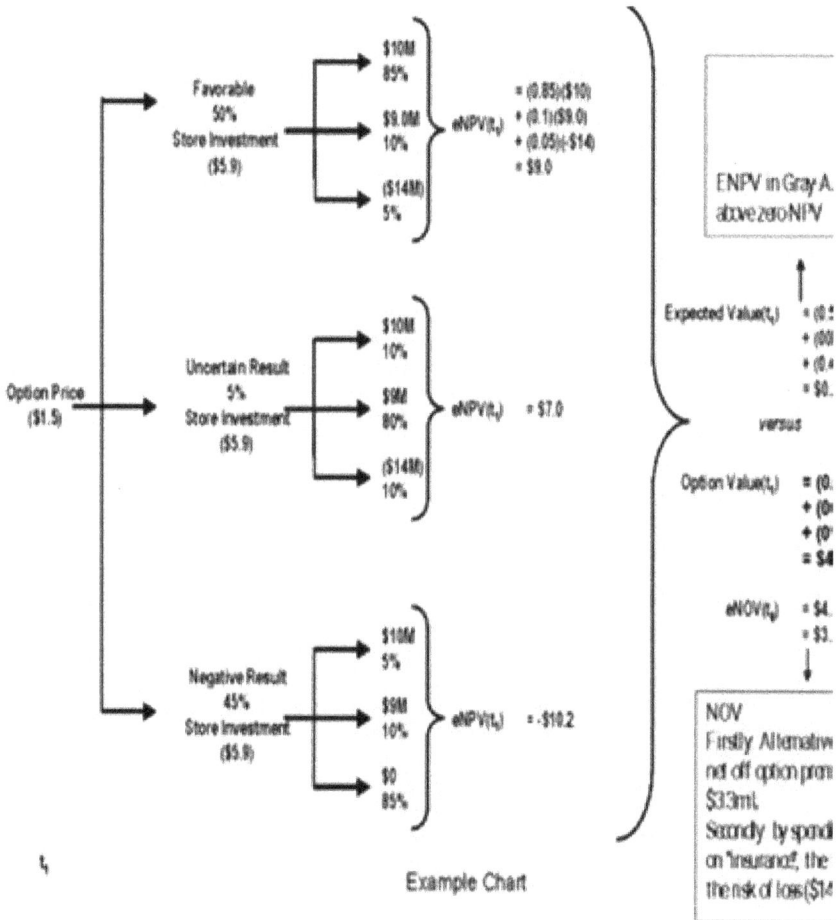

Example Chart

www.ingramcontent.com/pod-product-compliance
Lightning Source LLC
Chambersburg PA
CBHW040848210326
41597CB00029B/4775